KU-769-864

HIGHLAND PEARLS

HIGHLAND PEARLS

BY

BEE JAY

Author of
And It Came To Pass, 1963
The End of the Rainbow, 1964
Sunset on the Loch, 1965

BARKER JOHNSON
STRATH · GAIRLOCH · ROSS-SHIRE
1969

Copyright © S. Barker Johnson 1969

PRINTED IN GREAT BRITAIN
BY R. & R. CLARK, LTD., EDINBURGH

CONTENTS

Dedicated
to lovers of the superb settings
and way of life found in the
real Highlands, and which
should be preserved
for us
'richly to enjoy'.

CHAPTER I

A SAGA OF THE HIGHLANDS

THIS is a book of two parts. One section deals with Wester Ross; the other with the central and western seaboard of Sutherland as far north as Cape Wrath.

It is more or less a **Y** journey from Inverness, branching off at Dingwall (the county town of Ross and Cromarty) left to Wester Ross via the Torridons, Loch Maree, Gairloch and Ullapool; and right via Bonar Bridge (the Sutherland border), Lairg, Tongue, Durness, Kinlochbervie, Scourie, Kylesku ferry and Lochinver . . . taking in mountains of fame, Beinn Eighe (Ben Eay), Beinn Alligin, Liathach in the Torridon range, Slioch (Loch Maree), An Teallach (Dundonnell way), Canisp, Suilven and Stack Polly (Lochinver way); then in Sutherland, Ben Loyal—known as the 'Queen of Scottish mountains'—Ben Hope, Arkle, Ben Stack, Foinaven (near Loch Inchard), and of course many more. To say nothing of lochs; Maree, Shin, More, Stack, Hope, Loyal and Naver; and up in Sutherland lochans by the hundred appearing in all sorts of places, unexpectedly.

The peaceful, haunting beauty of Scotland's north-western coastline and mountains to which Bonar Bridge is the gateway to N-W Sutherland, and Garve the gateway to Western Ross, makes these regions of Britain the most memorable choice for visiting. Some people coming to a new place seem to like it so much, that they return again—and then are disappointed in it. But not so in the north-west territory.

There are few—if any—parts of Britain to which the adjective unique may worthily be applied, but unquestionably Wester Ross and Western Sutherland combine to more than satisfy this expression.

The whole book attempts to vividly capture Highland life—including the Clearances—amidst the ageless unsullied scenery of these fascinating parts of the Highlands, and should hold the readers attention, cover to cover.

In years to come QUIET will be priceless. Pearls . . . Highland pearls . . . of a great price scattered, if our so-called modern planners get more and more a free hand to do what they like. It will be a sorry day for the Highlands if large-scale developments ever come to pass; for then the magic of the Highlands extending back for generations—a land steeped in history at every corner, a land of exquisite beauty, a charm peculiar only to Scotland, together with its folklore, song, poetry, and above all its religious heritage—will vanish. Surely the Highlands, all the little villages, the wee stores, the wee Post Offices where one congregates to pass over news (and gossip), and the Sabbath, must be allowed to remain the grand way of life it is today? It is a truism that one has more respect for oneself in a small place, a village. You are really more of a person.

Some time ago, a politician said, 'the Scots are lucky to have such a vast holiday area in their midst'. We all know what politicians are like, but in this case he spoke the truth! He could have added, there is no prettiness in all the glens—only grandeur. And the air is free!

*   *   *

There is so much beauty in the north-west of Scotland, it's a shame to rush through it; and I shall adhere to that thought from beginning to end. In previous writings I am credited with the saying (or slogan) 'once you pass Garve, nobody hurries'. Whilst it is true that time seems of little account in the Highlands, some folk did not quite approve of this skit, and so in this current saga, I will compromise (this seems to be an age of compromise) by saying that when one passes Garve *en route* to Wester Ross, or Bonar Bridge on the way to Western Sutherland, you take off your wrist watch and put it in the glove box of the car, for no one knows the meaning of hurry or time. In other words you are coming into a land where calendars replace clocks. Some in isolated hamlets look to the newspaper checking the date. When you gaze on the Torridon mountains, you must recollect these are said to be the oldest range in the world; old before the Himalayas were born, older in fact—much older—than when the children of Israel saw Egypt. And you simply *have* to pause and think of the stupendous Corridors of Time standing before you in actual bold relief; and when the Creator made Time, He made plenty of it, they say in the Highlands. Certainly it is a commodity of which they have availed themselves to the full; and therefore it can well be understood, having been reared and brought up since their race saw the light of day, they are conscious of the Time factor. How could they be otherwise? Distance and difficult terrain still remain obstacles, and one should always remember distance is relative up in the Highlands. However, when all this grandeur of mountain, loch and glen were made, I feel sure He made and wished it to be peopled by the folk who inhabit it even today, for their especial care to be treasured as it was meant to be treasured in their own humble religious manner and with smiles, grace, friendliness and affection . . . the distinguishable marks of tranquility.

Indeed the Greeks say that when the Creator finished making the earth He had a barrow-load of stones left over; these were dumped into the Aegean sea, thus creating Greece's 1500 islands. But at least a fair amount fell in the North sea and the Minch, giving Scotland some 140 beautiful islands together with a host of lochs and lochans. So much for legend.

The Highlands and the Highlanders don't just shake you by the hand; they engulf you. The area can only be described by one word 'scenic'; the little bays (with their limitless stretches of clean golden sand—virgin white in some cases—and the uncrowded safe beaches), the tiny white-washed cottages and crofts scattered about like raisins in a cake. They have a way of life that is genuine, simple and good. With their close contact with the good earth, the solitude 'midst nature's unspoiled scenes, the ever-changing elements bring them nearer to God in his garden than anywhere else on earth. It is all imbued in their very soul.

> Ships and boats
> And things that float

run in their blood as the old sailor said about his wooden leg!

Their good nature is so noticeable that it can give these parts of Wester Ross and Western Sutherland an alternative name, 'The Friendly Counties'. The peace of the Highlands is not just a negative lack of noise; it is a primordial unseen force such as personality or magnetism which defies the sight but is deeply felt, just like on a Sabbath day up here, besides which the concerns of every day living appear trifling; something with which it is possible to dispense.

In the Highlands one becomes faced by one's own personality to a much greater extent than anywhere else in Britain, where the scurry and bustle (I dislike the phrase 'rat race') together with social custom and pretence seem to blanket the real feelings. Throughout the world each one of us at least seeks a peaceful corner sooner or later to come home to; to come home to roost. For the age in which we live can nowadays be described in more technical language than decades ago, namely the nuclear age, the jet age, the space age, the computer age. And as the centuries roll on, no doubt another 'age' will come to light.

But one thing so far has not changed in the Highlands though other changes come about, and that is the open-hearted hospitality of the people; a natural people in fact. At every turn you find the local folk ready to help and extend the gentle courtesies which add so much to the enjoyment of a Highland holiday. Perhaps, who knows, in another decade, a squee-gee roller will extend right across these two counties, squeezing out this old and pleasant existence right up, and overspill at Cape Wrath—another 'Clearance', and one that could never be reclaimed. Mayhap beatniks, and young irresponsible folk (possibly having the vote by then?) smoking marijuana cigarettes, cannabis and indulging in opium and a host of other drugs, peps and pills will take over?

For the present, however, one simply cannot and should not ignore the living beauty on our doorstep. Ireland may have its Killarney, and the Blarney Stone near Cork, but once you are up here in the far north you will say to yourself that this is *all* Killarney and more; and nothing between us and America but the foaming majesty of the breaking waves. The Irish have had their poets and song writers working overtime on such lilts as 'Galway Bay', 'The Mountains of Mourne', 'Killarney's Lakes' and so forth, but what grander haunting tunes and songs can there be than 'The Waters of Kylesku', 'Loch Dui', 'The Scottish Soldier', 'Morag of Dunvegan', and a heap more?

People and history; this surely sums up the Highlands in two simple words. A people of loving understanding, people who would welcome the stranger within their doors, who—when he departs—would have learned much with a wholesome knowledge he had made true friends and a strong wish to return.

MELIORISM, the doctrine that the world is capable of improvement, is not dead, and you would go away with this thought ringing through your head, 'We thank thee O Lord for the good things which still abound in this troubled world. Save us from magnifying our sufferings, and forgetting our blessings.' Above all, and all through their past centuries of sufferings, the Highland people have been loyal to their birth, as perhaps few others in this land have; and I would say their strength all through their trials and tribulations has been their enduring Faith and loyalty. And in this connection I bring to mind the advice given by the late Queen Mary to her granddaughter, Elizabeth—now Queen Elizabeth—which was as follows: 'Remember that life is made up of loyalty; loyalty to your friends; loyalty to things beautiful and good; loyalty to the country in which you live; and above all—for this holds all other loyalties together—loyalty to God.' Great words, great advice to be sure. Very akin to what Confucius said aeons ago, namely, 'To put the world in order, we must first put the nation in order; to put the nation in order, we must put the family in order; to put the family in order, we must cultivate our personal life; and to cultivate our personal life, we must first set our hearts right.' Great words too from this Chinese philosopher.

Peace and quiet in the Highlands, with just heather and sheep.

Half the young people in Britain today would like to emigrate. Two out of three want the return of hanging. More than half expect another world war. Three out of ten teenagers would send all coloured immigrants home. Less than two-thirds believe in God. But the Highlanders and the vast country they and the Hebrideans occupy look upon the Highlands as their own country—their heritage and will keep it so; and ALL believe in God.

By looking at the past and looking more into the future one

cannot but come to the conclusion of the bewildering tortuous roads that in olden days led to 'Highland predicament'. Looking back sometimes in anger and more often in sorrow one forms a picture of apathy, incompetence, indifference and muddled thinking that was really unbelievable were it not true. In the past the Highlands of Scotland have surely been a country in which general politics has expressed itself with flamboyant, ignorant extravagance. The picture was painted as a devastated countryside —a land of sheep and Highland cattle (beautiful beasts notwithstanding). Commissions, reports, white papers and documentaries galore in the past have all borne the stamp of a lacking purpose; just pious platitudes, a sense of helplessness. No small wonder the Scottish Nationalist Party have come to the fore of late! The year 1968 marked the 40th year the S.N.P. has been in existence. Since the children of Israel were forty years in the wilderness before coming into their inheritance, if one believes in omens the S.N.P. tell us they could be nearing the dawn of a new and exciting era for Scotland? Today there is a greater emphasis *inter alia* on transport and communications, and of island needs. 'Tis as well, for it makes for disturbing thoughts for the future if this be not so. However, much has been done in the matter of roads. They are all good; awkward corners, bends and such like have been straightened and ironed out, and there is no need whatsoever for anyone to be doubtful of a 'safe journey' all over the two counties. The days of rough tracks are over. Tarmacadam has seen to that; and I take off my hat to the grand work done by the county road workers. So now, there is no excuse for not paying us a visit, is there?

The jacket of this book depicts a waterfall. A waterfall can hold your interest and fascinate you for a long time. There are very many up north, all different in behaviour. A turgid, yellow-peaty-brown waste of water, no rocks in its path to stop it tumbling down, to stem its irresistible advance. A sparkling Highland torrent, its banks verdant with say early summer foliage, stretches of jet-black pools tipped at times by cascades of white. A waterfall. Or in winter, its waters fettered and its voice calmed by ice and snow; its fall spear-tipped by gleaming icicles with overhanging snow. A waterfall. In effect it can be many a mountain Highland stream rising in desolation miles up the glen, finally merging into a loch.

Sand, sea, mountains, loch and lochans, friendly folk, comfortable places to stay in, good Highland fare, the fun of exploring new areas, peace and quiet—a complete change from everyday routine; and romance? These are some of the ingredients of a Highland vacation. The water lipping the beaches, the gulls crying their morning welcome to the fishing boats as they return with the night's catch. The hotel, inn, guest house or B. and B. houses offer the happy combination of comfort with charm and the prospect of a day's pleasure—providing it is not raining straight up and down Highland rain!—stretches temptingly before you as you waken in your bedroom. A cluster of rock pools in whose depth lurk crabs and shrimps. The sun and breeze makes the face tingle. All this, and more, can be found in this favoured land of the north-west. The romantic west coast; the headlands and beaches that give infinite variety to the coastline of the off-shore islands. *Contrast*, is the operative word, in regard to scenery everywhere. Villages differing in character, one with another. Is all this not enough? The Highlands, where the old days never die, for they are constantly being reborn.

Up in the Highlands you can be certain you're not motoring and being kept back for long enough (as you are on the main roads of Britain—or along Loch Lomond side) sitting at the wheel gazing at the back of a 'Smith's Crisps' van, or one declaiming 'Removals are our business', all the way from say Hull to Wakefield or Carlisle to Glasgow! You have left all that well behind.

Along these vast Highland areas with moorland on all sides, the danger of fire is always present in the summer and dry spells, and one is constantly being cautioned on the radio as to exercising care; not throwing cigarette ends around, or when picnicing seeing that the kettle fire is under control, for once alight the heather burns readily and can cause untold damage. Along these particular routes there are many little wired 'boxes' having improvised brooms made of birch branches and handles which enable one to damp out any small fire unwittingly arising. They are indeed very handy. A child on seeing these stacks of birch brooms at varying spots by the roadside, once exclaimed, 'look, mummy, witches car parks'!

At a risk of repetition this *is* a land of rugged mountains, wild moor, green glens and of crofts. A land of incredible variety (and it is variety that keeps one's mind fresh); a land soaked in the romance of a vivid stormy history and redolent of the old tales of the Highland clans; a land with a fantastically fretted coast-line on which the North Minch has attacked and nibbled in its own sweet time; a land of big sea-lochs biting even far in to the mountains; a land of a thousand and one picnic spots; a land straddled by straths. Pearls, pearls and more pearls.

And you can take out a wee boat in any of the bays spending hours afloat if you are so minded, and if it is a calm day and whilst you're rounding Cape Wrath you'll feel you are sniffing the ozone off Cape Horn and visualising the welcome home awaiting you at Portsmouth! As you read on, you will learn of the roving Vikings of old who came skimming the seas and plunder was their family hobby! They left behind them many Norse names. There is so much to see and drink in (and I am not alluding solely to whisky!) that a short sojourn up in the north-west is far too little; and even a month will slip by as a yesterday. The artist's easel will need to bare the strain of working overtime, and the painter so engrossed as to forget he had a bottle of midge lotion handy! And if you are sitting by the side of a lochan you may see highly coloured dragonflies flitting in and out of the reeds, and given sufficient imagination you will go back home and tell your friends that there *are* fairies in the Highlands.

'Here's tae us, wha's like us', say the Scots; but do they shout as loud as they should considering some of their splendid accomplishments? Not the least being the scenery and background of their own country—the Highlands in particular. This book from the pen of a Colonial Englishman who has known the Highlands and Highlander for over fifty years and lives quietly amongst them—modestly attempts to throw as much light as possible on their surroundings and way of life. It can fittingly be a companion to *And It Came To Pass* and *Sunset on the Loch*, the author's two other Highland books; as well as *The End of the Rainbow* which was a true story bound up in Faith.

Many a cynic says, 'What can you expect of a day that begins with having to awaken?' But in the Highlands to wake up every day is a great beginning in more ways than one. When one thinks of scones, Scotch broth, Angus steaks, crowdie, oatcakes, pancakes and the rest, I find myself asking 'why does anybody emigrate?' By Parkinson's Law we know that the

more facilities we create, the more we shall need, until eventually
we have destroyed what we have been seeking to find—peace
and quiet. However to be honest, one can say that snow may be
found in the Highlands in any month of the year—somewhere
and on some mountain. And the pounding pulse of the Scottish
Highlands is to be found *in* the Scottish Highlands; and nowhere
else.

Those of us who live here, daily accept—let alone *expect*—the
crimson glories of a sunset; and the distant horizon so brilliantly
lit up, beckons us like a sea-waif in the Carribean Seas. The
camera is quite inadequate to capture such scenes. It is as if
Nature, having created a day of sparkling beauty, wants to show
she can still enhance it as the day closes.

> . . . Mirrored against the glassy waters
> The rugged sentinels of nature
> Drift into the shadows of the purple evening
> And fade softly into night. . . .

One special pleasure you find in the Highlands is the autumn.
There's a hush, in every sense of the word, that comes with
September, when the country turns gold; the season of the
turned leaf—tints of indescribable variety. And there's elbow
room too!

*   *   *

And so I will continue this saga, chapter-by-chapter, dealing
first with Sutherland. Wester Ross comes along later (page 85).

Though Scots—who emigrated over the seas during the
Clearance days—be far away. . . .

> . . . yet still the heart is Highland, and we in dreams
> behold our native land . . .

and many long in their hearts to return and re-live their days
'midst their old surroundings. Their Reverie might be poetically
put thus:

> How is it that the call of glens,
> And yearning thoughts of rocky bens
> Encompass all my life, forbye
> It is because my heart doth lie,
>   In Scotland.

How blood of Highland men, long dust,
Sings in my veins and says 'I must'
Return to all I hold most dear
Before my dreams with age are sere,
    Of Scotland.
For mountains, burns and lochs and wood,
I thank my God and pray I could
Be granted leave to end my days
'mid splendour wrapped in pearly haze,
    In Scotland.

The following acrostic spells out more truth than even poetry; facts every true-blooded Scot is proud of and cherishes. It could significantly be called SCOTIA REGNUM.

Scotia's mountain, moorland, fen
Colour in her woods and glen,
O'er her lochs, celestial light
These are her pearls, sparkling bright
Land of beauty, virtue, grace
All God's great gifts so interlaced,
Never shall some other race
Dominate this stately place ...

    *   *   *

And so we will go along together in search of these pearls, these jewels which can be found in the north-west, especially in the untrammelled space of Sutherland; this wilderness (and wildness) of moorland should never be spoilt—merely tamed to its surroundings.

I remember when travelling from Colombo to Hong Kong once on a French liner some 35 years ago, we touched in at Saigon, which was then French Indo-China; today it is now South Vietnam and devastated by war. As we drew alongside the quay, the passengers—mostly French—told me they called Saigon PERLE D'ORIENT, pearl of the East. It was indeed a beautiful place, and as the ship tied up, the galaxy of fashion in that outpost of Empire even in those days was extraordinary. The whole port seemed aglow with the prettiest of women— young and middle aged—decked up in the latest Paris creations. It was really overpowering. Today, how different it must be. But the phrase 'pearl of the East' has always stuck in my mind.

In this, our present mood, we can fittingly term the Highland gems we are about to discover as PERLES D'OUEST . . . pearls of the West, which I feel sure will create a breathtaking impact on our very souls, should one be able to fully appreciate moments of quiet out of this world, amongst a people still living out of this (troubled) world.

> No diamond ever shone so bright
> As Scotia's waters, oh! the sight
> To see them rushing o'er the leas
> To kiss the coasts and meet the seas
>   Of Scotland.
> Not for me the pallid pleasures
> But for me, the gold and purple blaze
> Of moors, light veiled with gilded rays,
>   In Scotland.

The people one lives amongst up here, are like oneself; seeking the same delights of life; contentment and happiness. Happiness is something we create in our mind, its not something you search for and so seldom find; for in making others happy we will be happy too, for the happiness you give away, returns to shine on you.

> Love is the language every heart speaks,
> and Love is the answer to all that man seeks.

> This is my story,
>   This is my song . . .

SUTHERLAND

... (for its own special beauty
Sutherland has no rival)

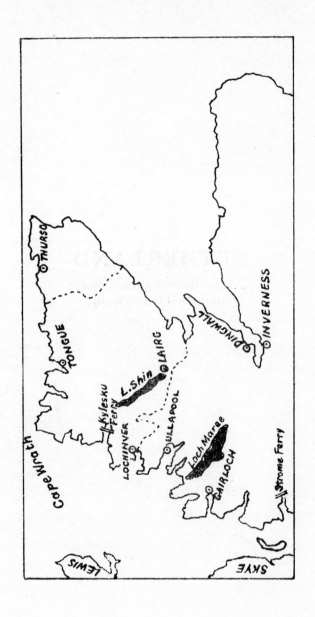

Sutherland

CHAPTER 2

WESTERN SUTHERLAND

WE now start on our travels from Inverness, branching off at Dingwall to the right, making for Bonar Bridge, where we cross over the boundary to Sutherland. Sutherland is really 'The South Land'; strange in a way for it is one of Scotland's two most northerly mainland counties. The name comes from the Norse, as in early days this region was colonised and ruled by Scandinavians. It is the most sparsely inhabited area of Britain; it has an area of 1,297,000 acres with a population of only 13,500 (compared with Ross-shire's 1,977,000 acres and population 57,500). Its rateable value is but £192,000 and a 1d. rate per £ only amounts to £750. So the county cannot be said to have a great deal of money for vast improvements. The north-west part of this county seems to be a land of dykes (stone walls) acting as dividing lines to various owners of crofts and moor. These walls—miles upon miles of them—are perfectly built and shaped, and is surely a dying art these days. In Wester Ross it is mostly barbed-wire fencing that is used for demarcation. One comes across similar stone walls in the Yorkshire dales.

The period of Norse influence on what later became 'Scotland' began in the 8th century A.D. and continued for almost five hundred years until the Treaty of Perth in 1266, by which following the defeat of the Norse at the Battle of Largs in 1263, the Hebrides passed to the Crown of Scotland. The Shetland and Orkney islands continued for some two hundred years longer to be Norwegian possessions until they too passed to the Scottish Crown.

The Vikings were seafaring traders and warriors who sailed forth in their 'long ships' from the fiords of Scandinavia to make long and perilous sea-voyages down the coasts of Western

Europe and around the British Isles. At first they appeared as isolated bands, making sporadic raids on foreign shores, but later they began to settle in some of the lands they visited. It was towards the end of the 8th century that the Viking sea-raiders first made themselves felt. In A.D. 794 they attacked many islands round Britain. The next year they plundered Iona and Skye. In A.D. 806 Iona, already attacked several times, was severely assaulted and sixty-eight monks were massacred. The Abbot of Iona withdrew to Ireland and the headquarters of the Celtic Church in Scotland moved from Iona to Dunkeld.

There is evidence that long before these piratical ventures, Scandinavian voyagers had visited the British Isles for purposes of trade. It would appear also that sometimes their attacks on the land communities were no more than attempts to obtain fresh provisions. Going ashore, they would round up the local live-stock, kill the animals on the shore and replenish their ship-larders with fresh meat, dealing roughly with any of the 'natives' who resisted them. This procedure was called 'strand-hogg' (shore-depredation).

The Vikings soon discovered that a much easier, quicker and surer way to wealth—even though more dangerous—than labouriously tilling the ground, fishing or even trading, was to steal other folk's property. It was soon discovered also that the numerous monasteries around the coasts offered rich spoils—vessels of gold and silver, jewels, ornaments and fine garments.

Before long the Vikings began to make settlements ashore, at first temporary ones whence they raided far and near; then permanent settlements on headlands and islands.

Scandinavia was a bare and bleak country, hard to make a living in; so with increasing pressure of population upon very limited natural resources, there had to be migration, seeking new lands, new homes, and new sources of livelihood. The Norsemen who were fishermen as well as farmers developed the art of boat-building to a high pitch. In particular they developed the keel, without which long sea-voyages in rough seas would have been extremely perilous. They were also highly skilled in navigation. Thus under strong pressure from within, because of natural and economic circumstances, and with the skill to make and navigate ocean-going ships, the Norsemen ventured out. They developed a type of ship, a method of navigation, and a frame of mind which enabled them to face the sea and made them the most intrepid seamen the world has yet seen.

There was no doubt much killing and much misery, but there is no record that the Norsemen wiped out the people they found in the areas they took over. They certainly made themselves masters and overlords, but they needed the natives as slaves or serfs to till the land and row the galleys; and they needed the native women as wives. The very high degrees of Norse occupation, indicated by the very high proportion of Norse place-names met with in Sutherland, does not mean that the previous inhabitants were necessarily driven out. It simply means that these areas were previously very thinly peopled.

So much for the Vikings . . .

* * *

Inverness, from where we are presently starting off, claims the proud title 'Capital of the Highlands', and with a population of about 32,000 makes it by far the biggest Highland town. It is a market town and a cultural centre, and has a broad river flowing through it, curving towards the Moray Firth and on to the North Sea. It has this advantage over Edinburgh and there are pretty walks round the river Ness. The city prides itself on the purity of its speech and intonation. There is an airport, Dalcross, about seven miles out of the town. Going northwards on our way out, there is a fine wide vehicular traffic bridge which was completed in September 1961 and formally opened on the 28th of that month by Provost Allan Ross, deputising for the then Scottish Secretary, Mr. Tom Johnston (who was ill). It was a day of pouring rain! It replaced an old suspension type bridge, totally unfit for the ever-increasing heavy traffic of the day, and it was costing a great deal of upkeep. Townfolk were saying the trouble with the old bridge lay, not so much in keeping it up, as in getting rid of it!

There is a very notable castle situated on a high mound overlooking the Ness, which in olden times served as a watch-tower. The castle stands on or near the site of Macbeth's Castle. The modern structure of today serves only as the administrative centre of the county. It is supposed the first Castle on this site was built in 1057. During the 1715 rising, the castle was, for a short time in the hands of the Jacobites, but was recovered for George I by

Rose of Kilravock, and Simon, Lord Lovat. On the mound standing boldly in front of the castle entrance is the statue of Flora Macdonald, whose name, as all must surely know, was so closely linked with Bonnie Prince Charlie of the 1745 rebellion. The inscription on the monument is in Gaelic and English, and reads:

> As long as a flower grows on a field
> So long will the fame of the maiden endure.

Flora Macdonald was the most illustrious woman the Highlands and islands have produced. Flora (or Funivella) of immortal memory.

It may be of interest to recall that in September 1921, His Majesty's Cabinet met in the Council chambers there to discuss the Irish question, and a framed document bearing signatures of Prime Minister Lloyd George and the other members of his Cabinet hangs upon the wall of the room.

Before saying farewell, *slàn leat*, to Inverness, and digressing a little more (and readers will find this is one of my faults—or is it?—in not sticking to any strict itinerary in the Highlands) one must remember Inverness is closely associated with the renowned *Caledonian Canal*, which was a tremendous engineering feat constructed by Thomas Telford who started making it in 1803; and nineteen years later (1822) the sloop *Caledonia* was the first ship to traverse the sixty miles from Corpach, Fort William, to Clachnaharry at Inverness. Of these sixty miles, about twenty are artificial; the remainder being composed of the three lochs, Loch Lochy, Loch Oich, and Loch Ness. The canal has twenty-nine small locks, controlled by the Ministry of Transport. These used to be hand-operated, but now all are hydraulically worked. The project originally cost 1½ million pounds. The main object was to save fishing boats the slow and often perilous journey right up the west coast of Scotland to the top of Caithness through the Pentland Firth ('twixt the Orkneys and Caithness) and down to the east coast ports. The canal was originally surveyed by James Watt. All this, while the Sutherland Clearances were getting under way!

We will now leave Inverness and make for Dingwall (population 4000) twenty-two miles north, passing through Beauly and Muir of Ord, both small towns in comparison. Just as one enters

Beauly one catches a glimpse of Beaufort Castle, built originally
in 1882 (and is really the thirteenth to be built there), the modern
seat of Lord Lovat, chief of the Clan Fraser.   Beauly takes its
name from the French *beau lieu*—beautiful place, Mary Queen of
Scots being responsible for the name;   and here is the legend.
She stayed at the Priory House for one night in the course of a
journey to Dingwall in 1564, and it is said that upon waking up
in the morning, she looked out on the vista from her window and
exclaimed 'c'est un beau lieu'.   This legendary link with the ill-
starred pearl of the Scottish monarchy appeals to the romantic
in us all, and no doubt the Queen did in fact so describe the
inspiring view which greeted her eyes that morning, but history,
in that case, can only give the incident the credit of a charming
coincidence.

   We now come to Dingwall, the branch off of our letter **Y**
to Sutherland direction.   Dingwall is the county town of Ross-
shire;   or to be more precise of Ross and Cromarty.   It was
called in Norse THING-VILLE, 'Field of the Thing';   the Norse
General Court of Justice.   Dingwall was therefore in those days
the centre of the Norse administration in Ross-shire.   For its size,
it is really a very busy market town, with cattle sales almost
weekly.

   Onward then to Sutherland, the most desolate and emptiest
county in Britain;   and where in some parts only the voice of the
wind answers a man in the empty expanse.   At times you can
travel miles and only see a ruined house, with weeds and shrubs
growing amongst the stone walls;   derelict landmarks.   Crofters'
snug clean homes once filled the land.   But in the late 18th and
early 19th centuries, the prospect of greater gain from sheep-
raising caused wholesale eviction of the people by the landowners
... The Clearances ... Houses were burned down and furniture
thrown outside about the poor old crofters' heads.   All these
displaced, despised crofters were forced to eke a living along the
rocky shores far away from their old homes;   homes which their
fathers and their fathers before them had occupied.   They had to
tramp and carry all their (meagre) personal belongings miles and
miles, on their backs, like snails.   Their boots looked as if a
blacksmith had made them, and for laces they used wire.   What
an inhuman pitiless, savage, merciless, barbarous treatment befell
them.   More of this later.

Leaving Dingwall we carry along the main road skirting the Cromarty Firth and shortly after passing through Evanton take the main left road at the fork not far from Alness where one commences to see a little of the moorland, but not until you reach Aultnamain do you really come to anything to whet your appetite for Highland-fare; you are then climbing the Struie (which attracts much snow, ice and fog in the winter), with Struie Hill 1082 feet on your far right. Dropping down the Struie you get a wonderful panoramic view—if it be a clear day—from a vantage spot made available by the A.A. of the Dornoch Firth. I once heard an American calling it 'a million dollar view'. You are looking across at SPINNINGDALE and SKIBO Castle with DORNOCH town away on the far right. At the small village of Spinningdale, a spinning mill was built at the end of the 18th century in an attempt to bring industry to the north, and was fairly successful; but it was burnt down in 1808 and never re-built. It was originally put up by a man known as 'Honest George Dempster' of Angus, who appeared to be a man of wealth, for he owned fishing fleets, built lighthouses, and the man who introduced packing fish in ice for transport. He was said to be a pioneer in central heating even in those days! The A.A. plaque points out the general lie of the land, and at this point you are 600 feet above sea level. Here with still half a dozen miles of Ross-shire road between you and Bonar Bridge (the gateway to Sutherland) the roadway falls steeply till it reaches sea level. From the Struie 'watch-tower' you may catch a view of Ben More Assynt (3273 feet) away to the west keeping guard over Loch Assynt which is Lochinver-ways. Of course you may find a capricious cloud blanking out the mountain! Proceeding the few miles more you reach the Sutherland boundary crossing over the impressive bridge into BONAR BRIDGE itself. This modern bridge was erected after the old stone structure built by Telford in 1812 was washed away in the memorable and tragic floods of 1870. (The name Bonar means 'the end of the ford'.) There are now plans to throw a new bridge across the Firth lower down at its narrowest part.

The broad and expansive county of Sutherland is now at hand. Its rivers abound in trout and salmon—more so than in Wester Ross—whilst the huge tracts of mountainous country, dense forests and wind-swept moor, are the haunt of the red deer. The roads all through Sutherland and to the north-west where we are going are without exception excellent; it is a pleasure to motor over them. Once across the towering bridge at Bonar, we turn sharp left, making for the west, viewing the lovely Kyle of Sutherland and on to Lairg and Tongue, but for the moment I am proposing to slip along the road (to the right) to Dornoch 14 miles away, which is the County Town (pop. 1000) and if not mentioned I feel it might be slighted, being so historic, as well as world famous for golf and also a further 15 miles onward to Brora (pop. 1700) as I would like to bring to notice the renowned coal mine there.

As to Dornoch, I particularly wish to mention the Cathedral. It was said to have been erected by Bishop Gilbert in the first half of the 13th century, about 1250 A.D. and was burnt down in 1570 by the Master of Caithness and Mackay of Strathnaver, and the ruin was further destroyed by gales in 1605. A certain amount of reconstruction was undertaken in the year 1616, otherwise the building remained in a ruinous condition until 1835, when it was rebuilt from the foundations with the exception of the central tower resting on lancet arches springing from shafted pillars, the old windows being more or less preserved. The church contains the tombs of the Sutherland family, relics of Sir Richard de Moravia, brother of Saint Gilbert, and a statue by Chantrey of the first Duke of Sutherland. This imposing statue stands at the west end of the nave. The full size monument in Carrara marble is a wonderful specimen of Sir Francis Chantrey's sculpture.

During the years succeeding the Reformation, the cathedral entered on a new phase of its history, and for the past four hundred years it has continued its spiritual function as the parish church of Dornoch. On entering the church the atmosphere is one of simple dignity. Its fine proportions give the building a suggestion of more space than it actually has. There are twenty-three stained glass windows. One on the south wall by Francis Spear of London erected in 1952, commemorates the life and service of Brigadier General Sir George Paynter, K.C.V.O., C.M.G., D.S.O., Lord-Lieutenant of Sutherland. The main subject is St. George, patron saint of soldiers, slaying the dragon. Also in the window are St. Andrew for Scotland, St. Peter for fishermen, St. Hubert for huntsmen and St. Gilbert

for Dornoch. An organ was installed in the north transept in
1893.

This cathedral has a clear power of communication that tells
better than recorded history, 'here surely has been the cradle of
religion in the north'. In fact Dornoch itself is a corruption of the
Gaelic for 'the holy place'. In its present state the cathedral is
still a beautiful edifice, endowed with beautiful proportions. For
over seven hundred years now, it has withstood the ravages of
time, an abiding witness to the glory of God and of the per-
manence of things spiritual amid the transience of all things
earthly.

*   *   *

And now we come to Brora, and its famed coal mine. Apart
from its coal mine, there is in this village a thriving and well-
known woollen mill (Brora tweeds are known all over the
world, as tweeds which will never wear out), a distillery and a
brickworks. The existence of coal here was known in 1529 and
its working began in 1598 (opened by the Countess of Sutherland)
chiefly to provide fuel for the production of salt. But this is no
ordinary coal mine, for it is now operated by the miners themselves as a co-operative enterprise; that is why I am giving it
pride of place. This mine went into voluntary liquidation in 1961,
and it seemed to many people in this small town, that the colliery
had closed for the last time. There had been many fires in the
workings. The miners—twenty-eight of them—approached the
then 'Highland Fund' for aid, and this enabled them to take over
the pit. Since then each miner became a shareholder, each buying
5s. shares per week to pay off the loan. The coal from Brora is
around £4 per ton cheaper than the N.C.B. coal. It is one of
the world's longest-worked coal mines, and it has now been
given a new lease of life, for the workers struck a new seam in
1968; and the Highland Development Board have granted the
miners a loan of £100,000 to develop this seam, estimated to
hold eight million tons of coal. The pits' future is now guaranteed
for at least forty years. In 1961 at the time of liquidation, the
men with the £10,000 given them from the Fund mentioned
above, bought the mine for £4000, £3000 went for working
capital, and a further £3000 for a new fleet of lorries. They pay
themselves a weekly wage of £22, and they have still been able

to pay themselves a bonus twice a year and put a substantial amount of cash into reserve.

The present output is 8000 tons a year, which is expected to be doubled within a few years, possibly by 1971. This mine provides another thirty jobs at the nearby brickworks. The coal finds its main market to distilleries in the Highland area, and local homes. It also provides coal to Dundee power station.

This is just an instance—and a compelling one too—showing what local enterprise, and a co-operative one at that, can do, which those at National level cannot do; and I take off my hat (as I did when I went down the mine a few years ago, for they made me put on a special coal helmet) to these twenty-eight gallant men and their engineers.

Whilst coal is generally referred to as 'black diamonds' and not pearls, I feel I am within literary license to include this mine as one of the many Highland 'Pearls'.

*   *   *

Returning now to Bonar Bridge, we leave for Lairg, Tongue Durness, Kinlochbervie, Lochinver and the rest of the north-west pearls of beauty. The road winds along the Kyle of Sutherland under the well-wooded slopes of Balblair to Invershin. This is a pretty wee spot, and just near the viaduct carrying the railway which goes on to Lairg, there is a very cosey, popular hotel which has been in the hands of Mr. and Mrs. James Black for some twenty years; and what they don't know as to making guests feel at home isn't worth knowing. I have stayed there many times, and Mrs. Black looks on me as a 'regular'. Invershin is only about eight miles from Lairg. There are two roads to Lairg, the upper and the lower one; this latter is the prettier run as it follows the Shin closely and in a few miles you come to the Falls of Shin, which one must not fail to visit. There is a path down to the Falls and when the river is in spate, you can spend hours watching the spectacular salmon leap there. The Falls and the gorge look formidable enough for these fish to attempt, but attempt it they do; and if at first they don't succeed in getting up the Falls, well—they just keep on trying. It is a beautiful sight with the white foam of the rushing, surging waters, adding their quota of beauty. Here is a set—indeed a string—of pearls you will not readily forget. The Shin runs

south from Loch Shin at Lairg, to join the Oykell before entering
the Dornoch Firth at the Kyle of Sutherland. The higher road
I have mentioned on the east bank of the river quickly attains a
height that commands an excellent view of central Sutherland—
on a clear day of course!

When at Invershin you see before you Carbisdale Castle,
towering—literally towering—like a Rhine schloss over the steep
slopes where Montrose was defeated by royalist troops in 1650.
The castle was built early this century by a former dowager
Duchess of Sutherland, and is known locally as the Castle of
Spite. It is now a Youth Hostel. It stands as I have led you to
believe on a spur of road overlooking the Kyle of Sutherland
at a point where the steep hills draw back, leaving a narrow
passage, through which road, rail and river pass. From the
entrance hall comes the lower gallery with the dining room at one
end and at the other the wonderful wide carved oak staircase lit
by a stained glass window depicting the successive titles of the
family of Leveson-Gower, Dukes of Sutherland. On the floor
of the upper gallery and ballroom are the rooms in which King
Haakon and Prince Olaf of Norway slept in 1942 as guests of the
late Colonel T. E. Salvesen, after their flight from Norway. Now
for a little history.

In the presence of a large and representative gathering the
foundation stone of Carbisdale Castle was officially laid in 1910,
although its north wing had been very nearly completed. The
dowager Duchess of Sutherland whose permanent home it was
to be, died in 1912. It then became the property of her daughter
Countess Bubna who lived there with her two daughters until
1933, when through ill health she sold it to a Mr. A. R. Mackenzie
of Invergordon. He in turn shortly afterwards sold it to Theodore
Salvesen (mentioned already) of the well-known Leith Shipping
family. I chanced to meet one of his charming daughters in
Edinburgh during the war and she told me much of their family
history. They were very wealthy. Theodore died in 1942,
whereupon the castle passed to his son Captain Harold, who in
1945 presented it to the Scottish Youth Hostel Association.

The inside story of the building of this castle is a long one, so
I may be excused if I confine myself to a few significant details.

The dowager Duchess whom I have mentioned was the
second wife of the third Duke of Sutherland. She was a Mrs.

Blair, a widow of a captain in one of the Highland regiments. Later on, she married again and was 'Lady Rollit', but she retained the title of dowager Duchess, as perhaps that sounded better. After marrying the Duke of Sutherland she made herself a nuisance to that household; and she selected Carbisdale site in order to spite the family. In those days the Sutherland's had their own private train (motor cars were almost unknown then) and naturally every time they crossed the Kyle at Culrain they could not help seeing this aggressive structure. The Duke was an old man when he married Mrs. Blair, and when he died, his family and friends, wanted to dislodge her from Dunrobin Castle; and so she determined to pay them out and denude the estates as far as possible. The Duke had left everything to her not entailed. When quitting Dunrobin she took away everything she could; it even amounted to vandalism. Her stepson forced a legal action and she was sentenced to six months detention. This then made her more determined to build a castle for herself which would put Dunrobin Castle to shame; but she could not purchase a suitable site in Sutherland. Accordingly she obtained Carbisdale estate just outside Sutherland and just inside Ross-shire. The old Duke, her husband, was said to have left over £300,000; and the Duchess of course had, when marrying, come into priceless jewellery. Much litigation ensued over estate papers and documents, which she was supposed to have burnt, and again for all this she was sentenced to six weeks in Holloway Jail. Poor Duchess! She was released in May 1893. The people of Sutherland exhibited little sympathy for her. It was fairly general talk that whilst the Duke's first wife was still alive, and whilst Mrs. Blair's husband was alive, they were constantly together, in fact it was said the Duke took her for a cruise to the West Indies. Whilst on this escapade the Duke's wife died suddenly in London. Poison through a broken heart it was said. Back in Dunrobin again, Mrs. Blair and her husband were the Duke's guests. Captain Blair was accidentally shot dead whilst the party were out shooting. In the spring of 1889, the Duke— four months after his wife's death and about a month or so after Captain Blair's sad (?) death—married Mary Caroline Blair. The Duke died in 1892; three years of glorious marriage? The Dowager died in 1912 as I have recorded. For all the litigation and abuse thrown at her, her vindictiveness took material shape in

B

Carbisdale Castle. And this, more or less, is the story of the
Castle of Spite. In olden days it was called Corbiesdale.

*   *   *

Onward now to LAIRG. There is a road to the left not far
from Invershin that takes you to Lochinver via the Oykel river,
Altnacealgach, Inchnadamph and Loch Assynt; but we will leave
this out meantime. The little town of Lairg (pop. 1000) figures
quite prominently in the north, for no less than five roads con-
verge here; they come from Tongue in the north, from Laxford
Bridge, Lochinver* and Ullapool in the west, from Golspie,
Dornoch, Tain and Dingwall in the east. Stone Age men must
have fished Loch Shin for there are many relics of the period still
to be seen. It has a good hotel and is a busy distributive centre;
in fact it is really the road and rail centre of Sutherland. It has a
great reputation for cattle sales, drawing buyers from all over
Scotland and northern England. At Achany on the low road we
took from Invershin the North of Scotland College of Agriculture
has a demonstration farm. Cupped at the end of Loch Shin
(18 miles long) now harnessed for hydro-electricity, Lairg lies
pleasingly in the summer sun—when of course the sun is out—
and has a great advantage in being on the threshold of the varied
storehouse of the north and north-west. All posts for these
extensive areas operate via Lairg. A mile or so out from Lairg
going north, the main road forks at an A.A. box; left goes along
by Loch Shin, Overscaig, Loch More, Loch Stack estates belonging to Anne Duchess of Westminster, to Laxford Bridge (which
used to be a change house for the horses; Laxford means 'Salmon
River' in Scandinavian), and from there either to Scourie and
Kylesku ferry (left) or Rhiconich, Kinlochbervie and Durness
(right). The road straight on from the A.A. box—to Tongue,
37 miles.

This is a fairly straight, wide macadamised road, and whilst
the scenery is good, it is not so entrancing as the run to Laxford
Bridge. You travel for miles without seeing anything but moorland until reaching Altnaharra, which stands as a lonely hamlet
at the head of a lonely loch—Loch Naver; you are then in the
Clearance country of Strath Naver mentioned in a later chapter,
a strath that more than most, was made to sup of the bitterness of
the evictions. The land near the lochside is still the most fertile

for many miles, but the people are gone—'Cha till mi tuille'. This large estate is owned by Mr. Marcus Kimball, M.P. for Gainsborough, Lincolnshire, who is a very co-operative, enterprising landowner, and is wishful to make Altnaharra more of a community. Achness at the south of Loch Naver was once the church of a populous area. It is said it was dismantled to provide stones for the hotel at Altnaharra. This hotel is a supreme fishing hotel, ably managed by Mr. Chas. MacLaren and his wife. Mr. MacLaren holds the world's championship record of sixty-four yards for a cast for a salmon or trout. What a phenomenal distance! Am afraid if I cast only twenty yards and didn't catch the hook in my trousers' bottom, I'd feel elated. There must be a trick somehow?

As you motor along this exceptionally good wide roadway you see many posts by the wayside, spaced only a dozen or so yards from one another. They are not passing place posts. They are there to let one know in the winter time, when the thoroughfare is snowbound, exactly the line of the road, and as a help until the snowplough should come along. Touring one summer, I recollect a lady passenger drawing my attention to these posts, saying 'My! there's an awful lot of bus stops on this road!'

Forward then, with TONGUE, fifteen or so miles away. This is the country of the Mackays, whose chief is Lord Reay. We pass Loch Loyal lodge on the shore of beautiful Loch Loyal with Ben Loyal—the Queen of Scottish mountains as I have said (2500 feet) on the left and seen for miles around. A magnificent sight —a rough many-peaked granite mass; then smaller Loch Craggie, and soon when on top of the Brae Kirkiboll you look down on a beautiful panorama—the Kyle of Tongue, with Tongue itself (a Norse name meaning 'a tongue of land') lying snugly below. On a good day it is really a great view. The land around is green and rich and well-wooded. Out to sea in Tongue Bay are islands known as The Rabbit Islands. If you are lucky, and the air is clear, you may see deer grazing peacefully on the far hillsides, and not too far from the road either. Only in Scotland and in the north-west, is it peaceful enough for such gracious creatures to roam around undisturbed and minding their own business. The air smells wooingly. Castle Varrich, an ancient peel—a fortified tower—of the Mackays, stands out vividly, on a promontory west of the village. In the village you will come across

Tongue House, now a seat of the Duke of Sutherland (one of his many) which was built in 1678 by Lord Reay, head of the Clan Mackay. It still bears an ornamental shield in the spacious dining room, the motto 'MANU FORTI'.

I have lived in Tongue at odd times, and find it to be a most hospitable friendly village, quite oblivious to 'rush'. In one of the hotels I stayed in, the Ben Loyal Hotel—a very cosy recently re-constructed building—I was amused one day to see the land-lord's small daughter using a Hoover dustette on the lovely labrador dog (obviously a great pet) 'shampooing' it, taking out the dust and stray hairs from its coat. The dog loved it all; it just sat, turned and lay down as she ordered it. Am sure it took half an hour to groom it!

A very imposing scheme for Tongue was sanctioned by the Government in October 1968, namely making a causeway and bridge at a cost of £500,000 to link Tongue with Melness just across the Kyle of Tongue. The bridge which will span a half mile stretch of water will save a 10-mile detour round both sides of the Kyle and will thus provide easy access for both tourists as well as the locals. It has apparently been pressed for by residents in the area for many years. The new causeway and bridge will play a big part in opening up this part of northern Sutherland. Whilst I am all for improvement I seem to think this new and costly development will take away a lot of the scenic travel round the Kyle; but of course those who have Time on their hands—and there must be many surely—can still take the curves and the bends at leisure and enjoy the pleasant journey in motoring along the former, and by no means narrow way, which has served the people so well for many years now.

It may be recalled in the early summer of 1968, a large number of whales (a 'school' I think is the correct phrase) came into Tongue Bay and in to the Kyle of Tongue. The shallow waters of these 'Kyles' quickly ebb, leaving nothing but sand, and most of the whales were stranded and many died. One or two seemed to live, and experts from the Flamingo Park Zoo, at Pickering, Yorkshire—who have mobile emergency equipment to deal with transport of anything rare—were told of this unique event many days later. They dashed up, but it was too late, as all but one—a whitish coloured one (albino)—were dead. It was transported to the swimming pool at Wick on the east coast,

there to spend a few days convalescing. Unfortunately it was
past revival, and died before anything more could be done. I
happened to be speaking to a young Canadian fellow who was an
expert on this subject and had come from the Hudson Bay district of Canada to join the zoo authorities. He was touring the
northern waters and villages to interest the locals in such matters,
begging them to inform the zoo *at once* of anything special they
might chance to spot in the bays. He was a very likeable, and
obviously very knowledgeable person who was grieved at learning these whales had gone to a watery grave, all through a Time
lag.

Looking across from Tongue you can see a group of crofting
townships that owe their origin to the evictions from Strathmore.
Melness is the chief village, and quarrying of flagstones used to
be its industry. From that peninsula you can walk, when the
tide is out, to the Rabbit islands in the estuary along the sands that
once held fast the French sloop *Hazard* with gold for the Jacobite
cause in 1745. Many legends still exist since this vessel was
wrecked over two hundred years ago. 'Tis a small wonder
the locals are not digging for gold 'in them there sands' even
today?

*   *   *

One day in the late autumn of 1968, which had just finished its
phenomenal Indian proportions (no rain for five months) and
whilst living in Tongue I took the car and went round the Kyle
road to the Melness area, got out, and as the sun was still shining
brightly even in October, I lay down on a nice patch of heather
that was still in bloom, though fading from its spilt claret colour,
and ruminated on things in general. I thought how peaceful it
was in this far northern 'Garden of Eden', and hoped the new
bridge to span the calm waters would not bring in its wake
traffic depreciating beauty.

I have already said, this country is a land of dykes (stone walls
acting as fencing) 'drystane dyking' is I believe the technical
calling. The art was handed down from father to son; aye, even
from grandfather too. One man I spoke to, told me that when he
lifted a stone, he already had a place for it to go. In this 'profession', trial and error never seems to enter into it. He said, 'I
just pick it up and put it in its spot, and there it will remain for a

hundred years or more'. These dykes seem to survive rain and frost, apart from forming shelter for sheep and cattle in the storms; for these beasts have wise heads on them, make no mistake. In the Highlands much good land is littered with stones. If they were taken off the fields and dykes built with them, it would be a big help to the economy; for once ridding a field of stoney matter, the plough can then take over. But alas, there are only a handful of such craftsmen living today in Scotland.

There is only one church in Tongue, but it's well worth a visit, for it is enveloped in history. From the outside the structure is built in the form of a huge triangle and reminds me very much of the style of missionary churches seen in the hinterland of South America or Ceylon.

The north and north-west of Sutherland is the portion of the great Mackay country and here is the historic Reay forest; and both families played a large part in the Church of Tongue. They typified the fortitude, ability, dignity and self-reliance of their people. One such worthy name of this century was that of Alexander Donald Mackay who died in December 1958. He had lofty aims, a sense of duty and dedicated to his noble name. His grandfather, William Ur suffered eviction twice at the time of the Sutherland Clearances. William's mother, Jane Mackay, was a niece of Rob Dunn, the celebrated Mackay bard, of which personality you will read later on.

Writings on the early religious history of Tongue and district, are practically non-existent but there is sufficient evidence to show that the region came under the influence of Christian religion at a very early period. At Balnakiel near Durness and at Skail in Strathnaver there were churches at the beginning of the 13th century. Towards the end of the 16th century, the Mackay chieftains became prominent in the religious struggle then prevailing and especially Donald Mackay of FARR (about twelve miles east of Tongue, on the coast), afterwards First Lord Reay. He was born in 1590 and succeeded his father as Chief of the Mackays in 1614. In 1616 he journeyed to London and was favoured with an audience by King James VI, and there and then in the presence of the Prince of Wales (afterwards Charles I) the honour of knighthood was conferred upon him—this young Highland chief. He was entrusted by the Privy Council of Scotland with various

duties on its behalf in his northern home. Later, he was em-
powered with the consent of Charles I to raise troops for the
service of Count Mansfeldt in the name of King Christian IV of
Denmark. He served with his Highlanders in Holstein from 1626
to 1628, and returned to Scotland to raise fresh recruits. In 1626
he had been created a Baronet of Nova Scotia, and in 1628 was
raised to the Peerage of Scotland as Baron Reay of Reay. Then,
for several years he was engaged in raising regiments for the
service of Gustavus Adolphus, King of Sweden, who had taken
the place of King Christian of Denmark as the Protestant Leader
in the Thirty Years War. Upon his return to this country he
was employed in carrying out commissions in the name of King
Charles I for the maintenance of law and order in Sutherland.
In the initial stages of the dispute which arose between the King
and the Covenanters, the conflict between Reay's sense of loyalty
to the Monarch and his Protestant religious convictions must have
been severe, and very real. Whilst at Tongue, he received a letter
from Montrose requiring him to come to Inverness where he
reluctantly signed the National Covenant. Within months, the
rift between Reay and the Covenanters widened. In 1640 civil
war broke out. Meantime in 1641, Montrose changed sides and
was actively supporting Charles I. (What intrigues?) At this
time, Reay crossed over to Denmark; then later—back in
Scotland—and following the surrender of King Charles to the
Scots army in 1646, Reay sailed from Thurso to Bergen. On
learning that King Charles had been executed, which affected him
profoundly, he died a few weeks later at the age of 59. The
Danish Government sent Reay's body in a ship of war to Tongue,
and it was interred in the family vault at KIRKIBOLL—the old
Church of Tongue. This old church was partially rebuilt about
1675.

Early in the 1600's, lofts and galleries became a feature of
church structures, installed principally for the aristocrats for their
own use. The loft fronts were usually enriched with carved
details. Lord Reay, at the rebuilding of the Kirkiboll church
had a family loft erected there; but because of its dangerous
condition, the loft was taken down in 1951. The congregation
intended to re-erect it, but as this was found to be beyond their
means, the Clan Mackay Society had the fragments taken to
Edinburgh, where they are today in the Museum of Antiquities.

This was agreed to by the General Trustees of the Church of Scotland, and the Presbytery of Tongue.

To commemorate the Reay family in Tongue Church, a framed photograph of the loft and a plaque, bearing the following words, were presented to the Kirk Session:

> MANU FORTI; the Protestant religion was firmly established in the district early in the 17th century by Donald Mackay, 1st Lord Reay. The family loft of the Reay's was removed to the National Museum of Antiquities, Edinburgh, 1960. . . .

The Presbytery of Tongue was set up by the General Assembly on 11th May 1726. Of the seven parishes then united to form it, EDDRACHILLIS, DURNESS, FARR and REAY were taken from the Presbytery of Caithness. To these were added the Parish of ASSYNT and KILDONAN, which had belonged to DORNOCH; and the new Parish of Tongue was established at that meeting of the Assembly in 1726. Kildonan, however, was given back to the Dornoch Presbytery on 18th May the following year, and on 19th May 1736, Assynt also was put again under the jurisdiction of the latter court. However, in September 1961 (only a few years ago, really), following approval by the General Assembly of the Church of Scotland, Dornoch and Tongue Presbytery united to become the 'Presbytery of Sutherland'. And the Rev. D. Macmillan of Aultnaharra, was appointed the first Moderator of the new Presbytery. This Presbytery is the largest in area in Britain, with ministers at Helmsdale, Brora, Golspie, Dornoch, Bonar Bridge, Rosehall, Lairg, Rogart, Lochinver, Scourie, Kinlochbervie, Tongue, Bettyhill, Melvich, Melness, and Aultnaharra. The only vacant charge is at Durness, and that is served by the minister from Kinlochbervie.

It was in October 1726, that the first Presbytery of Tongue met in Tongue. And the first statistical report of that parish gives the date of the renovation of the church as 1731. In many cases throughout Scotland, kirks have been entirely rebuilt except for a single aisle, containing the tombs of the founder's family. There is little doubt that these churches were arranged with a pulpit on the south wall; and the readers desk—the LATTRON— was in front of the pulpit. For the Lord's Supper, the table was set up usually on the long axis of the building. A sand-glass also formed part of the fixtures. At Tongue Church, the wooden

benches were made locally. Later on, pews to seat 520 worshippers were purchased by the congregation. The total cost of the
renovation was £208 odd and the work completed in less than
six months. The wages of a labourer was at the rate of 1s. and
two pecks of meal weekly, with 2s. to buy shoes. Tradesmen received 3s., with two pecks of meal weekly. (Those were the days?)

In 1788, and again in 1862, the church was repaired. At the
later date new doors were added, and in 1920 the pulpit was
lowered to the level of the adjoining window.

From an early date, the burial ground of the principal members of the Mackay family was at Tongue Church. In 1727 the
present vault was built over the graves of the earlier members of
the Mackay family. In 1907, a plaque with the following
inscription was placed on the vault:

> In the vault beneath this church are deposited the remains of the
> Right Hon. George, 3rd Baron Reay, 1748. The Hon. George
> Mackay of Skibo, 1782. The Hon. Sophia Aylmer, died 24th
> September 1866, wife of Charles Arthur Alymer and daughter of
> the Rt. Hon. Alexander, 8th Baron Reay, and other members of the
> Reay family. Erected in 1907 by the Rt. Hon. Donald James, 11th
> Baron Reay.

The Rev. William Mackay was minister from 1727 to 1728
only.

The Rev. Walter Ross was minister from 1730 to 1761.
During this time the '45 was in operation, and the function of the
church life of Tongue was greatly upset. It is generally believed
that as the Mackays were anti-Jacobite, the north of the county
was more or less free from any effects of this troublesome period.
The previous Rising of 1715 did not greatly effect the district.
In March 1746 in view of this 'unnatural rebellion', the Kirk
Session decided the Communion Services could not be held.
Another interesting item at this time, was that of the French ship
Hazard already mentioned, which, having been pursued from the
Moray coast through the Pentland Firth to the Kyle of Tongue,
the Frenchmen deliberately grounded near to the Narrows of
MELNESS. The *Sheerness* man-of-war, which had followed the
French ship remained in the deep water and fired shot after shot
at the stranded ship. The Frenchmen, believing they were among
friends, carried their cargo to the house of William Mackay of

Melness, where they remained overnight. Mr. Mackay's son, George, made arrangements to escort the Frenchmen (including 120 soldiers), to Inverness, where they hoped to join the army of Bonnie Prince Charlie. Meantime Lord Reay hearing of all this, laid a trap for them. Some were killed and the remainder taken prisoners. The French captain endeavoured to dispose of his gold, throwing the contents of his wooden boxes (containing about thirteen hundred pieces) in the sea. In Dunrobin Museum there can be seen samples of the gold pieces found in the Kyle of Tongue. This actually took place the day following the battle of Culloden at Culloden Moor, 16th April 1746, where the fate of the House of Stuart was sealed; but had the Frenchmen landed their valuable cargo at Inverness prior to the battle, who knows, the result might have been a victory for the Prince?

At the manse in Tongue can be seen one of the cannon balls fired by the *Sheerness*. On 1st May 1746, the Presbytery of Tongue sent an address to the ('bloody') Duke of Cumberland congratulating him on his victory at Culloden.

The Rev. John Mackay was minister from 1762 to his death in December 1768. At that time there was much martial blood amongst the inhabitants. Though Protestant, they were headstrong, and not at all inclined to submit to the minister's standard of Christian morals. Many of them had passed a wild life as soldiers on the continent, and had returned to their native parish, wild and reckless. Many had never entered a church and they usually avoided a minister. One of such men, when on his death bed, was persuaded by the Elder to accept a visit from the minister. When the minister came in, he found the old man half sitting, half reclining in his bed; and yet, amidst all the feebleness and decay of his old age, there was still in his look traces of the bold, fearless life he had lived. Beside him on his bed lay his big sword, which he never parted with day or night. 'I have sent for you, minister,' he said, 'in order you can give me some comfort as I lie here, a helpless, miserable dying wreck.' The minister quietly spoke to him of Death and of the only 'deliverer in death'. 'Death, do you think I care about death?' Then waving his sword about his head, he bent forward in his bed, shouting out, 'Death by the sword is the only death for a man'— and then fell back dead.

The Rev. William Mackenzie was minister from 1769 to 1806.

After the '45 rebellion, an economic change took place in the Highlands, and landlords came to accept as part of the inevitable order of things, that rents should rise at each re-setting. The rents on the Reay Estates were doubled between 1761 and 1792. The tenant eager for land had either to submit and pay to the best of his ability—or emigrate. Some of the tacksmen (rent collectors) acted in a humane manner towards their sub-tenants but the greater part behaved otherwise. Towards the end of the 1700's the sea fisheries along the northern coast of Sutherland were let to an Aberdeen company. Many of the local people hoping to augment their meagre earnings, entered into contract with the company. They did not have the necessary capital to buy boats or nets, so the company agreed to advance capital on the basis of two shares to the company and one share to the crew who, in turn were obliged to dispose of their fish at any price offered by the company. Outwith this legitimate fishing business, the company was in league with vessels engaged in smuggling contraband. This particular business was in the hands of a Lewis group. They demoralised themselves and all with whom they came in contact, as at every creek along the coast, large quantities of gin and brandy were openly discharged and disposed of by traders as far south as Inverness. It became common practice for drunkenness and fighting to take place during the Sabbath outside the church, where cattle were openly sold as worshippers left after service. The Presbytery and the minister Mr. Mackenzie had to take stern measures to suppress such heathen conduct. One of the chief offenders eventually became one of the most outstanding Elders in the congregation. He was 'born again'.

The Rev. Hugh Mackay Mackenzie became minister from 1806 to 1843. It was his father whom he succeeded. He was a Tongue man born in the village in 1771. The *Reay Fencibles* were raised in 1794, and while these men were serving in Ireland, another regiment of militia was raised which brought into its ranks all the able-bodied men of Tongue and district. Each regiment brought credit to its village and area, especially the *93rd Foot* (raised in 1800) who, whilst stationed at Cape Town formed themselves into a congregation, elected office-bearers and paid their own minister from their paltry wages. The example placed the parish of Tongue high in the estimation of all Christian people.

The Lord Reay of this period used questionable methods to raise soldiers from his estate to satisfy his personal interests. He was a degenerate son, who accidentally got the power to do so. Despite sound advice, he forced his estate to be sold and the large fortune from the sale he spent in London; so that his brother, Alexander, 8th Lord Reay, was left destitute.

Mr. Mackenzie was minister at Tongue at the period of the Disruption of 1843. He then adhered to the Free Church, but he was so infirm that his son, the Rev. William Mackenzie was at once appointed his colleague. The account of the two ministers of Tongue—father and son—attracted much attention. The family had occupied the manse for about eighty years. At the age of seventy-two the elder Mr. Mackenzie afflicted with asthma, had to leave the home and send his family to Thurso for the only accommodation he could get for himself and his son was a small room and bed-closet in a poor cottage, for which they paid four shillings weekly. The son was attacked by a fever and both died—the father on the 30th June, and the son on the 26th July 1845. To their blessed memory is erected a monument in Tongue churchyard. It was said at the time, that the memory of these two men would live fresh in the minds of the people of Tongue for generations to come. At the Disruption of the Church in 1843, all the people in the eastern district of the parish (about 1400 of them) adhered to the Free Church. The congregation at first worshipped in a tent. Churches were then built at Melness and Eriboll. The Established Church at Melness, being empty, was converted into a school; and later the proprietor gave the manse to the people.

According to church records of 1871, the 'tread of organised church life was resumed after a long and dreary gap of fifty-one years'. This had been caused by the great Sutherland Evictions at the end of the 18th century into the 19th century. The Rev. Mr. Sage was the seventh and last in succession of the missionaries appointed to officiate at ACHNESS. In one single day, this devout missionary with sixteen hundred of his people were evicted wholesale.

The Free Church continued to be supported by a majority within the parish of Tongue, but round about 1900 a section of the people formed a congregation of the United Free Church of Scotland. In 1929, the U.F. congregation joined with the Church of Scotland, with the Parish Church of Tongue as their principal place of worship.

In 1923 it was found necessary to extend the burial ground at Tongue, and so a piece of land to the north of the existing ground, between the manse burn and the public road was taken off the glebe in exchange for a piece of hill ground of twenty-five acres. The Heritors, or landowners, in the parish were obliged to hold in trust and maintain for the community the church, churchyard, manse and glebe, and to pay the minister's stipend. They had the right to pews in the church for themselves, their families, tenants and servants. By the Church of Scotland (Property and Endowments) Act of 1925, the buildings held by the Heritors were transferred to the General Trustees of the Church of Scotland.

Regarding the pews, apart from the owners enjoying traditional rights as I have said, many local families also have rights to the square pews, whilst they are living in the parish. Outside the churchyard, and on the wall by the road as you enter the gates there is a notice board, which reads:

> The Church of Scotland, St. Andrew's, Tongue; worship 11.30 a.m.
> The present church was built in 1724 (1728?) on the site of two former churches, and is the burial place of the Reay family, chieftain of the Clan Mackay.
> The Church is always open to visitors . . .

Inside the Sunday School room (the right wing) there has been inserted into the wall, a stone, from the original building— part of the Reay tombstone. Over the door of the right wing (south) on the lintel is the inscription 1680.

And so from details I have managed to gather together, I conclude the history and description of this most interesting church . . . Tongue Church.

The present minister is the Rev. Alfred McClintock, B.D., living at St. Andrew's Manse, Tongue. He has been at Tongue since August 1967 and his parish includes Tongue, Melness, Skerray, and Eriboll. I am indebted to Mr. McClintock for much of this information.

This church at Tongue may well be considered as one of the pearls of the north.

*   *   *

We have now come a far cry from Inverness and Dingwall. We have much further to go, and much more to see; west of Tongue, down the north-west coast from Durness and Cape Wrath to Laxford and on to Kylesku Ferry.

It is therefore better to make all that the subject of another chapter.

*   *   *

I have already remarked on the spaciousness of Sutherland; in fact it is a place where instead of putting out bread for the birds, you put out shoulders of venison for the eagles! One might say the Highlands is a country where that great visualiser Lloyd George saw dawn break over a land fit for heroes? In the early days, the roads were rough, narrow and grassy: the grass often gave the sump of your car an overdue wipe!

The tourist to the Highlands is attracted by the beauty of the beaches, and more often than not, seeks the sun and the sea. But we do well to lift up our eyes to the hills; they can give refreshment and health to those who are obliged to spend their working days in the towns. 'Mountains', said Ruskin, 'are the beginning and end of all scenery.' The birds sing sweeter, the flowers bloom brighter and the burns sparkle with more silver, in the bracing atmosphere of the hills.

Over the centuries the people of the Highlands have moved through many valleys, and Faith was the magnet which attracted all to the worship of the Almighty! Truly they are fortunate in their heritage. This bracing climate, pure air and the mountains are all around for those who care to enjoy same.

CHAPTER 3

WESTWARDS FROM TONGUE

LEAVING Tongue for the west is a delightful run round both sides of the majestic silver sweep of the Kyle, with a great deal of foliage to be seen, more than is usual in these parts, then crossing six miles of moor, known as the Mhoine (this road was originally made by the Duke of Sutherland in 1830) we come to the hamlet, Hope at the northern end of Loch Hope which is fed by the Strathmore river, with Ben Hope (3040 feet) towering inland. This mountain is noted for its rare alpines. Another mile and we find ourselves gazing down at about 700 feet on Loch Eriboll—a 10-mile sea loch—which to my mind is one of the prettiest anywhere around the north-west. I believe there are potash deposits around the loch. There are few crofting communities *en route* to Durness. Turning round the head of the loch at the small Polla hamlet, the ground drops almost to loch level; and we amble along regardless of traffic or Time. The scenery met with in the north-west and the general tranquility seem to give wings to Time. The next 'port of call' is Laid, followed closely by Portnancon—again two wee hamlets; the former just three or four cottages have wind-mills in their grounds for pumping water from their wells. At Portnancon there is still a good road down to the old pier which, in former days, was often used by fishing boats seeking shelter, for the deep sea loch of Eriboll is the safest anchorage on the north coast. About a quarter of a mile before coming to the pier turn-off, should you look closely at the roadside you will see two small heaps of stones which lead down a few steps to an ancient underground cavern, which leads about a quarter of a mile under the earth. It is supposed to have been a smuggling cave long ago. I have been in it for a short distance with a torch, but one needs to have old clothes on for it is a narrow, low, damp passage. From here it is not far till you come to the outskirts of DURNESS (accent on last syllable), a somewhat scattered village (pop. 400) on a promontory One passes many pretty houses, mostly with B. and B. signs up in the summer, bearing attractive names; one I particularly noticed CEOL NA MARA ('song of the sea'; or 'music of the sea'). Continuing along, one comes to SMOO CAVE, a big tourist attraction, being part of the odd architecture of the cliffs created by the endless pounding of wind and waves. Near by is a very snug, cosy, small hotel (Smoo Cave Hotel) looked after by Arthur and Molly Lewis, who charmingly attend to your comfort and needs. A little further on is a very nice, attractive café (The White Heather) with such a pleasing cheerful lady, Mrs. Clark, in command; you can also pick up a lot of souvenirs of the district here.

Smoo Cave takes its name from the Gaelic, meaning 'largest'. In olden times it was named 'SMJUGA' by the sea-rovers, for the name means a narrow cleft to creep through. You get to the cave by a zig-zag footpath. No charge is made for inspecting it. The cave is a limestone cavern with three compartments; the entrance is 53 feet high and resembles a Gothic Arch, with high spreading pillars. The first compartment (200 feet long and 110 feet wide), has a vaulted roof with vertical aperture to the open air above; its second compartment is 70 feet long, 30 feet wide and it also has a vaulted roof with vertical aperture, contains a deep pool and receives a waterfall of 80 feet in leap. The third compartment is 120 feet long, 8 feet wide and from twelve to forty feet high. This cannot be seen without a torch. A small pebbly bay adjacent to the cavern, serves only for small rowing boats. The waterfall mentioned comes from the waters of the Smoo Burn, and when this burn is in flood, tongues of swirling vapour rise upwards from this cauldron.

In ancient days it was believed these caverns, or 'black holes', were tenanted by evil spirits and formed the entrance to Hell. It is said that yet another cavern can be reached from the small third compartment, but with great difficulty. According to local tradition the first Lord Reay, when young, had entered it. His boatman became so nervous that he attempted to hurry back for 'he was assailed by the spirits of the place' and was almost overcome with fear; but hearing a cock crow, he took courage and went back for his passengers. There are a number of weird caverns in the north-west of Sutherland, but Smoo Cave appears to take precedence. There are no stalactites; only the slippery limestone, green with stranded weed; no fairy piper, only the harsh gossip of gulls vibrating eerily from unseen ledges in the watery dank.

It is only a matter of a few minutes by car, before we enter DURNESS. Still basically Gaelic (its name means 'The Deer's Point'), Durness is a very pleasant unspoiled village and has strong tourist appeal; it has good salmon, sea-trout and brown trout fishing in the district. On entering, you come into a large square with a tidily kept green in the centre; and it has a very convenient clock at the roadside; good stores and hotel. In fact it seems Durness lacks for nothing. I like Durness; the houses are strung along the roadside like a necklace that takes on a brightness from the sun, glinting on the small croft fields. Two roads lead out of Durness; one to the left takes you to Rhiconich (branching off there to the Kinlochbervie district), Laxford, Scourie and Kylesku Ferry; straight through to BALNAKIEL— where there is an Arts and Craft village—Balnakiel bay and an ancient ruined church.

Starting at the end of this road, Balnakiel bay is an immense 2-mile sweep of white sand with sparkling blue waters rolling in with an outlook to the Atlantic and Faraid Head jutting out at the point. The waters are shallow, and one can wade out quite a distance safely. Here, you are far away from the madding crowd. (I can only liken it to another wide bay in the north-west, near Lochinver, at Achmelvich; but this beauty spot is spoiled in the summer by caravans and campers dotted right down almost to the water's edge. At Balnakiel, these temporary homes are situate more inland.)

Here standing right beside the bay is an ancient burial ground with its roofless church of great antiquity. It contains the resting place of the Gaelic bard Rob Dunn and other notables. It was a Catholic church built in 1619 on the site of an older one which was attached to Dornoch monastery. Doubtless long before this date there was a still older cell of the Celtic church on this spot. The ruined walls and the crow-stepped gables are all ivy-covered. Inside there still stands an old circular font. Close by the church is a bald mansion-house of Balnakiel which was once the residence of the Bishops of Caithness who came to hunt the deer; and this residence later on came into the hands of the Reay family. Now it is a farm house.

The memorial to the Reay Gaelic Bard, Rob Dunn (or Doun) otherwise Robert Mackay of Durness is a very imposing one. The tall sculptured erection was put up at the expense of a few of his countrymen, ardent admirers of his native talent and extraordinary genius in 1827. There are suitable inscriptions in English, Gaelic and Latin around the monument. It is still well preserved; and all lovers of Celtic literature will stand before it in deep reverence. Although he could neither read nor write, he composed Celtic poems and melodies which were kept alive by tradition and handed down by word of mouth from generation to generation. He was born in Strathmore at Altnacaillich at the foot of Ben Hope near the ruined tower of Dornadilla. He inherited the gift of poetry from his mother. His wife, Janet, had a musical ear also and a good voice. Although he was not actively engaged in the Jacobite '45 rebellion, he was what one might call a 'Jacobite poet' and composed two political songs, one praising Prince Charlie, and one on the shame of the Act which forbade the wearing of Highland dress. He was a fine shot, and his gun was so dear to him, that when he was growing too old to tramp the hills, he filled the barrel with deer tallow, climbed leisurely to the top of Ben Spionnaidh, taking a fond farewell of his beloved weapon, and buried it among the summit rocks so no other hand should henceforth touch it. He died in 1778, aged only sixty-four. He was, at heart, a clean-living man and sang the praises of religion; in fact he was appointed Assessor of Session in his native parish. His poetry reflected the social life of his time in songs of the shieling, the harvest, the wool-walking and the drove road. His love songs were pure and tender. It was only fifty years after his death before the first edition of his poems was printed. It is indeed a handsome monument that was erected.

Before leaving this time-honoured burial ground, I must tell of a strange tomb, built into the south wall to the memory of one Donald MacMurchey and the inscription above it can, after the passage of all these years, just be made out, viz.:

> Donald Makmurchov heir lyis lo,
> Vas il to his friend, var to his fo,
> Trve to his maister in veird and vo. 1623.

He was a remarkable man. He was a MacLeod from Assynt (near Lochinver) but was always known as Donald MacMhurchaidh Mhic Iain Mhor—or translated 'son of Murdoch, son of big John'. As a reward for some service he did for the chief of the Mackays, he was given the life-tenancy of much land near Hope in the parish of Durness and was therefore a vassal of Mackay. He settled at Hielam where one can ferry across Loch Eriboll. The tombstone inscription 'trve to his maister' must obviously refer to Mackay. Notwithstanding he had a dreadful reputation, a 'Rob Roy' of the north, with at least eighteen murders to his credit! Accordingly he had many enemies, and he learnt that some of them, daring not to touch him whilst he was alive, talked amongst themselves of taking vengeance on his dead body. At that time, 1619, the Balnakiel church was being built, so he used his friendship with the chief of the Mackays to have a place prepared for him in the wall, where no foe could get at his corpse, or trample over his grave. He is supposed to have paid a thousand marks (about £50) for this 'privilege', and tradition has it that all that side of the church was built at Donald's expense. By then he was getting an old man. A new minister, Rev. Alex Munro came to the parish in 1620. About three years later Mr. Munro was at Tongue, which was then the residence of the chiefs. The then chief, the son of the former chief (the 'maister') named previously had a premonition and gave Mr. Munro an armed guard to escort him on his homeward journey. Coming to Hielam he thought it his duty to call on Donald whom he had heard was very ill, thinking that a few words of the gospel might yet affect a change in his heart and save him from eternal punishment that was surely awaiting him on his death. But the old man was still fierce even on his death-bed, and only sheer lack of strength prevented him from laying violent hands on his minister; who in sadness left and journeyed on. Donald had two sons, wicked but not quite so courageous

father. The minister was not long away when they came
the house. Donald ordered them to go after him, kill him
ing back his heart. They hurried out and soon caught up
with Mr. Munro, expecting to fall upon one man alone; but
when they spotted the guard of the chief's men, they were afraid
to act. Instead they killed a sheep, cut out its heart and brought
it back to their dying father. But the old die-hard recognised it
for a sheep's heart, but did not wish to chastise his sons, and merely
said, 'I always knew the Munro's were cowards, and no wonder
now I see its sheep's hearts they have.' He died shortly after he
had spoken those words, and was duly buried by the Rev.
Munro according to his wishes in an upright position in the wall
of Balnakiel Church. What a story; what an end. It may be
mentioned that one of Mr. Munro's descendants became a
President of the United States of America, who promulgated
the Munroe Doctrine.

So we say farewell to beautiful Balnakiel bay and its ancient
church. Retracing our steps to Durness, about a mile away, we
pass the Balnakiel Arts and Crafts village. You cannot mistake
it for it is fenced around, and if there were a man in uniform at
the entrance you would say it was a secret Naval or Air Force
Establishment. It was, in fact, an Air Force personnel base in the
last war. All the buildings have this concrete-type appearance
and could now be improved by some colour splashed around.
There are seventeen occupied buildings including a fine artist's
studio, set up by the talented Miss Kathleen Wylie; she also has
a studio in Edinburgh in High Street near St. Giles, and one at
CARNAN in South Uist, just south of the island of Benbecula.
The new car-ferry steamer calls in at South Uist at Lochboisdale,
and to the north this Macbrayne steamer calls in at Lochmaddy
in North Uist. So her studio is easily accessible. A nominal
rent of £5 a year is paid for these various buildings. This village
should in time prove to be a very valuable asset to Durness.
Included in its confines is an hotel, the Far North Hotel, a bakery
and a coffee house. Apart from all this, and tweed shops, there
is a Worm Farm! operated by Mr. Frank Lynam. This 46-
year-old Englishman's *piéce de résistance* is soil reclamation.
Wriggley's Worm Farm is the correct designation, and he is
producing worms for an assault on the north's one and half
million acres of peat. He is known as an ecologist. He has

prepared the large building for breeding worms, and has to import worms from the south to help in the process. Apart from

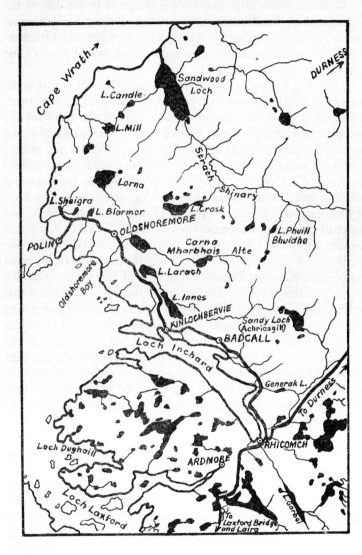

peat, he maintains he could turn all the unsightly colliery bings seen near all the coal pits in Midlothian and England, into productive areas, as well as developing waste lands. His idea is to put life

into what is regarded as barren waste. And worms, he says, are
the answer.

We now leave DURNESS, taking the road to the left at the
Green, making for Rhiconich (Re-co-nick) and the Kinlochbervie
district, Laxford and Scourie; and as this area has many interesting places and features, the map reproduced should serve of use
to new voyagers to these parts.

(However before leaving Durness I would mention that at the
1968 Mod held in Dunoon, 14-year-old Fiona MacRae of Durness,
who suffers from rheumatoid arthritis entered the Mod for the
first time and won the James C. MacPhee Memorial Trophy, the
premier award for beginners aged 13 to 16. Well done, Fiona.)

Barely two miles along at Keodale Farm there is signposted on
the right 'Cape Wrath' and 'Cape Wrath Hotel' (an imposing
building with a beautiful position looking on to the golden Kyle
of Durness), and it is only a matter of a few minutes before you
come to the end of this road where a ferry-boat takes you across
to Achiemore and the ten-miles of tortuous hilly road, with one
small river to ford, to Cape Wrath lighthouse; one of the most
inaccessible places in Britain. A sketch of this is shown at the
heading of this chapter. The Kyle of Durness is so shallow that
only a small motor boat can be used as a ferry, carrying pedestrians
and cyclists. The small pier at this Durness shore end is only in
use at high tide; at other times the boat has to ground on the
sands a yard or so from dry land, and then the stalwart ferryman
Donald Morison carries you pick-a-back to his boat, taking you
by mini-bus on the far side to an untouched wilderness of rocks,
rushing streams and utterly secluded beaches and the highest cliffs
on the north-west mainland. The ferry boat leaves about 9.30
a.m. and at frequent intervals thereafter throughout the day. The
fare (exclusive of ferry) is 12s. 6d. return. This ferry-minibus
operation is conducted by father and son Hugh who drives the
bus to the lighthouse which latter directs the traffic round the
'turning-point' which Cape Wrath means in Norse *hvarf*. Its
light is more than 200,000 candle power, and a year's supply of
paraffin is kept in stock. Should there be dense mist, then its
foghorn comes into play, and should that not be enough, its
radio-beacon gives the sailor opportunity to check his position.
What a sight this must have been when Norway's King Haco
took his fleet of over a hundred craft round this cape 400 years

ago to fight the Battle of Largs, which he lost, and with it control of the Hebrides.

Life on a lighthouse must at best be a very boring existence, and I am reminded of the enterprising keeper who brought a horse with him, hoping for occasional rides on the rocks! The poor old thing died of lack of exercise and its epitaph may be seen today over its grave:

> Here lies a lighthouse-keeper's horse
> Which was not ridden much, of course,
> How patiently it waited for
> The lighthouse-keeper's leave on shore!

This grim bulwark against the Atlantic storms, 523 feet high is the most north-westerly point of the Scottish mainland.

We now continue on the main road, known as the Gualin road to Rhiconich, and about four miles from Rhiconich is a big house, Gualin House, facing the famous salmon river, the Dionard river which empties into the Kyle of Durness, having travelled many miles from the interior via Strath Dionard, Loch Dionard and Meall Horn, (2548 feet) going towards the Strath More area. On the way you pass a specially built water-trough, with clear, clear mountain-stream water flowing in, and over the trough is the inscription dated 1883:

> As a mark of gratitude and respect
> to the inhabitants of Durness and
> Eddrachillis for their hospitality
> while protecting this road, this inscription
> is placed over this well by their humble servant
> Peter Lawson
> Surveyor.

We now soon come to catch a glimpse of Loch Inchard, and then to Rhiconich Hotel standing right at the head of this extremely pretty loch. Nearby the hotel you will invariably see three notable characters—donkeys; Jack and Jill and their new baby. They are very tame and love being stroked, and will poke their heads into your car, trying to nibble the steering wheel—and any chocolate you may have handy. The road to the KINLOCHBERVIE district turns off to the right not many yards before reaching the hotel. We will now take it. The mails brought by Michael's van from Lairg to Durness are transferred to Charlie's mail van at

Rhiconich; those for Scourie *en route* from Lairg, change hands at Laxford Bridge. Oh! yes, all these postal affairs are carried out and distributed with clockwork precision—unless of course snow-drifts hold up everything or one of the drivers has measles! The same clockwork procedure takes place all through these Highland districts, and it is hoped the Government sees to it that both the small Highland post offices and the mail drivers are well paid—for it must all be worked to a schedule, and in the winter it is none too easy. And everyone connected is doing an essential job.

Continuing on this lovely stretch of wide, macadamised road skirting the loch, the first village of any size is Badcall-Inchard joining with Achrisgill. It has a beautiful view over the loch with Foinaven 2980 feet and Arkle 2580 feet in the distance. There are two or three lovely trim croft houses down near the water's edge which I covet, but these 'great, little folk' will never sell-out their old homes. Up on the main road there is a most up-to-date well-equipped general store—'London Stores'.

Pressing on we soon drop down into KINLOCHBERVIE, the real hub of this north western area, for it is a big fishing port with two piers. On the way and standing on a little knoll is the war memorial to those who fell in the first and second wars; thirty-two names in all, mostly from the Argyll and Sutherland Highlanders and the Royal Navy. Beneath the column are the words 'More than conquerors'. At the back, the memorial looks on to a small loch, Loch Innes. Above the piers at Kinlochbervie there stands a fine modern hotel, the Garbet Hotel, delightfully situated over this fishing harbour Loch Clash.

There is a big fishing fleet operating at Kinlochbervie, and it has brought much gain to the village of population 450. The fish is landed at the Loch Clash pier, where there is an up-to-date ice-plant.

You can spend many an hour on a pier, watching the fishing fleet coming in, the unloading, packing into cases, weighed and iced and labelled for despatch to the buyers in Aberdeen, Hull and as far as Billingsgate in London: apart from listening to the special jargon these fisherfolk use. The boats at anchor are clearly reflected in the mirror of a calm, placid water. The scene conjures up two thoughts—peace at making harbour safely, and security. Peace which is an experience foreign to many of us today.

The fishing industry is of increasing importance in Scotland

and particularly in Sutherland. It is not widely enough known that Lochinver (south of Kinlochbervie by some 16 miles or so) and Kinlochbervie together land more fish, and indeed, separately land more fish, than any other port in Scotland except Fraserburgh and Aberdeen. They are the two most important inshore ports in Scotland—more than £1m. worth of fish is annually landed. Both these places are being developed even more, with money from the government. At Kinlochbervie the entrance channel is to be deepened by at least ten feet, and when this is completed it will mean that the large fleet of seine-net boats operating out of Kinlochbervie will be able to use Loch Bervie at all states of the tide. At low spring tide the water in the channel is only four or five feet deep. The Grosvenor Estate own the piers, and their subsidiary company Messrs. Pulfords (Scotland) Ltd.—reference to which is made in a subsequent chapter—are the local fish salesmen. They purpose building up a viable community at Kinlochbervie, by further improving the port faciletes and to attract the fishermen to make their homes there. At present these men live away on the east coast mostly in Banffshire and so have to travel all that distance by road in their own cars at week-end leave; which is generally from Thursday evening to Sunday night, for the boats never set sail again till the early hours of a Monday. Messrs. Pulfords (who are also allied with the Sutherland Transport and Trading Co. Ltd.—see later chapter also) are behind another project forming the Kinlochbervie Shell Fish Co. Ltd. who are operating a 40 feet boat, the *Silver Cord* in an experiment in lobster farming and shell fish marketing. This is a revolutionary experiment in lobster fishing. There is a team of five ex-divers, led by a Lt.-Cdr. Futcher, who have started up this prototype farm, the idea being to improve the natural surrounds for lobsters when they are most vulnerable to attack from predators, especially when they are shedding their shells. The team will provide artificial cover for them when they are at this vulnerable stage, and thus hope to keep the population of adult lobsters in maximum numbers. Cdr. Futcher himself has had many years diving experience all over the world, and was in charge of diving operations at Lake Coniston after Donald Campbell's fatal speed-boat accident there. Once this scheme gets under way, the diving team will provide artificial cover in selected areas, so these 'farms' can then be cropped on a systematic basis. If this completely new idea is successful, Kinlochbervie will be leading the world in lobster farming. According to scientists, the stretch of coast from Dounreay to Ullapool is the largest area of underfished lobster ground left in Scotland.

I now come to relate a very sad story for Kinlochbervie; the saddest that has befallen the community for many a long year—the loss of the Banff fishing boat *Refleurir* on Wednesday the 3rd January 1968 with a crew of five on board, just outside the harbour during a gale-driven blizzard in the North Minch. It was a tragedy that swept over the entire district. The *Refleurir* lies wrecked at the bottom of the sea. The 58 feet boat made her last radio call when she was only ninety minutes from harbour, where she was due at 1 p.m. Then there was silence; and as darkness fell, fears mounted for the 50-year-old skipper, George West of Gardenstown and his crew. The boats that had already berthed in harbour were virtually locked in from going out to help, for the tide was then too low for their boats to sail through. The Lochinver lifeboat was launched in the gale. The R.A.F. said they would send an aircraft to help search at first light if weather permitted. The *Refleurir* put to sea at 5 a.m. on the 3rd January, when the North Minch was described as being like a mill-pond. Subsequently the weather became violent and atrocious and it was thought the boat would have sought shelter in one of the many bays around the coast. The following morning grief was tinged with frustration when all hope for the crew was abandoned. As the boats were unable to get out, the men felt they were robbed of at least a slim attempt of saving their fellow men; and for the time being, until the tide was suitable, they could only wonder frantically if some or all of that crew were hanging grimly on to life. Twenty-five boats were in harbour, because the rocky entrance was so shallow for them to get out. The next morning there was still a little armada of twenty-five boats, and a Shackleton aircraft from Kinloss combing the area, and coastguards and volunteers, some sixty in all, were searching the rugged coastline—but in vain. Oil flecks and bubbles were spotted five miles west of the entrance to Loch Inchard. It was the *Refleurir's* first trip of the New Year. Wives and sweethearts mourned behind drawn curtains all along the Banffshire coast. The disaster left six sons and daughters fatherless. Two young women who were married only a year have been made widows; a pretty girl who was to be married six months later lost her fiancé. This heartbreak story—so common with fisherfolk—was shared by all along the north-east coast. Over a hundred fishermen together with a host of people of the district, attended the memorial service for the drowned men, which was held in the Church of Scotland; Mr. Mathew Hopper their present missionary at the Loch Clash Deep Sea Mission conducted the service; and the local organist Mr. John A. Morrison rendered appropriate sacred music. Most of these fishermen belong to the Close Brethren, the religious sect whose members keep their own counsel and hide themselves and their grief behind closed doors. At this sad time in Gardenstown, a little village clinging to the side of a huge black cliff like a limpet, the streets were empty and silent. No dogs barked, no youngsters shouted. Only the sound of grey waves pounding on the jagged rocks provided a link with reality. One old man at the harbour stood facing the cruel sea, and said, 'Fisherfolk expect this sort of thing. God gives, and He takes away.' That was all; he said no more. Doors remained closed to any knocking. The small fishing fleet from this wee place is the most modern of fleets, and earns nearly £1 million in the course of a single year. Yet in Gardenstown, they show the world no joy when times are good —and no sadness when tragedy strikes. Another old man there said he hoped the men would be found, but, he added, 'they are in God's hands'. Like the old man at the harbour, he had nothing more to say.

There is another 'Cruel Sea' disaster which I may recall in connection with the wreck of the armed yacht *Iolaire* just outside Stornoway harbour fifty years ago. This terrible tragedy occurred at 1.55 a.m. on New Year's morning 1919, when 205 Lewismen going home on leave (the 1st World War) were lost when the boat piled up on to the reef of the Beasts of Holm just outside the harbour. On Hogmanay night 7.30 p.m. 1918, two hundred and sixty Lewismen were heading home from Kyle of Lochalsh. In full sight of crowds waiting at the harbour to weclome them, the *Iolaire* suddenly struck the reef and sank; and in one blow the major part of an entire generation of island men was lost. This was one of the worst disasters ever to hit a small Scottish community. Lewis was swept with grief; and it was communion week in Stornoway.

Following this appalling disaster, the Highlanders produced
an impressive, sad song; but so far as can be traced it was never
printed—merely handed down by word of mouth. The Gaelic
rendering was composed by one Hector MacKinnon (1886–1954)
from Bernera, Harris. The B.B.C. chance to have a recording
of it in their archives, and for those 'who have the Gaelic', I
reproduce the eight verses. As to the slightly different poem in
English there is no record; but I heard it sung at a ceilidh up
in N.W. Sutherland some years ago and later on, after much
research, managed to obtain it—again by word of mouth. It is
a most moving, sorrowful song. Here, then, is *The Wreck of the
Iolaire*.

1. On a cliff across the bay
    Just two miles from Stornoway
    Stands a cairn of stones, above a jagged reef;
    It's a tragic souvenir
    Of that cold and sad New Year
    When a host of Lewis sailors came to grief.

2. In the Queen of all the Isles
    Everyone wore welcome smiles
    For the armistice was signed across the foam;
    Young and old were full of cheer
    Celebrating this New Year.
    For the boys who'd been at war, were coming home.

3. Happy parents lined the pier
    For they thought their sons were near
    Till the mailboat *Sheila* tied up at the dock;
    Then the dreadful news went round
    That their brave sons had been drowned
    And the *Iolaire* was wrecked upon the rocks.

4. Some were standing on the deck
    Of that sad, ill-fated wreck
    When she struck the cruel rocks, so near the shore;
    Screams and cries soon rent the air
    Here and there a dying prayer
    For the friends and families they'd see no more.

5. Of two hundred men or more
    Only sixty reached the shore
    The 'flower' of Lewis perished in the foam;
    These boys who'd come so far

Through the dangers of the war
The irony of Fate denied them home.

6. In the history of the Lews
Never did such dreadful news
Bring those brave God-fearing people to despair;
Boy's who'd fought upon the sea
That their country might be free
Lost their lives in that disaster *Iolaire*.

And now for the Gaelic rendering:

1. Nuair dh' fhosgail i na ròpan
   'Sa sheòl i as a' Chaol
   An *Iolair* 'si bu luaithe,
   Dh' aindeoin luasgan muir no gaoth
   O 's iomadh oigear fuasgailt bh' innt'
   An uair sin nach do shaoil
   Cho goirid 'sa bha chuairt aca
   Gann uairean anns an t-saoghal.

2. Bha h-uile ni dol fabharrach
   Gus 'n tainig meadhoin oidhch'
   Sin bhuail i air na creagan grànnda
   Bu neo-bhaidheil grùnnd
   Fhuair an *Iolair* buille bhàis
   'S na ràin a' tighinn bho com
   'S ged bha fearann lamh rithe
   Rathad tearnaidh cha robh ann.

3. Cha b' fhada sheas a cliathaichean
   Ri Biastan biorach Huilm
   An *Iolair* chaidh i sios leotha
   Bha'n oidhche fiadhaich doirbh
   B'e sud an sealladh cianail
   Faicinn ciadan ghillean calm
   A' stri ri'm beatha dhion ann
   Am measg siantan agus stoirm.

4. An oidche ud ann an Steornabhagh
   O chruinnich móran sluaigh
   'S duil ac' ri na h-oigearan
   Air fòrladh bho'n a' chuan
   Bha athraichean is màthraichean
   Is pàisdean beag gun ghruaim
   Bha peathraichean is bràithrean ann
   Son fàilt chur orr' 'san uair.

5. Mo chreach mo chreach 'sa thainig
    Chaidh an gàirdeachas gu tùrs
    Mun d' éirich grian na màireach
    'S iomadh gàirdean bha gun lùths
    Chaidh naigheachd feadh an àit
    Gun robh na h-armuinn ris robh dùil
    Air cladach tir an àraich
    Air am bàthadh anns a' ghrùnnd.

6. Nach iomadh caileag àluinn
    Tha leannan gràidh 'ga dìth
    Piuthar chaill a bràthair
    Chaill am màthair mac a cuim
    'S iomadh bean an tràth so
    Tha le pàisde beag a' caoidh
    Na dh' fhalbh 's nach till gu bràth rithe
    'S an osann cràidh cha chluinn.

7. Tha Leodhas is na Hearadh
    An diugh fo sprochd 's fo ghruaim
    'S iomadh cridh' tha leòint ann
    Agus bròn air iomadh gruaidh
    'Se dithis b' aithn dhòmhsa
    Dhe na seoid a chaidh thoirt uainn
    MacNeill Choinnich as an t-Ob
    'S Mac Dhomhnaill 'san Taobh Tuath.

8. Ach criochnaichidh mi an t-òran so
    Bho'n sgoideach cainnt mo bheul
    Cha bhàrd gus deanamh oran mi
    O's brònach tha mo sgeul
    Ach innseadh na tha beo an diugh
    Do'n òigridh a thig 'nar déidh
    Mar thachair dha na seoid
    A bha air bord an *Iolair*.

*   *   *

    After leaving Kinlochbervie we rise a little over the moor
coming down to little places called Oldshoremore, Polin, Blairmore and finally to Sheigra where the road ends. I have spent
most pleasant times at Oldshoremore in one of Mr. Kenny
MacLeod's bungalows. He and his sister live in a beautiful home
'Smithy House', and have been very enterprising in putting up

several stone-built bungalows and chalets, all with modern conveniences,. for renting. They see to it, you have every comfort. It is not always you can get whilst on holiday, fresh *creamy* warm milk straight from the cow, on your doorstep early each morning, and fresh eggs too. This lovely little spot has a sheltered mile-long stretch of sandy beach, completely safe and so private. The Gaelic name for Oldshoremore is *asher* meaning 'old shore'. There is a very well-kept little cemetery on a raised piece of ground overlooking the bay, and one day whilst gazing around I was very much taken by the following verse written on a tombstone in memory of a 23-year-old girl, Isabella Duncan, who died 26th March 1894:

> Remember me as you pass by
> As ye are now, so once was I;
> As I am now, so must ye be,
> Prepare in time to follow me.

Should you want a moderate afternoon's walk, there is a rough road turning off near Sheigra and Blairmore which will take you to Sandwood Bay—another pearl of beauty. To visit its isolation is to come to understand where local legends of mermaids get their credibility. The story of the Sandwood sailor goes something as follows: Sandwood bay is a seven-mile stretch of sand and dunes about five miles south of Cape Wrath. It is completely deserted. There is no road, or even a footpath between the bay and the lighthouse and this area has since long ago been called the 'Land of the Mermaids'. Late one summer afternoon before the second world war, a crofter from Oldshoremore, set out with a horse and cart to gather driftwood. He and his son were the only human beings on the beach as it grew dark. Suddenly the figure of a sailor in uniform appeared from nowhere and commanded them to leave his property alone. Terrified they dropped their load of wood and fled. Sometime later on, a farmer from Kinlochbervie was searching for some of his sheep in that self-same area with three local men. It was getting dark and the moon came out, when they saw the outline of a man on the rocks. Thinking it might be another of their village pals they went towards the figure, but as they drew near they realised he was a stranger who looked like a sailor, and as they watched, he disappeared amongst the rocks. Several weeks later there was a severe storm off the coast there, and an Irish vessel went aground at Sandwood bay. A number of bodies were washed up on the beach, and one of them was recognised by the four Kinlochbervie men as the sailor they had seen amongst the rocks, for he was a heavily built black-whiskered man, such as they had so closely observed before.

About fifteen years later, when three Edinburgh men staying in a B. and B. house nearby to Sandwood Bay, decided to have a picnic there, and whilst halfway through, they felt they were being watched. On top of a hill was this mysterious sailor, who fled when they shouted out. They ran after him but he had vanished leaving no signs of footprints. This was in broad daylight, remember. Now here is another peculiar 'twist'—if you can call it such, for I heard of a visitor and his friend fishing in the bay only two years ago. Suddenly they heard a shout and looking up they saw a very tall six-foot odd man standing knee deep in the waves. He, too, was heavily built. As he was waving and shouting vigorously, they hurried along and saw he was in seaman's uniform. Just before they came up to him, he vanished into thin air, although the water at that spot was so very shallow! The next time I am up there, I shall take a walk to Sandwood Bay . . . but not alone!

*   *   *

Before leaving this charming part of the north-west, I must tell you of a story concerning a young fellow, Calum, who was working as a handy man with a crofter in Kinlochbervie. He went along one day to a farmer at the south of Loch Eriboll asking for a job. 'I thought you were working with a Mr. Mackay near Kinlochbervie' the farmer said. 'I was, but I left him', Calum replied. 'And why did you leave him?' he was asked. 'It's a long story, sir,' the lad said. 'But long story or not, I must know the reason,' said the farmer. And so the boy explained. 'You see, sir, when I went to Mr. Mackay's there was only he and his wife and their old granny. A little while after being there, the old cow died, and I was sent over to the stores at Durness for salt; and for three months we fed on salt beef. Later, a pig died and again I went for salt, and we were eating pork for weeks. After that an old sheep died, and the same thing happened; salt and more salt. Last night the granny

died, and I was asked to go and get more salt. And so
And you'll now know the reason why.' The Kinlochberv
is owned by the Exrs of Mrs. L. H. Neilson (Garbet Hotel
the Ardmore district by Lt.-Gen. E. A. Osborne, C.B., D.S.O.
We now carry on from Rhiconich, making for Laxford Bridge,
Scourie and Kylesku Ferry. We pass by the turn off to Ardmore
(mentioned in the Clearances chapter) and Skerricha another wee
hamlet down to the sea, to Laxford, which is just a bridge with
the Duchess of Westminster's factor's house there, lying secluded
and pretty beside Loch Laxford. Turning right, is the road to
Scourie. When I was last over there, the road was under heavy
reconstruction, but possibly by now, it may be reasonably
passable. You pass through typical West Highland scenery.
Before reaching Scourie, there is a road on the right leading to the
village of Tarbet from where you can take a small boat across to
Sutherland's most famous island, HANDA, the bird sanctuary.
The island is uninhabited except for the raucous music of kitti-
wakes, razorbills, fulmars, guillemots and many others in their
thousands. Ornithologists can stay in an old bothy on the island,
whilst exploring. The cliffs of Handa, some 300 feet sheer, are
of a rusty-looking sandstone, stratified in horizontal shelves,
eroded into tier upon tier of balconies, all packed with vociferous
birds—a veritable snow-storm of flying fowl. Throughout the
long day, tumult reigns supreme, and when one suddenly dis-
turbs all these creatures it is like a feather bed being shaken.
Around Handa there are also seals, porpoises and basking sharks;
all having a great time. Handa once supported seven families
and was ruled by a 'queen'. The island was evacuated after the
potato famine in 1845. One of its legendary heroes was Iain
Beag who slew Judge Morrison, the hated representative of
James VI in the Outer Hebrides.

Reluctantly leaving Handa, we come to SCOURIE, a small
village with a very good fishing hotel; and then take the 11-mile
tortuous narrow road to Kylesku Ferry. Although only 11 miles
it will take you one hour motoring; and in it you see wonderful
scenery and bays notably Badcall and Eddrachillis. The latter is
particularly beautiful with its myriads of islets; and nearing the
ferry at Kylestrome the home of Lady Mary Grosvenor, you see
the many-peaked form of QUINAG 2653 feet looming ahead. The
Kylesku *free* ferry takes you across Loch Cairnbaan (Loch of the

C

Fair Cairn) to Kylesku Inn (said to be haunted at certain times).

One of Scourie's famous sons was General Hugh Mackay (1640–92), whose defeat at Killiecrankie failed to tarnish his reputation earned in the Low Countries and Ireland. Court intrigues by a Highland rival are said to have cost him the expected title of Earl of Scourie.

The other lochs the Kylesku ferry crosses apart from Loch Cairnbaan are inland lochs Glencoul and Glendhu, and this wonderful safe anchorage must have formed pleasant shelter for the Norse galleys years ago. At the head on the south shore of Loch Glencoul are the renowned EAS-COUL-AULIN waterfalls ('the fall of the beautiful hair'), which are the highest in Britain, 600 feet. They really are magnificent, and can be reached and seen best by small boat, by contacting the boatman at Kylesku (phone Kylestrome 408). Kylesku on a summer's day is very beautiful, being sheltered by the surrounding mountains, and the still blue waters lying tranquil in their unique setting.

KYLESKU FERRY . . . and that brings to mind the lovely romantic tune of *The Waters of Kylesku* (I am not sure who composed it, so am unable to pay due acknowledgement for penning the verses).

> By Clebrig and Ben Loyal and the bonnie Kyle of Tongue
> The roads we'd often travelled in the days when we were
>   young,
> There's magic and there's beauty in those hills when passing
>   through
> There's many a mile from Melness to the waters of Kylesku.
>
> O'er all of bonnie Scotland, I dearly love the west
> Its bens and glens in summertime, they surely are the best,
> There's grandeur and there's beauty in those hills when
>   passing thro',
> There's many a mile from Lairg to the waters of Kylesku.
>
> By Craggie pool and Loyal and the Coldbackie sands
> I thought of them when soldiering in far off foreign lands
> I dreamt I saw the sunset o'er the hills of Castle Dhu
> In fancy I was wandering by the waters of Kylesku.
>
> There's beautiful Achfary on the shores of Loch More
> Where winter waves are breaking like the seas of Skerryvore
> By Laxford and Rhiconich and the bonnie cave of Smoo
> There's many a mile from Durness to the waters of Kylesku.

By Ledmore and Loch Assynt, from Lochinver down to
  Stoer
You can view the wild Atlantic from its cold and rocky
  shore
The clear and sparkling rivers here, the salmon are but few
There's many a mile from Oykel to the waters of Kylesku.

Another grand lilting song is 'Lovely Stornoway', the opening
lines of which are 'make your way to Stornoway, on the road
to Orinsay'.

From Kylesku, you can take the high coast road (very narrow
with many blind bends, but extremely pretty) over by Nedd,
Drumbeg (hotel overlooks the loch of same name), Clashnessie
(where off-shore there is Oldany island with its old burial ground),
Stoer, dropping down to Lochinver. But we will now come
back to Laxford, taking the road to LAIRG, from where readers
will remember, we originally set out (for Tongue).

At Laxford, we come into the country owned by Anne,
Duchess of Westminster, who has her big house at Loch More.
The run to Lairg, about 40 miles (the same mileage as to Tongue)
is even prettier than Lairg to Tongue, for you travel along so
many different lochs, the road more or less bordering on these
lochs. You first come to Loch Stack, with Ben Stack 2364 feet
behind you, a conical peak, the peak of Arcuil, named after its
possible similarity to the Ark. Loch Stack is reputed to be the
finest fishing loch in all Scotland. On a wee island in the loch
you can see a monument, which was erected to the memory of
one of the Duchesses of Westminster who loved to picnic there;
and I believe her grave is there also. Then looking right across
Loch Stack you see the monster called Arkle standing 2580 feet
by himself, towering all alone. A fine curved mass rising very
like Gibraltar. Arkle of course is the name of the famous race-
horse owned by the Duchess of Westminster; a wonder horse,
an Irish thoroughbred bay gelding. In thirty-five races it won
twenty-seven times. It will never race again, however, for it
had a bone fracture of the pedal bone on the off-forefoot, and
although it was mended and satisfactorily too, it has been thought
unwise to risk any further break in which event the horse might
have to be destroyed. So he is now leisurely eating his head off
in far away Ireland, and is now twelve years old. At the time of
the accident it was feared he would be lame for the rest of his

life. His favourite tit-bit is Irish chocolate which has whisky in the blend! Legends have grown around him making him the most famous horse since Troy. He seemed to love crowds, and applause, and used to take his eyes off the course to acknowledge his fans in the grandstand. And when being photographed he would prick up his ears and smile toothily wherever he spotted a camera, and as soon as he heard the camera click, his ears flopped. And yet people say animals have no sense. He is only 16½ hands, but he has a heart twice as big. One jockey accused Arkle of 'laughing' as he loped ahead. It was on December 27th 1966, that the world's newspapers carried the headline 'Wonder horse Arkle may never race again'. It happened in the King George VI steeplechase. It was thought he had hit a guard rail, and he ran on with a broken hoof. The leg was six weeks in plaster. During that anxious time his bran, hay, oats, flax seed, and grass meal were all flown in from Ireland. Even his drinking water came from the Emerald Isle for it had the preferred content of limestone. His daily liquid consumption of a gallon of water was laced with as much as three pints of his favourite stout. Could one ask for more? The day of the mishap saw 16,000 people on the Kempton course. He even got hundreds of 'get well' cards sent; and gifts piled up in a room near his stall. There were sugar cubes by the thousand. A well-wisher from Australia put a telephone call through to enquire how he was getting along. In February 1967, he was flown back to Ireland.

When the horse left, his trainer had to put up a bar to his special hay-box 'not for Arkle's sake, but because while he revels in the attention, all the other horses in training are becoming nervous wrecks with such unexpected crowds.' He was supposed to have won about £100,000 in racing. So much for this wonder horse. I must apologise for dilating at length on this subject; I am not interested in racing, but I *am* fond of animals.

We next come alongside Loch More where the Duchess has her Scottish home—Lochmore Lodge. Just before reaching this you pass through the tiny village of ACHFARY, a beautiful little spot which the Duchess has made for her tenants, and there is also a small primary school for the children. In the gable wall of one of the farm buildings there is a tablet to the memory of the 1st Duke of Westminster, Hugh Lupus Grosvenor who died on

22nd December 1899, aged 74. It was put up by the people of
the district in affectionate memory of his kindliness and of his
constant desire to do all he could in helping all his tenants.
Passing onwards and at the end of Loch More, at Kinloch, there
is a private road on the left where shortly before coming to a big
house at Aultanrynie (which by the way was demolished one
winter by a heavy landslide), you come to an old burial ground
where there are some twenty or so shepherds, foresters and
farmers of the Westminster Estate buried. Some of the grave-
stones bear dates of 120 years ago. This small walled-in ground
is enveloped in mobriettia, which in mid summer provides a riot
of colour.

We now come to Loch Merkland where the Duchess's estate
terminates (going inland), and at the far end, Merkland Lodge.
Then after passing another loch, Loch Ghriama we come in sight
of Loch Shin, 18 miles long, which more or less dominates this
itinerary to Lairg. The road follows the loch all the way.
Shortly we come to OVERSCAIG and the hotel there, where the
enterprising owner, Mr. D. A. Good, is hoping to establish a
real worth-while community. With his wife, they are interested
in the land and developing the farm they have, apart from the
hotel business. They are wishful to start local home industries,
such as knitwear, carving and horn work, which would help to
keep people in the area. Overscaig is only 14 miles from Lairg
(about half hour run) which is a fairly convivial centre for young
folk. Visitors to the district (and it is a great fishing hotel), are
always looking for something genuinely local. It must be
appreciated that in all these Highland hotels their greatest difficulty
is in obtaining the right sort of staff, for there is little or no employment for them once the season has finished, and that being
so, everybody is paid off. Whereas if there was something worth-
while for them to do, and houses to live in, they would be quite
happy and content to stay on throughout the winter. Without
accommodation it is impossible to attract or even retain, people
in such a remote district. The hotel provides its own milk, butter
and cream from a Jersey herd, and there is also an Aberdeen-
Angus herd for beef production. When I was last there, Mr.
Good told me he had just completed reseeding a 15-acre park,
and before that, had finished two other reseedings. He was
erecting a cattle shelter on the hill, which would be used for

lambing. I understand the Sutherland Development Committee
are very sympathetic towards all these proposals, and doubtless
the Highland Development Board may come to be interested.

We now come back to Lairg and so have completed a grand
circular tour (as the coach people are so fond of saying) of the
north and north-west of Sutherland . . . Westwards from
Tongue, and discovered I am sure, very many pearls. The
following chapter will deal with the journey to Lochinver (again
from Lairg) via the famed fishing Oykel river and valley,
Inchnadamph and the Assynt country.

Legends

In travelling around the Highlands, I have heard many out-
of-this-world stories. Some are far-fetched; others not so.
Some of these are connected with places mentioned in this and
the next chapter, and I think it will afford more than passing
interest, if I tabulate them for easy reference.

1. This is connected with Invercalda House, near the ruins of
Ardvreck on Loch Assynt (vide next chapter). I have said earlier,
this house was burnt down, only one person, a piper surviving.
The legend says the Mackenzies carried their merrymaking well
into the Sabbath morning, and the piper much against his will,
was forced to play on after midnight. Assynt people believe to
this day, the fire was a manifestation of Divine wrath for breaking
the Sabbath, and that the piper was allowed to escape because his
intentions had been good. The remains of those who perished
in the fire lie to this day in the crumbling family vault in Inchnadamph churchyard. If you look through the tiny entrance, you
can see fragments of bone, pathetic reminders of the tragedy
still lying on the floor of the vault. You should not venture in,
for a drip of water falls from the roof of the vault even in good
weather, and people round about say that anybody hit by it is
sure to die within the year. Another grim legend about this
house is still unfulfilled. Coinneach Odhar the famous Brahan
seer, saw it as it was being built and remarked that 'the day would
come when the trees would grow from the roof, and when
they reached the height of the chimney, there would be bloodshed
in Assynt'. Last year, 1968, I noticed that the tallest of the little
rowans growing high up in the gable end of the ruin had reached
to within a few inches of what remains of the chimney top.

2. If you carry on a few miles further from Invercalda ruins, you come to the base of Quinag. One fine autumn afternoon about a hundred years ago, a cattleman was driving his beasts home along a track high up on the side of Quinag, after spending a few weeks at the shieling. Suddenly he noticed a funeral winding its melancholy way along the side of Loch Assynt, but he couldn't think whose it might be. Stranger still, when he got home, he found that nobody in the neighbourhood had passed away. Only a week or so later, he himself took ill suddenly and died. His remains were carried in a procession up the side of the loch, to Inchnadamph churchyard. On the way there, many of the mourners noticed a man driving a herd of cattle high up on the slopes of Quinag, but nobody ever found out who he was. It could have been his own funeral, he had seen a few weeks ago?

3. Since the first motor car appeared on Sutherland roads some sixty years ago, there have been numerous instances of phantom cars and ghost headlights in the Inchnadamph area. One of the owners of the hotel at the time (Miss Morrison), was very startled one dark night while motoring down Loch Assynt side, to see a pair of powerful headlights sweep over the brow of a hill close by, and vanish as suddenly as they had appeared. Another instance is of two local people walking along the road one evening at dusk some years ago, when they saw what they took to be the dipped headlights of a car at a passing place just near them. As they approached the lights suddenly disappeared, leaving no trace of a car. Inchnadamph has also a phantom pedestrian, a 'red lady' who appears at times on the road—again near Invercalda House—and vanishes as anyone approaches her. She was seen twice in recent years by the Lochinver bus driver, who is not a man to imagine things.

4. The most recent tale of the supernatural in the Assynt area, is only about six years ago. A young shepherd who lived by himself in a lonely cottage near Inchnadamph, was found drowned in a shallow pool of water up the glen near the foot of Ben More. He had apparently slipped on a stone and had been knocked unconscious. Only a few nights before he had been sitting gloomily in the hotel kitchen. When one of the maids asked him why he wasn't his usual cheerful self, he said, 'I had a bad dream last night that I can't get out of my mind. I dreamt

I saw my own bones lying out on the side of Ben More.'

5. Between the tiny hamlets of Tarbet and Fanagmore over-looking Handa, is a pass called 'the pass of the old men', and in earlier years it was said to be a favourite haunt of the devil; and even today there are folk in the district who are afraid to go near the place on a dark night.

6. Near the Kylesku ferry there is a large shooting lodge, where there were at least two eerie forerunners of death, both of them in the 1920's. In the first instance, a maid trying to open a door, found it stuck. She tried to force it but couldn't move it. The girl called for assistance, and several sturdy people put their shoulders to the door, but it would not open. They could get their hands in only as far as the light switch, but the light bulb seemed to have fused. Yet a few hours later, the door swung as easily as ever on its hinges, and the light worked perfectly. The staff forgot about the affair, until a few weeks later, when some-one died in the very same room. In the self-same lodge later on, two maids were lying in bed. One was fast alseep, the other lay awake, gazing into the shadows. Then suddenly she thought she could see a great dark patch hovering about her room-mate's bed. As she watched, it became more and more distinct, until she could make out quite clearly the shape of a coffin. Three weeks later the other maid died suddenly.

7. Near Lochinver, lies a small loch, beside which for years the locals used to see weird lights at night. Then one day some children were playing near its side, when two of them fell in and were drowned at the very spot where the lights had been seen. Since that day, the lights were never seen again.

8. Gualin Moor, the road we took from Durness to Rhico-nich, is also the subject of ghosts. Only two or three years ago, the Kinlochbervie minister at the time, accompanied by one of his Elders, was coming back from a meeting in Durness, when he saw a pair of lights sweeping towards him, and pulled into a passing place. The lights never passed him; they vanished suddenly. In the middle of this same moor, there is a lonely shepherd's cottage where a former shepherd, his wife and family often had their sleep disturbed by the noise of a car that never was.

9. Balnakiel churchyard. Here a man desecrated the great Gaelic Bard, Rob Dunn Mackay's grave, and stole a tooth as a souvenir. That night and for many nights afterwards, the thief

had no peace until he restored the relic to the skull of its former owner.

10. Durness. In a part near Durness called the Culkein, are two small circles of grass greener than any round about. The old folk will tell you a minister of the parish encountered the devil himself at this very spot. Satan wanted the minister's soul, but the latter was not prepared to let him have it. Repeating the Lord's Prayer, the minister described circles with his stick around himself and his adversary. Confronted with such a formidable formula, the devil was obliged to flee. The two green spots and the circles the minister made are the result seen today.

11. Tongue. Only a few miles east out of Tongue on the Thurso road, a side road takes you to Skerray. This minor road too, has known its phantom cars, the lights of which have dazzled many a driver; but before these days there was an interesting character of Skerray who possessed 'second-sight'. Although very popular, nobody in the village was very keen to walk along the road with him. When walking with people he had the disconcerting habit of often pulling them to the verge of the road to allow past a phantom funeral, that he alone could see. Once whilst with a friend, he met such a spectacle and recognised all the mourners except one. He puzzled over the stranger. Who could he be? Then all of a sudden it dawned on him; it was himself!

12. Drumbeg. During the last century there was a witch of the name of Mhairi-bhan ('fair-haired Mary'), who lived in this small hamlet of Drumbeg—on the coast road from Kylesku ferry. She appeared to be as good a servant of Satan as anyone in the Highlands. She was feared and hated by all the villagers. One night some young men of Drumbeg decided to put an end to her misdeeds once and for all. So they climbed on to her thatched roof, shouted down the chimney, and when she looked up to investigate, they let a noose fall round her neck and dragged her up the chimney and strangled her. But before she died she summoned up strength to curse her killers with her last breath. Within a year all these young men died.

13. Ullapool. I mention Loch Lurgainn coming from Lochinver to the Ullapool road in the next chapter. In the folk-lore of the North, we find few traces of the FEANS, that legendary race of warriors whose exploits have been celebrated by their

bard Ossian. Their native region was in the south-west of
Scotland and in Ireland. But at an early age, their adventurous
leader Finn was in Ross-shire. He was only young when he
came for a holiday with his grandmother, who lived near Garve.
One day he was out for a walk with the old lady, when they were
attacked by some giants, members of a savage tribe that had its
haunts around Strathconon. There were too many of them for
the lad to handle, for he had to see also that no harm came to his
grandmother, so he threw her over his shoulder, taking a good
grip of her legs, and ran. The giants had got between them and
their home, and so Finn was forced to flee westward. The men
came after him at speed, but young Finn managed to keep beyond
their reach. It was a terrible chase, through woods and burns,
and over hills and moorland. He ran about fifty miles and was
almost dropping within a few miles north of Ullapool, when the
giants gave up. Finn sank down wearily on the shore of Loch
Lurgainn, and then he found to his great dismay, that all he had
left of his granny was her legs. When he realised the situation
he threw the legs into the loch. From that day the loch became
known as Loch Lurgainn—which means in Gaelic the Leg Loch.

*   *   *

'Second sight' or 'The Sight' as it is called in the Highlands, is
a strange and sometimes terrible thing; a heavy burden to be
borne, made heavier by the knowledge that the possessor will
almost certainly pass it on to the children or even grandchildren,
since it seems to run in certain families. People have always been
most heatedly divided over the question 'Does it really exist?'
One is told that it is just superstition, a part of the Celtic Twilight.
But even today in the Highlands incidents still take place which
seem to suggest the existence of a sixth sense. I know of a case
of a man who was at a dinner party in the 1890's and among the
guests was the hostess's niece, whose parents were in India. In
the middle of dinner the girl sprang to her feet with a cry of
horror and fainted. When she revived, she said she had seen
her father being killed by a great white beast, in shape like a tiger,
but not striped. Later, it was learned that her father *had* been
seriously mauled by a tiger, but was recovering. He did, and
brought back to Scotland with him the skin of the beast a very
fine white (albino) tiger, whose pale cream stripes hardly showed.

In many instances Second Sight is held to be a worse curse even
than insanity. It is said seers could receive a widespread thought
present in many minds, such as war. St. Kilda was in mourning
for Queen Victoria when the ship sent to tell them of her death
arrived. So, too, when King George V died. In the autumn of
1914 the St. Kilda seer told the islanders that Britain was at war
and our army in retreat, for he had seen what must have been
the retreat from Mons. But he did not know with whom we
were at war, because although he saw and described the enemy
uniforms, neither he, nor anyone in the island knew to what
nation they belonged; so it was said by the first ship to call there
after war was declared. Strange? After the 'Clearances' many
people sought news from the seers of relatives overseas, often,
but not always, with success. A number of these seers became
utterly exhausted whilst 'in session', and eventually could say,
or divulge, no more, because they had reached the edge of 'the
Emptiness' beyond which they might not see. It was a sin to
try.

There is the story of a Wester Ross man who possessed the
'second sight' who was out walking one late evening along the
public road near his house, when he saw a spectre funeral as he
was about to cross a bridge. When he stepped aside he received a
severe kick on the leg from a horse that happened to be ridden
by one of the funeral party. There could be no doubt he got the
kick, for he felt the pain and actually limped home. He told his
wife what had happened, but on looking at his leg, neither of
them could find a mark of any kind that would show that he had
received a kick from a horse. He persisted in saying he *had* been
kicked and even complained of severe pain in his leg during the
remainder of the night. Next day, however, he was up and
about as usual and his wife laughed at him for his imagination.
He went out along the road and over the same bridge, when he
met a real funeral at the very spot where the spectre funeral had
passed him the previous day. He saw the funeral party was
exactly the same, and the same horse and its rider were there,
and then suddenly as it passed him, the horse shied, kicking him
severely on the leg in the exact spot where he had received the
kick from the spectre horse. He limped home, as on the previous
day, and then was obliged to keep to his bed for some time
owing to the severity of the blow he had sustained, but he assured

his wife the pain was no more severe than he felt after the kick from the spectre horse. Another person, a woman this time, in the same Strathcarron area, frequently saw the spectre of people known to her. On one occasion she saw the spectre of a person, then abroad, and sure enough some weeks afterwards, there came the news of that person's death, which had actually taken place on the very day the old lady had seen the spectre. On another occasion, she said she saw what looked like a human eye coming out of a certain house in the evening, and going along to the churchyard. And although there was no case of illness at the time, a few days afterwards a death occurred in that house, and the funeral took place to the churchyard indicated in the vision.

I know of a case given me by an Elder of one of the Gairloch churches, who when going home one night near Badachro, saw bobbing lights over the gates of a house coming *away* from the house and down the road before him—an indication of a death and of the funeral cortege going by road to the Gairloch cemetery. In those days invariably the coffin from the south side, would be rowed across the bay to the churchyard, for the road was so very rough and difficult; no more than a track. He couldn't quite understand all this, for the waters were calm and the occupants of the house quite well. A few days later a death occurred at that very house, a gale blew up and the funeral party simply *had* to take the remains in a cart by road to Gairloch. And who is to doubt the word of a well respected Elder?

Then, in a village carpenter's shop, whenever the planks of wood on the shelves move or vibrate, this is invariably an indication of an impending death and a coffin to be made. The stories are endless.

*   *   *

I am now about to relate two of the *most extraordinary stories* I have ever heard, given me personally and in all seriousness. They have never been published before and were told to me by a man in his late 60's whom I know living near Strathpeffer—still hale and hearty and of temperate habits . . . I will call him Mr. X. . . . One story he told me was given to him by his grandfather and is more of the legendary type; but the second one, is of his *own* personal experience, bordering well on, if not right on, the supernatural. I have not the slightest reason to doubt its truth, and am quite sure after you read what he told me that Truth *is* stranger than Fiction.

The first story bears on the Loch Maree side; the second and the most amazing has its location near Dornie (on the road to Kyle from Shiel Bridge). I will tell them more or less in his own words, for to do otherwise would rob them of their true worth.

First . . . 'In the old days the young men from Wester Ross tramped all the way to the east coast for fishing. Often I have sat and listened at the real old ceilidh's to the old men relating tales of those times. Not only the young men, but also the young and middle aged women used to go away to the lowlands to work at both fishing and harvesting; walking every step of it both ways. One particular tale sticks in my mind as often told by my own grandfather, before roads as we know them today were built. The people from Aultbea (*i.e.* about 12 miles from Gairloch) Gruinard and little Loch Broom had a track which they always used to go south or east. I myself walked over this track in the early 1920's and it could be followed at that time. I followed it from Kinlochewe, round by the north side of Loch Maree, passed Furnace and on near Letterewe, then up the hill and over the shoulder of Slioch; there was a fork before you came to Fionn Loch where the Loch Broom people went east and the Aultbea people came down between Aultbea and Laide. I walked every step of it. The tale as I heard my grandfather and other old men relate it was as follows. One time as a party of young men and women were returning home from work in the south, there was a dozen or more of them in the party; and when they had climbed up to the shoulder of Ben Slioch, the heavy hill-mist descended. They did the sensible thing; they sat down where they were, collected dry heather and bracken and started a fire. They had very little food with them, as they fully expected to be home that night, but the little they had, they shared, and afterwards they had a good ceilidh to pass the time. Just as they were having their sing-song, an old grey-haired man and his two dogs arrived and sat down among them. After a while the old man said that he had a bothy just a short distance away, and that if they cared to come with him, they could pass the night more comfortably. This they agreed to do, and they followed the old man and his two dogs. When they came to his bothy only a short distance on, they found what looked like a typical

Highland shepherd's bothy, but when they entered the place, it seemed to be much larger inside. They found a huge fire burning on the middle of the floor and a huge pot of porridge boiling on a crook. They were all struck speechless with amazement, but the old man told them to sit down round the fire. He then went out somewhere and came back with a dish for each person. He then proceeded to fill each person's dish with porridge from the pot. Again he went outside, and came back with a large pail of milk, which he also distributed. Afterwards when they were all fed and satisfied, the old man went out again and came back with a set of bagpipes and they had another grand ceilidh and dance. After that the old man went out again and came back with a small keg of whisky. He gave each and everyone who would take it a good dram. (Now this is the point to remember.) Some of the women or most of them would not take the whisky, and as it was now late and they were very tired, the old man told the women that if they went into the other end of the bothy they would find good dry heather and bracken which would make good and warm beds for them. This they did, and the men stretched out all round the fire and very soon they were all fast asleep.

'The first of the men woke just at break of day, and as he lay on his back he noticed the clear blue sky. He lay as he was for a while gathering his wits and rubbing his eyes. He then woke up all the rest of the men, and they just could not believe it. There was no sign of a bothy or house or old man or his dogs. They were just stretched out round the original fire which they had lit themselves when they had been caught by the mist. Of course the fire had, by then died out, but the remains were still smouldering. Each individual for a time thought that he or she had just dreamt the whole thing and were ashamed to mention it in case the rest would mock them. But little by little they came to speak about the occurrence of the night, and it became quite clear to them that they could not *all* have had the same dream.

'They searched the hills round about, but no sign of the old man or his bothy. Again they remembered hearing the old shepherd's dogs snoring as they lay near the fire. Where then did the old man and his dogs come from? Where was the bothy with its good fire and good pot of porridge? Where did the old man get the good pail of milk? There were no signs of cows, or cattle or goats, and where did he get the good keg of whisky? Each and every one of them remembered all those things, but now, everything had vanished. In a very sober frame of mind they all made their respective homes safely, and it was only many years later that this tale came to light. Some years later, my grandfather married one of those young women in that party, and she told him the tale of that night. He asked her if she would repeat it to their minister, which she did. Afterwards the minister got confirmation of it from some of the rest of that party. Well, Mr. B.J., that's the tale as I often heard my grandfather tell it. I remember once telling this tale to an Englishman whom I casually met, and I afterwards asked him, "Well, what do you make of it?" "Oh, that's easy," he said, "they all got tight on the old man's keg of whisky"; but I said, some of the women of the party did not touch the whisky. He could not answer that one, and neither can I,' he told me. . . .

Second . . . And this is Mr. X's true story of his *own* personal experience; and as before, I give it in his own diction.

'. . . During 1936, '37 and '38, I travelled very extensively all over the Gaelic-speaking Highlands and Islands. At that time I was a fairly well-known Gaelic singer. I attended the National Mods and had won most of the Higher awards going at that time, so I decided that I would "have a go" on my own. I made up a programme of Gaelic songs from various places. I also bought an old magic lantern (oil burning) but I changed that to gas burning (carbide) and so got a brilliant light. I then got a set of lantern slides from David MacBrayne's—just views of the Highlands and islands. I then gave a free show to the Dingwall Branch of An Comunn Gaidhealach, and this was so well received that I decided to go further afield. At that time there were very few Public Halls in the Highlands, so I decided to approach the Education Committees regarding the use of schools for my "Lecture Recitals". They took a very favourable view, and I was granted the use of all the schools in any Gaelic-speaking area, Ross-shire, Sutherland, Inverness-shire, and Argyll, including all the Outer and Inner Hebrides. I packed up all my equipment and a change of clothes and fixed two carriers on my push-bike, one fore and one aft and set off on my journeys through the Highlands. I did Sutherland first, then Wester Ross, crossed over to Skye, then over to Lewis and Harris, continued on down through North Uist, Benbecula, South Uist, Eriskay, Barra, then crossed over to Mallaig and did all the Prince Charlie country; then Argyll, Mull, Tiree, Coll, Islay, Colonsay right down the Mull of Kintyre; the whole trip took me about one year. I was not making a fortune, but I usually cleared £10 to £12 per 5-night week. I did this for three years, as I have told you Bee Jay. In 1939 I was intending to get a mobile cinema similar to what the Highlands and Islands Film Guild have; but the war came and put me out of business. Strangely enough I often see the B.B.C. showing views of Gaelic interest, while they have Gaelic singers singing the songs which I sang and produced in my own way thirty years ago. My programme ran like this: ¾ hour general interest, slides and comments by myself. Then ¾ hour of songs by Bards from the district I happened to be in, showing slides of birth places of Bards and possibly their burial places—and their songs. This usually took two hours. I then ran a competition for children, say singing a song by a local Bard, and I always gave a Gaelic song book prize. After which I usually got a few of the audience to give a song, or recitation. My programme rarely finished under 2½–3 hours. Now, with that history behind me, I must tell you of a startling, personal experience I had in 1952—not so long ago really. At that time I was working on the Hydro-Electric scheme at Glen Cnoich near Invergarry. I was a driver/chain man to the resident engineer there. I also showed films four times a week in the camp. Well at Christmas and New Year, the works closed down for ten days, and the camp was very near empty. At that time I was a widower, so I stayed on at the camp. Now the Highlands and Islands Film Guild Operator who usually did the Wester Ross circuit, fell ill, and I was asked if I could go up to Dornie, and give one show there. As I was free on that date I said I would go. So on the Friday evening before New Year, I set off with my van and equipment and arrived at Dornie— roughly half way between Glen Shiel and Kyle—about 6 p.m., had one glass of whisky and my high tea. After tea I went to the hall and rigged up my equipment. By then people were gathering, so at 8 o'clock I commenced the film show which finished shortly after 10 p.m. Now this was a special show that night, and after the films, the hall was got ready for a dance. After dismantling the equipment and loading the van, I went back to the hotel again, had another small whisky and another meal. Now Bee Jay, remember that's all the whisky I had that night, and that, hours apart. I went back to the hall and stayed at the dance for about two hours. As it was now after 1 a.m. I decided to set off back to the camp at Invergarry about forty odd miles away. It had been a lovely moonlight night up till then, but just as I was leaving Dornie it began to snow. Anyway I set off, and as you possibly know, shortly after leaving Dornie you come to a very, very steep hill climb; CARR BRAE it is called. I think it derives its name from the many turns and hair-pin bends (Carr meaning a twist or turn). Anyway by the time I reached the brae, quite a bit of snow had fallen. I managed to get round the first bend, but at the second bend—I stuck; and as I had no chains or any other means at hand, I saw that it was impossible to get any further that night, so I reversed the van back into a near-by passing place, locked it up, and left it there. I had decided to walk back to the Dornie hotel, and stay there until the road was clear. I set off at a brisk pace back down the steep hill. Now just as I came near the bottom of the brae, I noticed a man coming up the hill towards me. He was dressed in a long black cloak, similar to the Inverness cape, and had a black hat well down over his eyes. When we met, he spoke in the very best of Gaelic, so he said, "you did not get so very far after all?" "No," I said, "I got stuck on the second bend." "Oh," says he, "I heard you passing the bottom of the brae, and I knew that you would not get very far, so as I had some chains that someone left with me long ago, I decided to come up and see if I could help you to get over the Carr Brae." I thanked him, and then we *both* retraced our steps back up the brae to where the van was. When we reached the van, he put his hand into his pocket and drew out a bunch of short chains—not the usual kind of chains that go round the whole wheel, but some short lengths of chain with belts and buckles for tying. He handed me three chains and told me to fix them on the back wheel. He himself then went to the other side of the van and fixed more chains on that wheel. When we had fixed both wheels with the chains, he said, "Now I think you will get over the hill all right; but in case you have any more trouble I will come along with you for a short distance." With that I got into the van, and he got in to the passenger seat.

So we set off, and of course with the help of the chains, we got over the hill—nae bother. Now once over Carr Brae, the road then drops down through the village of Inverinate, and continues down to sea level, and once through the village the snow faded away, and as you know, Bee Jay, when running on a bare road with chains they make an awful racket. So when we were down near the sea level, I said that as we had now run out of the snow, we might as well take the chains off. He agreed to this, so I drew into a passing place—and stopped. Now during the time we had travelled up Carr Brae and along to where we now were, the man had been speaking quite naturally about current affairs, and all the time he spoke in Gaelic; and what excellent Gaelic he had; much better than my Gaelic, and certainly much better than the Gaelic spoken in Kintail at that time. I complimented him on the excellence of his Gaelic, and I asked him to which part, or village, did he come from. "Oh," he says, "where I come from, they talk much better Gaelic than they do about here"—but he did not say where that was. He then said, "We'd better get the chains off. You take them off your side, and I will take the chains off the wheels on my side." With that he opened the door and out he jumped. I lit a cigarette before opening the door and getting out. Then I took off the chains on my side. Afterwards I walked round to the other side to see how my friend was getting on, but to my surprise there was no sign of the man, or the chains. I thought perhaps he had gone off to relieve himself, so I dropped the chains which I still had in my hands; I dropped them just at the roadside opposite the wheel. I then went back and sat in the cab to wait for the man to appear, but after a few minutes I came out again, and started to whistle, and call out—but no reply. I then looked at the ground where only a few minutes ago I had dropped the bundle of chains, but there was no sign of any chains, though the moon was now shining quite bright as a full moon usually does on a frosty night, and I could see both up and down the road for many yards. But there was no further sign of the man or the chains. I sat once again in the van for about ten minutes, as I felt sure the man was just hiding and playing a prank on me; but after waiting, I came out again and walked back up the road a bit. By now it was after 3 a.m., but I kept walking on back up the road until I reached the snow line once again. Then I reached the place where the snow was covering the road. The tyre marks made by the van were quite plain and clear, but to my amazement there were *no* chain marks, which would show up in the snow. Well, I sat down on a stone, for how long I do not know; thinking, thinking and thinking. At last I got up and continued to walk back up the hill and over the top, then down the other side to where I had originally parked the van when I stuck climbing the Brae at the second bend. The marks of the van were there quite plain, but not the marks of the chains. I then followed my own footsteps down to the bottom of the Brae, to where I first met the man, but again my own footsteps were the only visible ones, although we *both* walked back up to where the van was. My own footsteps were the only one's there! Who, then, was the old man who helped me with chains to get over Carr Brae that night? Where did he come from; where did he go? I am still looking for an answer to those questions. With deep thought and mixed feelings, I retraced my steps back over the Brae again, and down the other side, all the time watching the plain marks made by the van wheels—but no sign then or since of the chain marks, or the old man. I know that it was a practical impossibility for a van, or any wheeled vehicle to climb the Brae that night without some aid. Nevertheless there was my van on the other side. Well, there it is, I got back to the van; I started up and made the camp at Invergarry about 7 a.m., turned into my bunk and fell sound asleep.' ...

So ends this amazing remarkable story; in fact I have never heard, or read of its equal. It most certainly borders on the supernatural.

The same Mr. X told me of another incident, this time bordering on 'second sight'. There was an old man Kenneth Morrison, who used to visit his old home at Aultbea years and years ago. A very respected man, he said, who was an Elder in the kirk. He came to the house one night and said, 'What a lot of lights are shining in Loch Ewe.' He likened them to hundreds of fishing boats all round the Loch and bay. We went out to look, but all we could see was one solitary light shining dimly on Isle Ewe across the bay. That was in 1910. What he actually 'saw' was the lights of all the Royal Navy vessels, for in the 1914 war Loch Ewe was crammed with naval craft.

*   *   *

And now perhaps, in order readers may have a comfortable, undisturbed night's rest, I will end these dissertations with a humorous story.

Kenny was a Wester Ross man, and about eighty years ago he was living with his aged mother in their cottage by the sea. He was a lazy fellow and generally short of cash. One evening he was feeling very dry, thinking how lovely it would be to be down having a beer at the hotel. But he had no money in his pocket. He knew his mother had a little money in the house, but she was dead against drink, so it was no use asking her for the price of a dram or a beer. He thought up an idea. He went out into the dark evening, got a ladder, climbed up to the chimney pot, and in a melancholy moaning voice, disguising his own, he called down, 'Be good to poor Kenny; be kind to poor Kenny for you won't have him in this world long.' They were superstitious days, and when the old woman, who was sitting beside the fireside, heard these ominous words, she was convinced it was a warning from Heaven. Kenny came down the ladder, put it away then went indoors, and dropped into a chair, saying faintly, 'I don't know what's come over me, mother, but I feel so ill these past few days.' His mother, with her mind still on the warning from the unknown, left the room and went to where she had her few savings. She came back and gently laid her hands on her son, saying 'here's two shillings from my small savings, son; go down to the Inn and get a drop of whisky for yourself, and I'm sure you'll feel better'. Kenny thanked his mother and hurried away to the Inn. As whisky was then only about 2s. 6d. a bottle, Kenny would certainly have had more than a drop for the two shillings. He came back feeling full of life!

CHAPTER 4

LOCHINVER AND ASSYNT

WESTWARD out of Lairg and before going north to Tongue and Laxford as per previous chapter, the main road takes us via Strath Oykel, Oykel Bridge, Altnacealgach (Alt-nar-kal-a-ger), Ledmore—the turn-off left being to Ullapool in Wester Ross—Inchnadamph along Loch Assynt, thence to Lochinver, about forty-five miles in all—again through beautiful stretches of country and good roads. As you approach Inchnadamph, Canisp 2779 feet and Suilven 2399 feet stand boldly on your left, and Ben More Assynt 3273 feet on the right. Shortly after Inchnadamph at Skiag Bridge the road (right) takes you to Kylesku ferry, which we have already crossed. You are then ambling along by the side of Loch Assynt about seven miles long, for Lochinver. In this journey trailing along the broad strath under ridges of crofting country to the pine woods of Rosehall and the forestry community at the foot of Glencassley—before reaching Oykel Bridge—you are striking into yet another mountainous wild of Sutherland. You pass a wee hamlet of Tuiteam, the scene of a bloody battle in 1408 between the Mackays and the MacLeods of Lewis. There is an ancient burial ground there. Onward to Oykel Bridge (and it is only a bridge with a famed fishing hotel) the route is that of the flight of Lord Louden and President Forbes from Dornoch to Ullapool and Skye after the Rout of May and the capture of Dornoch by Jacobite troops in 1746. As we continue, the road cleaves the hills to Benmore and Assynt. At Ledmore and a few miles left (to Ullapool) the boundary of Sutherland and Ross-shire is marked and whilst we do not take this road (we are going straight on to Inchnadamph and the west) there are two little villages ELPHIN and KNOCKAN that I would mention. Some of the place names in Scotland have a wonderful lilt. Elphin is one of them and conjures up visions of elves or the famous Wee Folk reputed to be still seen by some Highlanders. At the turn of the century,

77

these two villages nestling in the foothills of the Cromalt Hills together made up a busy wee township. Nearly 200 folk eked out a living from the limestone soil. Today Elphin and Knockan are 'ghost villages'. There are more houses than people; the combined population is now about twenty-five, most of them being old or middle-aged. The school which in living memory had more than fifty pupils at a time is now silent except at some week-ends, when pupils from senior secondary schools on the east coast stay there during mountaineering expeditions. In the 1920's there would be around 1500 sheep on the hills and over 100 cows in the byres. The social life is nil; though there is a weekly service in the tiny corrugated-iron church. Sheep and people have been displaced by trees. Those living nearby say they would rather have a piece of mutton to eat than a chunk of wood! Sutherland's 'ghost twins'.

However, we will proceed on our way to INCHNADAMPH, just at the commencement of Loch Assynt. The village—if we may call it such, consists of a church, shooting lodge, a hotel (well known for its fishing hospitality), and a few cottages. The hotel has been in the Morrison family for many years, and you can be assured of every attention. Around Inchnadamph there are many uncanny legends to be heard—and ghosts too. Just along from here you see the gaunt ruins of Ardvreck Castle built on its little peninsula jutting out into Loch Assynt. Erected towards the end of the 16th century it was the residence of Donald Ban Mor MacLeod of Assynt and his successors in the lairdship. In its day it must have been a place of considerable strength in which, even in those turbulent times, its inmates might sleep without anxiety. It is set strategically, and from its watch-posts a considerable extent of surrounding countryside could be kept in view. Ardvreck has taken its humble place in Scottish history principally as the prison for a short time of James Graham, Marquis of Montrose, after his capture by Neil MacLeod of Assynt, who betrayed him. Montrose's meteoric career was finally ended by the defeat of his army at Carbisdale, and from then until the time of his capture he was a fugitive in the wilds of Sutherland.

Romance has given the turncoat Montrose a reputation for gallantry and honour that he ill deserves, and has been less than just to Neil MacLeod. Writers, both for and against Montrose agree that he offered a large sum of money to MacLeod for his liberty and that MacLeod refused the bribe. The execration of MacLeod's memory came largely from the Jacobites of later times; and superstition has connected the ruin of the MacLeod's and their castle with Neil's 'treachery' towards Montrose. But nothing is said of Montrose's undoubted treachery to the cause of the Covenant of which he himself had been a signatory and to begin with, an ardent supporter.

The ruined walls of Ardvreck today are merely an interesting feature of a particularly pleasing countryside, a silent witness to the stirring days of long ago when Scotland was fighting to the death for her spiritual and civil liberty. In the cellars of the castle there still are to be seen two old cannon of that period.

Further along there is another gaunt, grey ruin, Invercalda House, which takes its name from the Calda Burn it stands beside. It was built by the Mackenzies who inherited Assynt in the 17th century, and was burnt to the ground with all its inhabitants, except one piper, early one Sabbath morning, only a fortnight after it had been occupied. There is a legend about this, which I have given in the previous chapter.

It is not far now till you come to Lochinver; we have seen the noted mountains *en route*, Ben More Assynt, Canisp, Suilven and Quinag. Suilven sometimes called 'The Sugar Loaf' is the most westerly of the Assynt mountains, and is probably the most remarkable of Scottish mountains. It is one of several isolated peaks in the north-west composed of Torridonian sandstone on pre-Cambrian gneiss. Conival is another high mountain (3234 feet) near Ben More approached from Inchnadamph. It is one of the 'Munro tops' in Sutherland. Another well-known mountain in Lochinver district—one which has a great sight-seeing draw with visitors—is Stac Polly (2009 feet), for it has such an intriguing look about it from all angles. Cul Beag is another 2523 feet mountain nearby; as is Cul Mor (2786 feet).

Assynt is a beautiful region of the west; indeed its very name sounds sweet music on one's ears. The poem by Norman MacCaig 'A man of Assynt' is particularly symbolic of the countryside; and I give a few significant lines though it is not in strict rhythmic verse:

> Glaciers, grinding West, gouged out
> these valleys, rasping the brown sandstone,

and left, on the hard rock below, the
ruffled foreland—
this frieze of mountains, filed
on the blue air—Stac Polly,
Cul Beag, Cul Mor, Suilven, Canisp—a frieze and
a litany.

and again,

Who possesses this landscape?
the man who bought it, or
I who am possessed by it?

*   *   *

We are now in LOCHINVER itself. It is a lovely little village,
compactly built round the head of the sea loch that resembles a
peaceful Norwegian Fiord, and provides safe anchorage for its
busy fishing fleet and other small craft. It was from Lochinver
that a great odyssey of Highland settlers took place in the mid-
19th century to Nova Scotia, thence to Australia, and finally to
New Zealand. The village and its surrounds are owned by
Mr. E. H. Vestey and lives under the shadow of Suilven. Over
the years I have spent quite a while in the village, and nearby,
and remember the first time on crossing over the narrow bridge
into the parish, catching my eye on a big black board with large
white lettering, the words 'Worms for Sale'! The village with
its white washed houses and cottages is built round and looking
on the loch, and follows pretty much the same pattern for these
Highland villages—paper shop, churches (3), well-equipped self-
service store, children's green, bakery, post office, garage and
bank; and of course the village hall cum-café, with the heart
warming notice 'High tea served at any time of the day'. In
mentioning the post office, I would say the same clock-work
procedure operates as I have indicated in other quarters. All
mails come from Lairg via Loch Assynt, and the Oykel region,
wet, fine or snow. I would like to pay my respects to a very
genial postie, Willie Dixon, who used to deliver my mail to me
in his red Morris P.O. van. He retired after 30 years service as
postman in January 1968; and at a social held in the Public Hall,
on 6th January, he was presented with a gold watch and a wallet
of notes. I hope he will have many years of happy retirement.
   The War Memorial is well placed and there are inscribed upon

it seventy names in the 1914–1919 war, and sixteen names in the 1939–1945 war; and finally of course the big Culag hotel at the end of the half-circle, facing the pier. The name Culag means 'a sheltered corner' in the ancient Highland tongue.

The hotel is not only excellently situated, but provides accommodation and fare of the highest order. It is a great rendezvous for fishers, and in this respect can offer some of the finest brown-trout, sea-trout and salmon fly-fishing in the north. The hotel controls some fifteen lochs, many of them with boats. Stalking can also be arranged by agreement with the estate.

When first erected, the building was known as Lochinver House. Its history is peculiar and worthy of recording here. It was originally built by a company from Liverpool as a house for smoking fish and herrings which after some years' trial proved an utter failure. They abandoned the place, and it was for years empty—a monument of foolish speculation, after an expenditure of over £2000 upon it. It was then purchased by Mr. MacDonald of Skeabost, Skye, for a mere trifle. He converted the west portion into a dwelling house and set going the curing of herrings and other fish at Lochinver, which he sent by his own vessels for sale in Ireland, and he made a financial success of it. He made it over in his lifetime to his eldest son, and went to Skye to look after his property. His son was speculative, took extensive salmon fishing along the coast, which eventually ended in bankruptcy. He sold Lochinver House to the Duke of Sutherland. His father had, at great expense, made the garden at Lochinver, which was originally a gravel bank: he carried earth from Ireland in his vessels to it, built a high wall to protect it from the sea, and made it a productive spot, which it continues to be to this day. He also planted trees on the hills behind and improved the place greatly.

In 1845 the Duke of Sutherland converted a great portion of the original house into a dwelling house, and planted a large area of land near it, and in the vicinity of Lochinver, adding much to the beauty of the place. His Grace and family resided there several years during the summer and autumn months, and made acquaintance with the Assynt people. Unfortunately, the house was almost wholly destroyed by fire. It was well insured, and the money was all expended in restoring, enlarging and improving it, along with many thousands besides, making it really a

Gentleman's residence, with elegant rooms and every necessary accommodation.

Having so many different residences, the Duke let Lochinver House to Mr. MacBrayne, owner of west coast steamers at a rent of £500, which continued for several years, but not to the profit of Mr. MacBrayne, who gave it up, and it has since been let as an hotel . . . the Culag Hotel.

*   *   *

This, then is Lochinver—charming and almost a Meditteranean picture afar-off. Small wonder this district of Assynt is the mecca of the artist and the art photographer. There are many pretty runs round and about; one, a most beautiful but very narrow and tricky road to Ullapool by the coast road, which takes you through Inverkirkaig—where you cross the boundary into Ross-shire—Inverpolly (warden's house), from where you see Stac Polly and a marvellous sight of Enard Bay and up by the road which then forks, right to Achiltibuie and the Coigach country, and left passing Loch Lurgainn to join the main road to Ullapool coming from Ledmore (Inchnadamph-ways). The other route out of Lochinver—again by the coast—is by Achmelvich (a large bay with a fine stretch of sand and a Youth Hostel at hand), CLACHTOLL village, where just before the hamlet, with tall rocks on your left and a lochan to your right, it is said you may see a black dog with a human face, howling as he passes you at night. Near the beach at Clachtoll you will see a huge rock on your left split right in two. This phenomena was forecast by the Brahan Seer, years before it ever happened, and it is recorded he said the noise would be so loud and great, that it would separate two cows, tethered together at ELPHIN—over fifteen miles away as the hooded-crow flies (a greyish crow, also called hoodie-crow, a detestable thing). This actually happened. The cows stampeded. Thence on to STOER village—a scattering of houses as is the case in most of these villages, CLASHNESSIE with its perfectly charming bay. A small boy once wrote on the sands there 'Goodbye Clashnessie', sad at having to leave for home in England. All these beaches have no bathing huts, no deckchairs, no ice-cream sellers, no Punch and Judy shows—just yourselves, and ample space. It's a rare thing today, becoming rarer every year . . . a beach where you can be alone, a seashore which has

not turned into a seaside, and in the north-west there are hundreds
of such havens, where you can relax with the morning paper
which is yesterday's.   Then DRUMBEG and on to Kylesku ferry.
So one therefore has two wonderful 'outlets' at hand from
LOCHINVER.   On the road to STOER, you can take a side turn to the
sadly depopulated crofting villages of CLASHMORE and RAFFIN and
the Stoer promontory.   You get a spectacular expansive view
from the lighthouse at Raffin, 100 feet high at least on the sheer
cliffs. Joan Prince has written a moving poem of Stoer Head,
and I give the first verse:

> At Stoer Head, the lighthouse stands
> Bold and white.
> At Stoer Head the four winds blow
> Day and night.

And so I say farewell to LOCHINVER and ASSYNT.   At the same
time I must recall that in journeying up to Lochinver on 2nd
May 1967, to a house I had rented, there was snow falling quite
heavily, but the sound of the cuckoo came over loud and clear!

*   *   *

This, more or less, completes my pearls of discovery in this
journeying of Sutherland.   Again I would stress not to under-
estimate the immensity of that county.   It is also more of a
fisherman's paradise than Wester Ross.

Fishing really is a great art.   Trout are always where boats are
not!   The presence of a boat on trout seems to have the same
effect as the presence of a minister has on people who haven't
been to the kirk for a month of Sundays; they scatter in every
direction.   Excuses given for a poor catch can be many; in-
sufficient wind; too much wind; a correct amount of wind but
from the wrong quarter; the level of the loch is too high; that
it's too low; it's too bright; too much cloud; the water is cold;
the water is too warm.   And so on, *ad infinitum*.

WESTER ROSS

('We're friendly people in Wester Ross')

Rubha Ré
Lighthouse

Gruinard
Bay

Laide
Ullapool

Melvaig
Aultbea
Loch Ewe
Dundonnell
Loch
Broom

An Teallach

Poolewe
Inverewe
Strath
The Gairloch
Gairloch
Loch Maree
Badachro
Letterewe
Slioch

Red Point
Beinn Eighe
Kinlochewe

Loch Torridon
Ben Alligan
Achnasheen
Isle of
Rona
Diabaig
Torridon

Applecross
Loch Monar

Loch Carron
Stromeferry
Loch Mullardoch

Kyle of
Lochalsh
Loch Affric
Kyleakin
Dornie

Isle of Skye
Glenelg
Loch Duich

WESTER ROSS

N

Loch Clunie

Sound of Sleat
Scale approx. 12 miles to inch

Wester Ross

CHAPTER 5

WESTER ROSS

OVER the past five years, I have written quite a lot on Wester Ross. It is easy perhaps to change, but incredibly difficult to improve. I cannot tell you of new mountains, new lochs, new glens and the like; I can only attempt to bring in some more details *en route*. The only thing new really, are the youngsters toddling around when I first saw Gairloch over fifty years ago. They are now grown up, married with children and grandchildren.

We now start on the left arm of the **Y** from Inverness, branching off at Dingwall to the left for Wester Ross (instead of to the right as we did for Sutherland). Ross and Cromarty—to give it is true name—is the only county in Scotland with a double-barrelled name. In Dingwall (the county town) there is a war memorial that was originally erected in France, and brought home to stand on Scottish soil in 1924. From Dingwall we go through Strathpeffer, five miles away. It is a very popular resort and centre for tours up further north, and is beautifully situated in a fertile strath. It has an equable temperature the year round. It used to be famous for its Spa waters, but this has greatly declined. The waters were of two kinds, chalybeate and sulphurous, bearing a strong resemblance to those of Harrogate in Yorkshire (again defunct) and Aix-la-Chapelle in France. It was really the discovery of the beneficial properties of the local sulphur water a couple of centuries ago, that led to the establishment of the then village as a Spa. The waters were at first looked upon as miraculous, and the parish minister had the Well fenced to protect it from cattle; but it was an Aberdeenshire doctor who popularised it by his articles in many periodicals extolling the virtues. Soon the local Cromartie family developed the Wells. A pump room was erected, and many hotels and houses were built to accommodate the flood of visitors who came for over half a

century for the waters. Of late many attractions have been
provided to make Strathpeffer a focal point for tourists. A new
Spa Pavilion in six acres of gardens, the largest and best equipped
ballroom in Ross-shire with ample provision for refreshments;
music and Highland dancing, pipe bands and so forth have been
created. In fact there is always something doing in Strathpeffer—
or as it is locally known as 'the Strath'. From Strathpeffer we
soon come to the village of Contin.

At Muir of Ord (after Beauly) you can take a branch road
across country to Contin. This is a pleasant run, and the road is
perfect, and runs through Strath Conon, through the small village
of Marybank, crossing the Conon river in to Contin. This avoids
main-road traffic and is more direct. (At Muir of Ord there is a
road turning eastwards to the Black Isle; Fortrose, Rosemarkie,
and Cromarty. Like many isles in Scotland, it is really a peninsula
and a very fertile one. It is termed the Black Isle because snow
seldom lies there, and is famous for its crops and cattle. In the
old days it was also said to be black because the greater part of it
was black moor, uncultivated.)

From Contin, in a mile or so, we pass the Falls of Rogie, a
famous beauty spot where the Black Water and the Rogie Burn
meet in a wild gorge and the water crashing over the black rocks
in a spectacular fall. Viewed when salmon are leaping in their
efforts to ascend the falls, the scene cannot easily be forgotten;
all in a setting of rock, heather and birches. To the east of these
falls and south of Dingwall and Strathpeffer is Loch Ussie, into
which loch it is said the Brahan Seer cast his divining-stone.

The Black Water loops north-west from these falls and soon,
following the curve of Loch Garve, we reach the tiny village of
Garve, set in the colourful wonderland of the north-west, among
waters and heights (Ben Wyvis 3430 feet, and rarely free from
snow, to the north-east) and moorland; unbelievably an astound-
ingly different country from which we have come only a mile
away at Contin.

Here at Garve, with a lovely snug hotel of fishing and food
renown the whole scenery changes like a flash; precipitous
mountains loom ahead midst rugged beauty; moorland stretching upon moorland, and if it should be September, the heather
for as far as the eye can see, takes on a colour of spilt claret. Loch
Garve with its wooded shores presents an incomparable picture;

everything now is so different; you seem to be entering a
completely new world, a break-away from the old.

Garve; the entrance to the colourful wonderland of the
north-west of Ross-shire. In the village, the old church and
manse were built on an island in the Black Water and tradition
attributes the burning of this old church with the women and
children of the Mackenzie clan, who had taken refuge inside, to
the Macdonalds of Lochalsh. The name Garve in Gaelic means
'the rough place'. The Romans, under Agricola explored this
area as there are recorded mentions of Uxellum Montes (Ben
Wyvis) and Portus Salutis (the Sutors of Cromarty). The Garve
Hotel—originally an inn—is said to be one of the oldest in Scotland. In the far-off days, the question of roads (or rather their
absence) was a serious problem; but in 1757 a military road was
made from Contin to Poolewe, but after about forty years this
track had faded away. In the early 1800's the Fishery Society
built another road, branching off a mile or so beyond Garve, over
the moors to Ullapool, where they had a prosperous fishing
village. Of course in those days, the 'drover's days', the men
driving their cattle did not take kindly to hard roads for they
said it injured their beasts' feet having to travel such distances
to the markets, and so they made their own routes through the
moors. In those days travellers changed horses at Garve. In
1870 the railway track came through Garve on its way to Kyle;
but of course for Ullapool, one needed to get off the train and
take the stage coach, as it was then termed.

What must be an unrivalled family link with the hotel business
in the Highlands is brought to light by the retiral of Miss Helen
Mackenzie of the Garve Hotel, and who died shortly after
retirement, at her home 'Hazelbrae', Garve, on 8th November
1966, aged 67.

I have a soft spot—a sentimental one in fact—in my heart for
this hotel. Helen was a good friend of mine and a great upholder
of the Highlands and everything Highland. And why a special
love for Garve? because I was married there; just that! At
this event she gave me the Freedom of the Hotel for the long
week-end I spent there in anticipation of the occasion. The
season had commenced but she had refused all bookings, so that
I could have the entire place to myself. How very good of her;
and I shall never forget it. That was only a year or so before she

D

died. Her own native village of Garve will long remember her, where her long years of service to the community will remain in abiding memory. She succeeded her father, the late W. D. Mackenzie to ownership. In March 1966 she sold out to Scottish Omnibuses Ltd. She was a member of many local committees, and an enthusiastic worker for every worthy cause. She was a devout member of the Free Kirk.

Her family's connection was managing not only the hotel (which dates back 118 years) but of the 28-acre farm attached. When she closed the doors of Garve Hotel in 1966, it must have brought back many memories to Helen of the thousands of distinguished guests she had catered for, so warm-heartedly; many of her closest were Americans. She had hotel-keepers on both sides of the family tree—the Mackenzies on her father's side, the MacIvers on her mother's. The men were also pioneers of public transport service in Wester Ross, dating back to the old four-in-hand stage-coach days. The family's link with the village, began in 1848, when Helen's grandfather—William Duncan Mackenzie—a Scatwell man, became tenant of what was then known as the Inn of Garve. He also became post-runner to Ullapool, carrying the mails there in saddlebags on horse-back. He gradually built up the hotel and the stage-coach (stand-and-deliver!) service to the west. His son, William Daniel Mackenzie, continued the business in the same high tradition.

Helen returned from London in 1928 to assist her parents in the running of the hotel, and became proprietrix on the death of her father. She displayed marked ability. The farm consisted purely of Jersey cows, and provided fullsome Highland fare for the hotel. The hotel was also famed for its fishings, with its own stretches on the Black Water and neighbouring hill lochs. Helen drew guests from all over the world, including many notables, as I well know. She used to show me the hotel register, with its eulogistic remarks, and even sketches by famous artists. A duke wrote of his most pleasant stay in verse as follows:

> Her friendly smile, her cheerful way
> Warmed many a weary heart;
> She has sent thousands on their way
> Refreshed to play their part.
> And Sassenach and Highland man
> Bless the name of Mackenzies' clan.

There is one secret (supposedly) that Helen took with her into retirement, namely how to make Athole Brose, for which the hotel was a legend. I am able to divulge it.

It is a traditional and energy-giving drink. The big drinking cup or quaiche was usually made in silver or wood. The recipe:

> 14 oz. medium-cut oatmeal
> 2 pints cold water
> ¼ pint Black and White whisky
> 4 dessert spoonfuls of heather honey
> and ¼ pint single cream.

And the safely-guarded method of preparation. Put the oatmeal in a bowl and pour over the cold water; stir well and leave the bowl for at least an hour, covered with a plate or board. Strain through muslin, then mix with the whisky and honey, and lastly the cream. Serve at room temperature.... Until her retirement she still operated the mail and bus passenger service between Ullapool and Garve. In 1912 came the change from horse-drawn mail coach to motor bus. That was an epic day for Charles Fraser, driver on the Garve–Ullapool route for 40 years. After a spell in the south, breaking in his new steed, he drove his new Albion bus into Ullapool with almost the whole population lining the route to cheer him in. Helen's other grandfather, Murdo MacIver in addition to his hotel at Achnasheen, was also in the mail-coach business. A man of stern Christian principles, he courteously, but firmly declined to carry mail for Queen Victoria on the Sabbath, when she was on holiday at Loch Maree. It was a refusal which Her Majesty was not accustomed to, but recognising the principles involved, she accepted it in good faith. Helen's interests included the W.R.I. and the Garve Works Society. She loved the hotel life, for it enabled her to meet so many interesting people from all quarters of the world. Helen's father, William Daniel Mackenzie took a deep interest in public affairs, and for over forty years—1895 to 1936—he represented the Kinlochluichart Division on the Ross-shire County Council; he was also a member of the Contin School Board, and the Contin Parish Council, and was chairman of both bodies for many years. He had the longest period of continuous service as member. Down the years Garve Hotel continued increasingly in popularity and success, and guests from a' the airts, including many who were notable in national life, relaxed and returned each year to its hospitable precincts. Helen entered her retirement with a rich store of memories during her chatelaine at Garve. It is a shameful pity she did not live long after her retirement. She was noted for her strength of character, richly endowed intellect, and a lively, wide-ranging mind. She was particularly fond of the songs and airs of her native Highlands. Of late years she did not enjoy too good health, but her clever hands were never idle, and she faced her last weeks of illness with the same resolute courage and evident serenity, which marked her life. She is survived by her brother, William Mackenzie of Inverness, and two sisters Mrs. Grant of Dores, and Mrs. MacRae in West Africa. The funeral service in the Free Church at Garve was largely attended, and many floral tributes were laid on her grave. Three ministers officiated, the Rev. Angus MacKinnon, Rev. Norman Morrison and the Rev. Murdo Macdonald.

At the time of writing, the hotel (of tender memories) is under the able management of Mr. Adrian J. C. Sewell and his wife, who—I know—are determined to carry on in the same spirit and tradition as Helen left it—and as she would have wished. Many improvements have been made, and all in all, I consider the Garve Hotel to be the finest hotel to the gateway of Wester Ross.

From Garve it is 46 miles to Gairloch, where I live and where no doubt a new chapter will be born; but owing to the narrow tortuous road it will take at least two hours careful driving. A certain difficult section of the Loch Maree road has been ironed out, but there are still other blind bends to be straightened. You may remember at the beginning of this book what I said about Time; that past Garve or Bonar Bridge you took off your wrist-watch? Well, you need to bear that in mind, and take things leisurely, for there is plenty to see and to interest you; so why speed? Just out of Garve, one road turns to the right; this is the way via Aultguish, Braemore to Ullapool—a good road on which you can make headway. Paying no attention to this turn-off but continuing straight on, you are on your way by Loch Luichart, Achanalt to Achnasheen ('Field of Storm') where the mails for Gairloch and Aultbea are transferred to the waiting mail bus under Alfred's protection; those for Kyle and Skye remain on the train till it reaches its terminus at Kyle of Lochalsh. All these mail operations are carried out with precision and ease.

just as I have indicated they do up in Sutherland; and whether the road or passes be blocked by snow or ice, Alfred and his various colleagues connected with Her Majesty's mail all over the remoteness of the Highlands, manage somehow or other to get through. I take off my hat to the postal services here. I also took it off to the road workers, so I'd better watch out I don't run the risk of getting a cold! If so, then it will mean a hot toddy at night and a Beecham's, with my hat hanging on the peg in the hall! In passing Loch Luichart you see the Hydro-Electric building at Grudie Bridge; beautiful in appearance, and particularly beautiful and intriguing inside as well. Visitors are welcomed and the charge-hand will be honoured by your signing the visitor's book. Everything is very spick and span. You may not hear the huge generators turning, but you might hear the Hoover polisher going over the highly polished red cement floors. We are now travelling through Strath Bran and by Loch Achanalt passing a house here and there, that's all, but plenty of real Highland country. From Achanalt you will see on your right a large mansion house, with turkeys, geese and such like, roaming around. It is the home of the Marquesa de Torre-hermosa, of Strathbran, whose late husband was such a well-known and respected landowner, and for many years a prominent member of the Ross-shire County Council. The Marquesa too, is an able lady and also a County Councillor.

You are journeying now with mountains towering in your midst, and through rugged country. To your left is Sgurr Vuillin (2845 feet), and in the distance Fionn Bhein (3060 feet), its lower slopes rising from the shores of Loch Rosque. There is nothing much to interest at Achnasheen; only the railway station and the hotel. Just out of Achnasheen the road to the left takes you by Ledgowan Hotel (beautifully set in its own grounds; most capably managed and every hospitality shown you), via Loch Carron to Strome Ferry and Kyle. (Note: the ferry at Strome does not operate on Sundays.) But paying no attention to this road, we carry right on to Glen Docharty, a gradual rise to 800 feet, and where at the A.A. box, it descends 1 in 12 to Kinlochewe. Just over this summit, suddenly and without any warning, there comes into view the majestic panorama of Loch Maree and the country for miles beyond—the great west country of Ross-shire.

Should you be fortunate to have a nice bright day, you will look down on this famous watershed open-mouthed, with miles of apparently molten-silver reflecting the morning's sun, with —it seems—scores of fir-clad islands floating on its waters, the haunts of much bird-life, gulls and grey geese whose homes are sheltered by the feathery trees rising from the loch itself; you will look down on all this and look up to Slioch on the right (3217 feet) and Beinn Eighe (Ben Eay) to the west (3309 feet)— a white quartzite mass. It is a dazzling view, this silvery setting, the more so I think because you are looking 800 feet down on everything. You may search the dictionary tumbling over all the superlatives you can find; search your mind for all the appropriate epithets, but none I feel sure can adequately or justly describe the sudden and terrific impact of the occasion. It is not as though you are on the edge of a precipice looking sheer down; nothing so frightening as that, but you are looking down and across to the great expanse of the west, and what it has to offer. A breath-taking panorama of that initial moment when every-thing appears before you fresh, new and shining; a herald of things to come; grandeur of stark simplicity. It beggars all description. The sight is compelling. At that instant you feel you have a sense of being a member of that company of original explorers and pioneers who opened up this country of the north-west. Of all the countless lochs in Scotland—or in Britain —none possess this commanding, arresting approach. A loch whose still and polished surface reflects as a mirror every detail of the enchanting scene, flawlessly. . . .

The Gaelic name of Glen Docharty is GLEAM DOCHARTAICH, and from the negative prefix DO and CARTACH—scoury or place of scouring—we get the term 'glen of excessive scouring', which describes it well.

Cruising down Glen Docharty (sometimes spelt Docherty) in third gear—there's no hurry, you know!—you soon reach Kinlochewe, a typical Highland village, with its neat little kirk erected by public subscription in 1878. Kinlochewe means 'the head of Loch Ewe'. There is a nice, cosy well-managed hotel there, with food at its best. A few yards beyond this hotel (the original part of which was built over 300 years ago as a posting house) the road divides; the left, or south-western branch enter-ing Glen Torridon and the renowned Torridon range, whereas straight on, the main road continues to the head of Loch Maree —thence to Gairloch.

*   *   *

Before leaving Kinlochewe, I would tell you of a cairn; a rough mound of stones on a hillside. Many such cairns are to be seen dotted here and there in the Highlands, built by children or a family as they romp the moorland. It is just something to do, something unusual to that of making sand-castles on a beach. But this *is no ordinary cairn*; perhaps not in design, but certainly in origin and in family memories.

In my last book *Sunset on the Loch*, I devoted much detail to this cairn; but since then, I have come across a sequel to that historical building of those rough stones, which (being one of the most moving stories I can call to mind) prompts me to again record what I had to say originally regarding the cairn, so those readers who may have missed that account, may now be *au fait* with the whole details.

On coming down to the bottom of Glen Docharty, and just before crossing a small bridge at a bend, a quarter of a mile from Kinlochewe village itself (and the bridge there, built 1843), should you look to the right, this cairn is seen a little way up the rocky hillside. . . . It is to the memory of one, Major Angus James Donald Macdonald, M.C., of the 1/6th Gurkha Rifles, who was killed in Malaya in June 1952.

Angus was born in Newtonmore shortly after his father's death, and his mother then brought him and the three other young children in the family to live in Kinlochewe, where he attended the village school and later went on to Dingwall Academy. He made the army his career, but always spent as much time as he could in Kinlochewe, roaming around Loch Maree and Slioch. He received the M.C. whilst serving in Burma in the Second World War; then he married. Going east again, he won his second M.C. in Malaya in action against the terrorists, and many times was mentioned in despatches; all of which the Kinlochewe folk greatly admired. His wife and two young sons were with him during the Malaya campaign, but in May 1952 she had to bring the younger one, Roddy (a babe in arms, who was stricken down with severe poliomyelitis) to England for special medical treatment and operations. The following month, June, her husband Angus was killed near Taiping, Perak. He was shot whilst leading and shouting to his men to attack a terrorist camp. His personal gallantry, to quote his commanding officer, far and away exceeded the call of duty; he had no thought for his own safety, only that for his men under him. He was a fine tall fellow (cut down in life at only thirty-five years of age), with Highland looks, dark hair and the bluest of blue eyes. In uniform he resembled the familiar Canadian Mounty.

His wish had always been, if anything were to happen to him in Malaya, for his remains to be placed in that cairn at Glen Docharty, so that he could for ever be near 'his' Loch Maree and Slioch. His wish was carried out in July 1953, the service being conducted by the Rev. Macdonald of the Church of Scotland, Gairloch. The cairn was built up more firmly by the village folk of Kinlochewe, who all loved and esteemed him; and then they hauled the heavy granite plaque up the hillside. The inscription thereon (headed with the crest of the 6th Gurkha Rifles) reads:

In memory of
MAJOR ANGUS J. D. MACDONALD, M.C.
1/6 Gurkha Rifles
Killed in action Malaya 3rd June 1952
Dearly beloved husband of Jean
and daddy of Andrew and Roddy
"If it be life that waits
I shall live for ever unconquered;
If death—I shall die strong
In my Faith and Free." . . .

Am not sure from where this quotation comes (it was suggested by Mr. Macdonald, ex-Chief Constable of Arbroath, now curator of the Clan Museum, Newtonmore) but almost the same words appear on the Scottish/American War Memorial in Princes Street Gardens, Edinburgh.

For myself, I could add these lines . . .

Softly the leaves of memory fall
Gently we gather and treasure them all.
Unseen, unheard, you are always near
Still loved, still missed and very dear.

The then babe-in-arms, Roddy, is now 17 years old; still having to be carried, still undergoing operations, yet still brave and courageous as his daddy, and nothing daunts him. His elder brother Andrew is 19 years of age, and is at Sandhurst making the army his career. They all live in Edinburgh. A long, long time since tragedy struck this Kinlochewe family in the jungle of Malaya in June 1952. Whenever I pass that cairn, I turn and salute, not only the bravery of the man whose ashes lie there, but the bravery of his widow and of his two sons, whom I know. As the French would say: ÇA DONNE BEAUCOUP À RÉFLÉCHIR ('it makes one furiously to think').

Now I come to the sequel. It began some 17 years ago, when Mr. Gerald Gillespie of Giffnock, and his wife were living on a remote plantation in North Malaya. One day a Gurkha patrol appeared from the jungle, led by a young Scots army officer. He was Major Angus Macdonald, and he and his men were searching for terrorists. The Gillespie's were thrilled to meet a fellow Scot so far from home, and for a day and a night he was their guest. When he left, they all promised to keep in touch. But though the Gillespie's waited for word from Major Macdonald, they never heard from him again. They couldn't understand why, and even when they returned home to Scotland shortly afterwards they often thought of him. Then in March 1968, Mr. and Mrs. Gillespie were making an early tour of the Highlands with their three boys. On their way down to Loch Maree, they saw a cairn on the hill at the foot of Glen Docharty. The boys begged their father to stop the car so they could all climb to the cairn—and a few minutes later they stood before it.

There, on the plaque, they read the simple inscription. 'In memory of Major Angus Macdonald, 1/6 Gurkha Rifles, killed in action in Malaya in June 1952'. Unbelievable, though it was, the question they had asked so often, was answered at last in the strangest of ways. Their friend had been killed shortly after he had left them. Now his ashes lie under the cairn, as I have said, looking out over the beauty of Loch Maree.

That, now, is the completed story. True, and stranger than fiction.

*   *   *

Ten miles brings us to Loch Maree Hotel—a very noted fishing hotel. The road along Loch Maree follows the western shore. Loch Maree is a gem if ever there was one; a real

Highland loch over 12 miles in length, 30 feet above sea level. Embracing beauty, romance, superstition, and of course—salmon and sea trout; mostly the latter. The Scottish Council of Physical Recreation, now runs a course of learning the art of angling at Loch Maree Hotel.

We stop at the hotel, which was built in 1872. From it one may see the loch is adorned by a number of wooded islands.

This hotel claims distinction on account of the visit of Her Majesty Queen Victoria who occupied the house from 12th to 18th September 1877. This visit called forth the reverential loyalty of all in Gairloch parish.

As we enter the doorway and look up we see a plaque bearing the translation of the Gaelic words on a boulder, 'Torridon Red' sandstone, Sir Kenneth Mackenzie, Laird of Gairloch, caused to be carved to mark the occasion, and which is to be seen just across the roadway from the hotel door.

The Gaelic inscription is as follows:

AIR AN DARA LATHA-DEUG DETH MHÌOS
MEADHONACH AN FHÒGHAIR, 1877, THÀINIG
BAN-RIGH BHICTORIA A DH'FAICINN LOCH-MARUIBHE,
AGUS NAN CRÌOCHAN MU'N CUAIRT. DB'FHAN I
SÉA OIDHCHE S'AN TIGH-ÒSDA SO THALL; AGUS
'NA CAOMHALACHD, DHEÒNAICH I G'UM BIODH
A' CHLACH SO 'NA CÙIMHNEACHAN AIR AN
TLACHD A FHUAIR I 'NA TEACHD DO 'N CHEÀRN
SO DE ROS.

And the literal translation thus:

On the 12th day of the middle month of autumn 1877 Queen Victoria came to visit Loch Maree and the country around it. She remained six nights in the opposite hotel and in her kindness agreed that this stone should be a memorial of the pleasure she experienced in coming to this quarter of Ross.

The hotel is beautifully placed in a sheltered bay backed by a hill called Sron a Choit, 970 feet high whose rocky tops rise above most beautiful natural birch woods. A small jetty was built in 1884 as a landing-place for the steamer which in those days plied up and down the loch, from Loch Maree Hotel to its western end near Loch Ewe, Tollie pier.

This steamer ceased to operate many years ago, but at the

time, afforded an easy comfortable way of viewing the beauties
of this 'Queen of Highland Lochs'.

The waters of Loch Maree are exceptionally clear, owing to
the rocky and gravel nature of the bed and shores. It never
acquires the dark and peaty tinge which very often characterises
Scotland's many other lochs. Loch Maree's greatest depth is
360 feet; mean depth 125 feet, and the volume of water contained in the loch is some 38,000 millions of cubic feet.

The steamer, *Mabel*, used to berth at the north-western
corner of the loch, at Tollie ('a place of holes') just near Tollie
farm, and you can see some of the jetty posts to this day, nestling
under trees and rock, beneath the rugged grey cliffs of this wild,
yet gentle beauty spot. This pier was erected in 1883; and on
leaving it, Fox Point is on the left; a low small promontory
terminating in grey-white rocks, deriving its name from some
legend of a fox closely pursued by dogs, taking to the water
here; either that or of some fox of unusual size being killed
there. Behind here, the river Ewe leaves Loch Maree, where
Inveran House and farm are situated. There are stepping-stones
across the narrow waters and legend calls them 'sweethearts
stepping stones'. Giant Fingal himself is supposed to have planted
them.

About half-way up the loch, the woods of Letterewe appear
('the Slope to the Ewe'). Near here may be seen the mouth of a
canal and on the hillside above, the track of a tram line which
brought limestone from a large quarry further up; now defunct.
Thence we see Letterewe House, a delightful setting, and used as
a summer residence by one of Britain's tycoons. Both in and
out of season, Mr. MacPherson, head gamekeeper and general
factotum, keeps the estate with its red deer under control. Just
beyond Letterewe, the Furnace burn falls into the loch; the
hamlet takes its name from the old iron-smelting furnace established there by Sir George Hay about 1605, using ore shipped
from Cumberland to Poolewe and brought down the loch to the
forest at Loch Maree which was burnt to make charcoal. In all,
seven iron furnaces were so situated until all the trees were felled.
The furnaces consumed over 100 acres of forest annually. 'Tis
good this is all defunct, for who would wish this countryside to be
labelled 'The Black Country'?

There is a story—still told to this day—of the first Presbyterian

minister who came one summer across to Letterewe to convert
the people there. The folk in the wee parish were so incensed,
they stripped him naked and tied him to a tree to be literally
eaten alive by midges. He suffered agonies and was half demented
when he was finally released one night by an old but kindly
woman. He fled as best he could, laying a curse upon the hamlet
to the effect that no godly people would ever inhabit Letterewe.

We then pass under Slioch's dominating gaze. Slioch,
composed mainly of Torridon sandstone, resembles, from some
angles of its conical shape, a spear-head and that is its Gaelic
meaning; an ancient spear or lance and also that of an ancient
flint arrow-head. As you sail close by and look up, it has the
appearance of a vast wall, a mighty Gibraltar in Wester Ross.
Cold, austere Slioch, whose blue, purple and grey flanks shimmer
in the heat haze, or stare vividly at you from the mist before
plunging steeply sheer down into the loch. Loch Maree is never
frozen over. The red deer are often seen to swim across from
their forest to the many islands on the loch, just for a few months;
then back again. From Letterewe and near by, the steamer
crosses over to Loch Maree Hotel, and as you tie up you get a
good view looking up the glen down which the Talladale flows
emptying itself into the loch. From Loch Maree Hotel, the
steamer wends its way along the south shores of the loch, passing
Slattadale, thence onwards till it comes to Tollie again; its
starting-point.

In Loch Maree, sea trout run up to 20 lb.; a record catch
for two anglers recently for one day was 17 sea trout weighing
79 lb. This trout season is from 1st July to 12th October.
Salmon in April and May.

There are twenty-seven islands in Loch Maree, all beautifully
wooded; the principal ones are Isle Maree (named after St.
Maelrubha, who came from Ireland in 671 to found a monastery
at Applecross (A.D. 673), below Torridon, and which has a ruined
chapel and burial-ground; and of which I will have more to say
shortly); Eilean Suthainn ('isle of fairies' or 'the everlasting
island') the largest, nearly 1 mile long and within it there is a
small loch with two tiny islands; Garbh Eilean ('the rough isle');
Eilean Dubh na Sroine ('the black isle of the promontory'); and
Eilean Ruaridh Mor ('the big island of Rory') and called after a
celebrated chief of the MacLeods. On this island, as well as on

some of the others, no doubt, the illicit distillation of whisky took place during the good old days of the 1800's.

There is much superstition up in the north-west country; this generally seems to be the case in most mountainous countries. The supernatural comes to light and takes on form in many ways: mountains and the weird shapes they throw out in the dark and closing mists; old gnarled and twisted trees; lochs with inky-black, deep, still waters; and the long drawn-out stilly nights— all go to make up legends, yarns and superstitions.

There was the belief that a draught of Loch Maree water was a sure cure for many a disease; in fact it is on record that many invalids had bottles of such water sent them in the certain belief of its curative powers. Nowadays I suppose it would be whisky from Loch Maree, should there ever be such a brand or blend! Recently I heard of an American millionaire who obtained a bottle of Loch Ness water by air mail, as he wished, in opening an old folk's home (whose Scottish ties were of the Caledonian Canal district) to give each resident a glass of real Loch Ness water. Verily there are no ends to ingenuity!

Among older superstitions was the Druidical sacrifices of bulls on Isle Maree which continued as late as 1678. The afore-mentioned St. Maelrubha, who brought Christianity over to these parts in the 7th century, allowed this, giving it a Christian aspect! In those later years the sacrifices seemed to have been connected with the resort to the island for the cure of insanity. This is recorded in the Presbyterian annals.

Yes, there are legends by the score: of a Wester Ross woman who had spent one year with the fairies; that certain peculiar noises and moving lights foreshadowed a death; that plants bedded when the moon was on the wane would never survive; that a stick cut from the bird-cherry tree prevents one being lost in the mist; that whales attack boats newly tarred, and that breaking of the Sabbath brings swift retribution.

On Isle Maree are the remains of a chapel, the successor of an early hermitage of St. Maelrubha. Close by is the sacred well long famous for its cure of mental disorders.

Queen Victoria visited Isle Maree on 16th September 1877, whilst she was spending the six days at the hotel. It was the Sabbath day and Her Majesty graciously read a short sermon to her Gairloch gillies. She then fixed her offering in the wishing-tree, it being understood that a wish silently made when making such an offering would be realised; and that should anyone remove or steal any such offering, a misfortune to the person would follow in its wake.

Near the celebrated wishing-well stands this oak tree studded with nails and hundreds of copper coins. To each of these was originally attached a piece of clothing belonging to some patient who had visited, or been brought to the spot. I must confess I have plugged more than one penny into that famous tree myself over the years.

In all probability coming to the island for the cure of insanity dates back to the time of the saint. The procedure was for the party to row several times round the island and those next to the afflicted forcing the lunatic three times into the water covering his or her head. They then stepped on the island, the patient knelt before the altar, then went to the wishing-well, drank some of the water, and finally attached some offering to the tree. They all then rowed back again to the mainland.

This well, so legened has it, lost much of its power later on, because a shepherd who had a mad dog took it to the well and pushed it headlong in. The following day the dog died, and a few days later the shepherd also died!

An American poet once visited this sacred well and was so impressed with what he saw and of the stories he was told as to the healing-powers attributed to the well that he wrote these lines:

> And who so bathes therein his brow
> With care or madness burning
> Feels once again his healthful thought
> And sense of peace returning.
> Of restless heat and fevered brain
> Unquiet and unstable
> That holy well of Loch Maree
> Is more than idle fable.

After St. Maelrubha's death, he became the patron saint of this district. His name is variously known as Malrubius, Murie, Mourie and latterly the corruption Maree. There can be no question but that this island and this loch bears the name of this saint.

In respect of St. Maelrubha's death, four parishes lay claim to the honour of being that in which his remains lie: Applecross,

Ferintosh, Gairloch and Farr.   There is no doubt he was the greatest of Celtic saints, and by whom throughout Scotland some twenty-two churches were founded around the north-west coast, Skye, Harris, Argyll, Islay, Loch Fyne and up at Lairg in Sutherland.

Fishing for legends in Loch Maree is a rewarding sport surely. All the world loves a lover, and many times have I told the following tale to visitors.   I tell it again, for I read of another version of the story in Brenda G. Macrow's *Torridon Highlands* (Robert Hale Ltd. 1953).   First, *my* story, which was told me by a Gillie some fifty odd years ago.

After St. Maelrubha's death at Applecross, 21st April, A.D. 722, the holy College of Iona appointed a successor to his hermitage on Isle Maree.   He was an aged religious man reputed to have great sagacity and piety, one to whom the local folk, as well as the Norse Vikings, could call upon frequently for ministrations of religion, as well as to obtain his wise counsel.   The Vikings held this district in subjugation, but to all alike, Celt or Norwegian, he gave his blessings.

There was a young Norwegian prince, Prince Olaf of royal blood, who was the chief of the Vikings in this part of the north-west coast.   Not only did this parentage warrant him being their chief, but his personal bravery and daring also enamoured him to his fellow clansmen to be their leader.

They all lived in the prince's war-galley, but during the winter months they would seek shelter and comfort in some of the islands of Loch Ewe.   The prince would oftimes come to Isle Maree to see the venerable saint and solicit his advice and blessing.

In due time our noble prince fell in love with a Norwegian princess, but he hesitated to bring his lady-love away with him to live on board a rough war-galley, as a life of that nature and in such surroundings was not befitting such a lady of rank.   He accordingly sought the advice of his friend of Isle Maree.   This blessed saint suggested the building of a high tower and enclosure near the west side of the isle, so that the prince could bring his bride there, surrounded in peace and quiet by her maid-servants and still be close to his royal highness's galley on Loch Ewe.

This was done and Olaf brought his beautiful fair bride to Isle Maree where they were married by the aged hermit.   The princess and her servants were enraptured with such a romantic secluded setting. Everyone was happy and life for the young lovers was one round of passionate delight.

His comrades, however, were planning another expedition and begged their leader to join them on board and sail away to plunder. His young wife was distressed beyond all measure when he told her he had to go and join his comrades and that he must leave forthwith. Shedding copious tears was of no avail to our warrior, who was impetuous and highly strung and so after hours of sorrow she allowed him to go off on this exploit.

But what if something dreadful should happen to him; or for that matter, if something should happen to her during his absence?

In talking over such grievous ideas they both thought of a plan to let each other know in advance how the other had fared.

When the prince was returning up the loch, he should hoist a white flag from his barge on Loch Maree should he still love her and all was well; if not, then a black flag would be flown.

This was arranged; and the princess too, when she saw her master's boat approaching was to leave her retreat in her barge and to fly a white or black ensign accordingly. Both then would know in advance each other's thoughts.

The years went by, as they do in all fairy-tale books, and in due course being victorious, the prince and his party returned safely and anchored at Poolewe. With feverish haste he got into his barge all ready for Isle Maree, raised his white flag of success and love, and urged his oarsmen to row fast to his beloved.

But all through these years, the princess had been filled with anxiety and foreboding. Did her lover, she wondered, prefer his exploits of war and plunder to that of the quiet and stillness of Isle Maree—their home where they could raise a family—or in fact was he really faithful to her when out of her sight? Was this exploit, and others too, a mere pretence for him to court the love of another woman? Under this spell of jealousy and distrust she thought of a plan to test her darling's affection.

When the prince's barge was sighted the princess and her maidens set off in her barge with a black flag amast; not only that but a bier was placed in the middle of the barge on to which the princess stepped, and reclining with the apparent sleep of death on her, a white shroud was spread over her still body. Then her attendants feigned utter grief in all this play-acting.

As Olaf's boat drew nearer he could see a black flag was waving from his beloved's barge—the flag of death; and he was beside himself with anguish and despair, being quite unable to control his agony of mind. When the barges drew alongside the prince leapt aboard, raised the shroud, and seeing that his dear wife was dead, flung up his hands to heaven, drew out his dirk and plunged it straightaway into his heart, dying instantly.

Now this was certainly not what the princess had expected, albeit she had assumed a posture so deathly real; full of grief and stricken beyond all measure, she drew the dirk out of Olafs' heart and plunged it into her own bosom.

She did not die until her barge turned back to Isle Maree, where the holy man was waiting at the slipway, and was able to administer the last prayers of comfort; then she silently passed away to join her beloved Olaf.

The two bodies lie buried in the grounds of the now ruined tower of the island; and a stone and two ancient crosses mark the grave to this day.

Truly a sad, sad story, but one that many old locals seem to have heard of in their bygone youth. We will treat the legend as true, for it will then lend a special air of romance to that lovely saintly island ('the eye of Loch Maree') set amidst the loch bearing its name—a gem within a gem.

As in J. M. Barrie's play, *Mary Rose*, there is one island in particular that 'likes to be visited, and where one never grows old'—and I would say that island should be Isle Maree.

And now I present Brenda's story: in it a Viking prince Olaf of Norway comes with his boat drawn across land to camp beside Loch Maree; and there he meets and falls in love with a Princess of Dalriada named Deora, who had a refuge on the island. However a rival suitor, a Scot called Red Hector, comes into the picture, and he fights and seriously wounds the Viking. Deora nurses the Viking back to health on the island, but has to leave whilst he is convalescing. An old hermit promises to go in search of Deora, and to show a red signal if all is well, and a black one if tragedy had overtaken her. To cut a long story short, the hermit flashes back a black signal, and this causes the Prince to kill himself. *But* it is the old hermit who kills Deora; he is Red Hector in disguise. One may recall that in Shakespeare's *Romeo and Juliet* story, a friar or hermit, was involved. Whatever it may be, the story is common amongst ancient legendary sources.

*   *   *

Loch Maree was probably once a sea-loch; the river Ewe which links it with the salt water of Loch Ewe is only 3½ miles long—doubtless the shortest river in Britain.

Anent Loch Maree, a story is handed down from generation to generation that one day after Culloden's disaster to Prince Charlie, a stranger with fair hair and clad in tartan, came to a wee farmstead near the present Loch Maree Hotel, asking for food and shelter. On the morn's morn he left and gave the wifey a gold piece. News that a stranger with gold was in the neighbourhood spread as fast as news *does* spread in the Highlands! The next night, a shot rang out in the stillness, and later on the dead body of the young man was found, robbed of everything. It was subsequently learnt that the young laddie was Prince Charlie's valet, who was carrying French gold pieces. A day or so before this event, two vessels had been sighted in Poolewe bay, and it was assumed they had come to pick up this man and his gold.

So much for entrancing Loch Maree, most of the northern side of which is privately owned and reserved.

We now carry on another ten miles to Gairloch, passing *en route* Slattadale, where we leave the shore of Loch Maree, and cross inland, through narrow Kerrysdale, where at Kerry Falls there is a small yet prettily built Hydro-Electric power station.

From here, skirting the Kerry river (said to be the Norse for 'the copse river'), passing the small stone Kerry bridge on the left (the turning off for Badachro, Port Henderson and Red Point) we soon come to the sign GAIRLOCH; then the factor's house, down the brae to the post office and the Old Inn (completely modernised and excellent accommodation) when we catch sight of the harbour and pier on the left, and Flowerdale House —for long, long years, the west coast residence of the Baronets of Gairloch, the Mackenzies—through a grand avenue of trees on the right. And you say to yourself 'so this is Gairloch!'

Having just mentioned the turn-off to Badachro (Bad-ack-roe) and Red Point, perhaps we should go back and take that road, which terminates at Red Point, 8 miles, and where the County Council have recently made a very attractive view-point. The road is perfect, though a little winding. It is a very pretty run lined with trees until reaching Badachro. Taking the journey on an autumn morning you will find the sun breaking up the mists hanging over the landscape, the bracken coloured red, yellow and brown; yellow birches and larches, a burnished old gold. Everything is still—a general hush prevails. The former Shieldaig Lodge—now a first class and well-patronised hotel, so much so that I think it has the longest season of any hotel in the district—comes suddenly to view, with its pre-possessing lawn rolling lazily down to the water's edge; a really beautiful, quiet, position. Passing a wee cluster of bungalows at Leacnasaide (Leck-na-saide), the road gives no distant vistas of hills or mountains until you start to rise further on, when you catch a glimpse of Gairloch bay and the mainland across, with the wee village of Strath bathed in a limpid light. This journey takes you on the south side of the Gairloch bay; and it is referred to locally as 'The South Side'. You then come down a brae into the village of Badachro and its beautiful, small, out-of-this-world, bay.

In days of yore, Badachro had a large fishing station where curers purchased the herring, cod, ling, etc., from the fisherfolk, and exported their catches in their own boats. It was said the cod fishery of Gairloch was historical. It was carried on by two firms who had curing houses at Badachro, Dry Island and Isle Horrisdale—isle of happiness. These curing houses no longer exist.

During the winter months there is, of course, little or nothing doing in all these wee villages in the north-west. But as spring approaches, the houses are freshened up by a dab of paint here and there, the accommodation signs put up and preparations are made for visitors. In due season there is a general air of restlessness; all on account of the foreign invasion! Cars and their human loads arrive, cooking carries on around the clock, and when these families leave after a week or so's holiday in the peace and quiet of these REAL Highlands—and it is exactly the same in all these wee villages up north—the rustle of pound notes can be heard changing hands. Sweet music! Yes, there is a deal to be done in these out-of-the-way places in looking after all the tourist's needs. The secret of cooking to them, is anticipation!

Cooking, baking and preparing meals, washing plates, cutlery and linen; peeling potatoes, clearing and setting of tables, besides attending to their own particular work in the cutting of peat, milking cows, collecting eggs, feeding hens, geese and maybe ducks; getting in the hay, looking after the cats and dogs and a hundred and one odd jobs connected with a croft/boarding house; late teas and cake, and then to bed for say a few hours only. Comes the dawn, then up again to this catering-cum-croft cycle. Feeding becomes the password, for they tell you that part of a Highland holiday is Food, with a capital F. And should you refuse a second helping, you are thought to be off colour! Surely Scotland is the best place to take an appetite—or to obtain one! Seldom have I seen so much put on so many plates so often and so willingly anywhere else in Britain. My! my! this is the life, you can hear the visitors saying to each other. If only we could stay up here all the year! God's own country indeed; fishing and feeding 'midst gorgeous scenery surrounded by lofty mountains, pierced by glens and lochs . . . relaxation to the full, and no worries at all. Could one ask for more? The breathing in of air that so refreshes the body, and the sight of the eyes that makes glad the heart. It is all so true; so real. There are no commercial fakes in the Highlands; it is just as Nature made it. And Nature knew what it was about in Wester Ross.

There is a post office at Badachro, with its well-equipped grocery store. There is a small inn right down by the edge of the shore, and a jetty. This picturesque old inn has a beer-only licence, and locals will tell you proudly there is no other such licence in the whole of Scotland.

Passing through this tiny village unspoilt by Time, and giving a glance to the right is the promontory known as Aird, where the few houses there look down on Isle Horrisdale and Dry Island. Whilst this latter island 'Dry' has nothing connected with alcohol, it seemingly takes its name from olden times; and from the fact that when the tide goes out one can walk across the stones or causeway to it; not always needing to take a boat to the one house there. To get across to the two or three small houses on Isle Horrisdale (official postal address, Main Street, Horrisdale!) you require to row over from the jetty at the Inn; in stormy weather one may easily be marooned 'at home' for a few days. But these little retreats—away from it all again—are only used as summer houses by their city owners.

Continuing along, we pass open moorland and a pretty loch

abutting the roadside—Loch Badnahachlish—and soon reach Port Henderson, where there is a farm, small stores, petrol pump and a telephone kiosk. Port Henderson is called by the natives PORTIGIL; Norse, port-gil (gate gulley); by others PORT AN SGÙMAIN (Haven of the stock). There is no 'port' now, but long years ago there was one Roderick Mackenzie, an elderly and much respected boat-builder. When young he went one day to a rocky part of the shore, and, whilst gathering bait, he suddenly saw a mermaid asleep among the rocks. He got near her and managed to seize her by the hair. She, in great embarrassment, cried out that if he would let her go she would grant him whatever wish he might ask. 'Rorie' requested a pledge that no one should ever be drowned from any boat he might build. On his releasing her, the mermaid promised this should be so. I am told by one living in the district that this is a true story—or at any rate the essence of it is true, for there is much superstition around these parts—that the promise was kept throughout Roderick's long life and his boats continued to defy the storms and seas; in fact I believe one or two of his boats are still afloat this very day; eighty years or so old.

From here, another mile or so brings us to Opinan ('little bays') where the sandy beach and sand dunes stretch for miles, and you always find yourself alone, or nearly so, looking right across to Skye with the tip of Rona Island and lighthouse showing. A post office and telephone, and another phone box further on near Red Point, completes the last link with the outside world. Opinan is a wee village which the stage-coach seldom visits! It boasted a school also, but that has now closed down, and scholars go over by bus to the Gairloch school.

The next small hamlet is SOUTH ERRADALE, a mile or so onwards; then comes the end of the road, Red Point, which has but a few crofts. In Gaelic, Red Point, AN RUDHA DEARG, means the dun or swarthy point. High up on the cliffs of Red Point one looks down on Loch Torridon, the islands of Rona and Raasay, and over them, Skye which seems so close at hand. On the far side of Loch Torridon, the Applecross Forest mainland one can see the pebble-whiteness of scattered cottages glistening in the sun in the various small villages of Fearmore, Fearnbeg, Kenmore and Ardheslaig. Further down Loch Torridon, but out of view, is Loch Shieldaig and Upper Loch Torridon, wherein nestle two other wee villages of Annat and Torridon, where the Torridon mountains begin.

Back now to Gairloch again, the post office with the Old Inn opposite. All the mails for this area come to the Gairloch P.O., where they are sorted, and the little red vans take them on their way; one lot to the Badachro (or South Side area) the other to Gairloch, one to Melvaig direction—then Alfred carries on with *his* area to Poolewe, Aultbea and Laide. Everything works out smoothly and dove-tails in perfectly. A grand old lady, Mrs. Mackenzie (now in her 90th year and still hale and hearty), was in charge of this post office for some sixty years. In 1953 she received the Coronation Medal in recognition of her services. Even today she may take a hand at odd times, helping her daughter who is now Postmistress. Old 'Mrs. Mac', as I call her, well remembers the penny post of Queen Victoria's day, *and* the relief of Mafeking, in the Boer War years 1899–1900, seems to her to be only yesterday! She would be around twenty years of age then. Even the Crimea War was only twenty-five years before she was born in 1879. Truly a great woman, and I take off my . . . oh! no, I can't take my hat off again, for I have a cold, and my hat is 'anging on a 'ook in the 'all!

I have mentioned the Old Inn. Long, long ago (when knights were bold, and monkeys chewed tobacco) this inn was just a change-over for horses and drivers of the stage-coaches. It is now very modern, capably managed and owned by my friend Donald Mackenzie and always choc-a-bloc during the season; Easter to around early October.

Quite a number of English folk look upon the Highlanders and crofters as being simple; but nothing could be further from the truth, as the following story illustrates.

As I have said, this happened many many years ago.

There was an old printer, Mathew Hardgraft who had a small printing press, antique and jewellery shop in Candlewick off High Street in Edinburgh. It was a dimly lighted street, as gas lamps were in vogue then. Mathew's name was not above the door, just 'The Printing Shop', for he thought people—seeing the name Hardgraft—might think he was a bit of a slave-driver. He had his nephew working with him, and the business consisted mainly of printing off religious tracts, betting slips, and a few bank notes. His nephew's name was Luke U. Wright. Mathew's

sister being married to a man Luke Wright. (I imagine he was
the originator of the school-children's highway code road-sense
in 'look right' before crossing the roads.)

Well, the nephew was a very smart lad, and spent much
time in the shop at nights in the back, designing the bank notes,
and printing them off for his uncle. One night the uncle went
in to see what Luke was doing and was shown a beautiful brand
new note, which the lad had just completed off the press. It
was an £18 note. Mathew gazed at it for a while and then said,
'Look you Luke, you're a very smart clever boy, and this note is
a perfect one, but I'd have you know there are no £18 notes;
only £5, £10 and £20 ones.' So what? 'Mark you, Luke,'
he said, 'we can't pass this off in Edinburgh, but I have an idea.
There is a stage-coach leaving for Gairloch tomorrow, so you
had better take it and go there with the £18 note, and as soon as
you get there look around for some old crofter or such like,
saying you have journeyed far and want some small change for
it is difficult only having a biggish note on you. Ask them to
change it for £1 notes. You know m'boy, they are a simple
lot up in the Highlands, and they'll think this is a new issue by the
Government.' So Luke came to Gairloch on the coach, which
stopped at the Old Inn. He went inside, and after talking with a
number of drovers in the inn, saw, whom he presumed, was the
owner of the hospitable resting house. He told him he had just
come from Edinburgh with no change in his pocket—only a
treasury note—and would he oblige him by changing it into
small notes for easy distribution. 'Sure,' said John (we've already
heard of Mathew, Mark and Luke you know!), 'let's have a
look at it.' Luke produced the faultless £18 note, thinking of
the fortune he was about to make. John looked at it, and in his
quiet Highland voice said, 'Yes, laddie, I'll be glad to change it
for you. Would you like to have three £6 notes, or two £9
notes?' History does not record the aftermath, or if Luke
returned to Edinburgh to his uncle's printing shop.

CHAPTER 6

GAIRLOCH

GAIRLOCH: the Gairloch of Wester Ross, the land of the Fàiltes and Slàinte Mhaths; a village and district possessing one of the loveliest settings in the north-west Highlands, a 'resort with a difference'—commencement of the real Highlands of Scotland, overlooking beautiful horse-shoe Gair Loch (with the islands of Eilean Horrisdale—sometimes spelt Isle Horistle—Dry Island and Longa; the Minch, the Cuillin of Skye, the wild Torridon mountains. And on clear days and nights, Stornoway in Lewis and the south end of Harris. Gairloch with its ever warm climate, even in winter, due to the Gulf Stream supposedly lapping its shores; limitless stretches of golden, sandy beaches (the safest imaginable), a small golf course—a village typically Highland and hospitable to the last degree; a hospitality that is not just a cliché, but a way of life. A coastline said to be the finest, not only in Britain, but in *Europe*; a friendly people with that old-world Highland courtesy and charm; a God-fearing Gaelic people who keep the Sabbath as few others do in this land of ours; and all this 'midst crashingly beautiful scenery, peace and quiet. The scenery is not merely viewed—but lived in. It is true there are no cinemas or dance halls, no bright neon lights, no rush of traffic, only one stretch of pavement, no No. 9 buses, no city germs (unless they're brought in by commercial travellers!); just Nature. An air of respectability, an air of difference and uniqueness—far away from the hurly-burly life of towns. The Scottish 'Wild West' in fact.

As I have said, when you pass the post office and the Old Inn, over the narrow bridge, the pier is on your left, and Flowerdale House on the right.

Discussions on the pier have been going on for years; it

seems it is in a state of collapse and the proposal is to build a new one across near Shieldaig Hotel, complete with ice-plant and all the ancilliary fishing facilities. But the all-important question of money arises. Most of the fishing fleet that puts in here, are from the east coast, and up to a year or so ago the men, after landing their catches on Friday evening, went back home returning here midnight on Sunday, to set out again for their fishing grounds. But since then, the fishing boats come in and unload their fish on the Sabbath—an unheard of thing anywhere else on the west coast, and I am told, anywhere else in Scotland. Even the fish look for a day's rest on the Sabbath. The condition of the pier is giving much cause for concern; but apparently so far no Government departments are prepared to make a grant for either repairs, or indeed for the building of a new pier, which would probably cost, when completed, little short of £300,000. And so the harangue goes on. Messrs. David MacBrayne are the owners of the pier, and unless repairs are undertaken on a big scale, MacBrayne's will have no alternative but to close the whole structure. So far as they are concerned it is isolated by sea and road from their current-day activities; and they say they cannot spend much, or any, money on it without getting a reasonable return. It has been suggested, since the pier was given to them many years ago by the Gairloch Estate, they should (or might) hand back the pier to the County Council. In short, as it stands today, the council have a ruinous pier on their hands, which is in imminent danger of being closed. If that came about, fishing operations in Gairloch would cease; and this would be nothing short of a calamity. The gross annual return from the pier is substantial.

The Minch has two herring seasons, summer and winter, together amounting to eight months of each year. The winter season begins in January, and apart from the Clyde, is the only British water in which herring are caught. Over the years the number of boats fishing the Minch has been increasing, and to facilitate the growth in landings, steps have been taken to develop Ullapool and Mallaig as major ports. In Gairloch the landings of white fish have been stepped up. In 1966 Gairloch handled over £300,000 worth of fish of all classes; Ullapool over £500,000. It would surely be a tragedy, if Gairloch lost this industry lying on her doorstep.

Two local fishing boats met one day, coming inshore to Gairloch. Robert in one boat shouted to Hughie in the other, 'Where did you get the herring tonight?' To which Hughie sarcastically replied, 'Where would you expect, Robert, but in the sea.' 'Oh! well,' says Robert casually, 'the few we caught were in the nets!'

Flowerdale House, as I have said already, is the west coast residence of the Lairds of Gairloch—the Mackenzies. Their east coast residence is at Conan House, Conon Bridge, Ross-shire.

Leaving the small bridge just beyond the P.O. and Inn, we rise up a small brae passing the Bank of Scotland—the only bank in the Gairloch/Aultbea area; the bank has a travelling van which allows the outlying districts to be conveniently served. Carrying on we pass the small 9-hole golf course (a lovely sporting course to play over, the greens and fairways being so well kept), the Church of Scotland; then the 2 cemeteries, a 300 year old one, the other comparatively new; on and up another brae at the top of which is the War Memorial and a pull-in vantage spot called CRASG, from where you get a magnificent view of the large Gairloch sands bay—a stretch of perfectly level, clean golden sand. You can wade out in this secluded bay a hundred yards or more, and still be only waist-deep in the clear, blue water. The bay is so extensive you feel alone, even during the peak tourist season. The unrestricted beaches here and around Gairloch— there are as many as nine superb safe beaches within easy reach in this *tir-na-mara* ('land of the sea')—are so spacious, so *un-cluttered*, that a few hundred or so people would hardly be noticed. And there are no deck-chairs with attendants pouncing on you for a 6d. or 1s. hire of chairs, as per the English coastal resort beaches.

At CRASG view-point, you see the whole of Gairloch's horse-shoe bay, and Skye; and possibly the fishery cruiser may be lying at anchor keeping a watch for any illegal trawling that might be going on. At night, when lighted up, the cruiser presents a most attractive and 'protecting' sight.

The War Memorial commemorating the First World War stands silently overlooking the bay, and has sixty-three names inscribed round its sides; men from Gairloch, Strath, Badachro, Red Point, Poolewe, Mellon Charles, Melvaig, Inverasdale, and

Kinlochewe. As you mount the twenty steps up from the
roadside, you read the inscription facing you:

Erected by
Sir Kenneth and Lady Marjory Mackenzie in memory
of their son Roderick I. Mackenzie, Lieut., Black Watch
and the men of Gairloch
who gave their lives 1914–1919

And on the base is the quotation:

'Be thou faithful unto death, and I will give thee
a crown of Life'.

Roderick Ian was buried in a private vault in Beauly Priory.
The inscription on the plaque there reads, 'Erected by Sir Kenneth
and Lady Marjory Mackenzie, in loving memory of their younger
son, Roderick Ian Mackenzie, 2nd Lieut. 1st Bat. Black Watch,
died 11th April 1915'.

Passing on, we drop down with the Free Church of Scotland
on our left, the manse on the right to Gairloch Hotel, a 3-star
55-room hotel erected in 1872, and enlarged over the years and
now equipped with everything of the latest. I have patronised
this hotel for nigh on fifty years; it has a most attractive front-
age; an unrivalled outlook commanding a beautiful situation
80 feet above and close to the edge of the large bay of Gairloch.
From all the front windows of lounges and bedrooms, wonderful
views are obtained.

The hotel is superbly decorated; has an attractive cocktail
bar and cellar bar; every comfort, with first-class food and most
efficiently managed and staffed. In truth an ideal spot for a
peaceful and contented stay; you are certainly 'away-from-it-
all' here. (During the Second World War it was taken over
by the Royal Navy as a hospital; for Aultbea, 15 miles further
on was a very important base in those perilous Atlantic convoy
days.)

Yes, quite a nice restful hotel. A number of the old and
faithful servants that I have known for many a long year, are
now living in the village, enjoying their well-earned retirement.
It is pleasing to see them—links and memories of those good old
days—and to talk to them of bygone times, and to wish them
all *Slàinte Mhath*. Upstairs to change for dinner; a good meal

and then to bed, and looking out on to a perfect bay, completes perhaps your journey for that day. If you chanced to hear the strains of a guitar playing O *Sole Mio*, you'd say you were in Italy.

*   *   *

Gairloch—the land of the *Fàiltes* and *Slàinte Mhaths*; and mentioned by that great geographer, Ptolemy of Alexandria, Egypt, who lived about A.D. 120. Its name is derived from two Gaelic words, *gearr* (short) and *loch*. It is a typical Highland parish; very large for it covers an area of over 200,000 acres, ranking as the fifth biggest in Scotland. It is larger than the county of Rutland in England, and bigger than Clackmannanshire in Scotland; but it has an extremely small population

In 1880 the population was over 5000.

In 1911 it decreased to 3300.

In 1951 the population again dropped to 1990.

In 1961 the census puts the figure as 1763, nearly 50 per cent decrease in fifty years; and today 1968, it will be still lower.

The parish has a tremendous coast-line, very indented and possesses innumerable and lovely sandy beaches—all unrestricted as I have said. There are more than twenty-five peaks of over 2000 feet in height; five of them reaching over 3000 feet.

Taken as a whole the people's livelihood may be aptly put as 'one foot in the sea, and one foot on the shore'; in other words, fishing and/or cultivating their bit of land.

In early days it was nothing for the young men to tramp on foot over to the east coast, Fraserburgh and such-like towns, to earn twelve weeks' money for the herring fishing; then tramp all the miles back again in time to fish at this side of the coast.

The northern-most boundary of Gairloch parish is at the river, Little Gruinard, thence it follows down the centre of that river to Fionn Loch (white loch) and Dubh Loch (black loch) and the mountains to the north-east of Loch Maree, including Letterewe, Loch Maree, Kinlochewe and as far as the eastern end of Loch a' Chroisg, the other side of Glen Docharty, almost adjoining Achnasheen. The boundary then follows in a south-westerly direction going across the ridge of Beinn Eighe and Beinn Dearg and coming out at the sea at Diabaig. From there, we have the whole coast-line Red Point, Longa Island, Melvaig,

Cove, Inverasdale, Poolewe, Aultbea, Isle of Ewe, Mellon Charles, Mellon Udrigle, Laide and back to Gruinard.

In short, from Gruinard to near Achnasheen, across to Diabaig (near Torridon) up all the coast-line, Red Point round to Gruinard.

The parish is governed by the District Council of Gairloch, the District Clerk's office being at Poolewe (he is also the Welfare Officer); and comprises six elected Councillors and two (*ex-officio*) County Council members. All serve for a term of three years, whereupon an election to the whole Council takes place.

I have already said the name Gairloch is composed of two Gaelic words. This sea-loch which gives its name to the parish is appropriately called 'short' as compared with Loch Broom, Loch Ewe and other more deeply indented arms of the sea.

As regards postal affairs for this region in the olden days, it is impossible to fix the exact date when a system was established.

Originally a 'post runner'—a man on foot—came from Dingwall by Strath Bran and Glen Docharty to the head of Loch Maree, the same way as we travelled. Then along the east side of the Loch to Letterewe and on to Poolewe. If necessary he would come on to Flowerdale when the Laird of Gairloch was in residence, which would be the summer and autumn.

Sometimes he might have gone by the west side of the loch to Slattadale, then over the pass by the Kerry falls to Flowerdale.

There was no post at all during the winter months. Even in summer the runner only came to Gairloch once a week, but when a second runner was employed, the post bags were brought twice a week.

After construction of roads the mail came by horse and trap three times a week, and in 1883 the post office authorities granted a daily mail, except, of course, Sundays.

There were no roads in Gairloch until the military roads were made, which took nearly the same course as the present county roads and can still be traced in places. It was all part of the system of military roads constructed under the supervision of General Wade in the first half of the 18th century, *i.e.* around 1745. By the following century these old roads had become virtually impassable by wheeled vehicles.

The potato disease commenced in August 1846, bringing havoc and untold hardships to the crofters of Wester Ross. The road at the upper end of Loch Maree and Slattadale was begun

the following spring. A Destitution Committee was set up in
Edinburgh with the primary object of road making as a means
of helping the out-of-work crofters. Nearly £3500 was spent
on the Loch Maree road; and the Committee also assisted in
the making of other roads on the north and south sides of
Gairloch.

Elsewhere in this book I draw attention to the superstitious
characteristics in these northern parts of Scotland. The Brahan
Seer had (as a gimmick we would call it nowadays) a perforated
blue divining stone whereupon he became gifted with second-
sight to a very marked degree.

Such a stone, charm or spell is called the *sian* and not only
can such a charm help predict the future, but it could by means
of a certain incantation render any object that it was wished to
conceal, invisible either for the time being or for all time, subject
then to brief periods of visibility recurring either at the end of
every year, or as was more usual, at the end of each succeeding
seven years. I may say there are quite a few people around
Gairloch who still believe in the *sian*.

There is on record the case of one Alastair of Charleston
Gairloch (a wee house situate near the pier, and to this day the
name still appears, although the building is not that of centuries
ago) who was a dealer in illicit whisky and was frequently
engaged in shipping cargoes of it between Gairloch, Skye and
Longa Island. At this time a certain Captain Oliver was commissioned by the government to put an end to this smuggling
business, and he cruised up and down the Minch keeping a
constant vigilant watch on any strange craft. Apart from his
main vessel he had a smaller one which was utilised mainly for
the sea-loch observations, so that Gairloch, and any other loch
Captain Oliver might be watching, was veritably blockaded.
When our smuggling friend Alastair was afloat and he was
approaching a government vessel, he would pronounce the magic
words and with the aid of the *sian* his ship would become
invisible to anyone else; and so it would seem our Captain
Oliver was always thwarted!

Another time, he brought casks of whisky down Loch Maree
and when he reached the narrows where the Tollie burn dis-
charges into the river Ewe he landed and hid the casks in the
moorland near Tollie farm; and making certain signs with his

hands made the casks in their hiding place invisible. Later on when requiring the whisky he sent his men over from Gairloch —those who had been with him when he buried the casks—to collect them and bring them to him. But his men searched high and low, unable to discover their whereabouts, and it was not until our charming charmer Alastair went along himself that the casks made themselves seen to him and his men!

During the rule of the Pictish kings (the Picts was a name given to a race that settled in the Highlands of Scotland, so named because they tattooed themselves) the Norwegian Vikings made continual raids upon the Highlands, at first as lone pirates and later on as followers of Harald Haarfagar, the first king of Norway. These Vikings with their unique and gaily decorated boats used to put in during the wintry months to small islands off the western seaboard, laying up their craft for that stormy period. The Island of Longa, in Gairloch bay, exhibits the Norwegian suffix *a*, meaning an island.

It has been thought that the Danes scarcely ever came across to the west coast, but those Danish invaders who were here were driven out in 1040. There can be little doubt from records made at the time, that both Norwegian and Danes intermarried with the women of Gairloch. One can discern certain Norwegian/ Danish characteristics in some faces of the Gairloch people even to this day.

It will no doubt come as a surprise to many that amongst Highland glens and landscape such an industry as ironworks could have existed. But such is the case. Iron ore was worked from very early times (there is evidence as far back as 1500) and the remains of blast furnaces—slag and dross—can still be traced, as well as charcoal deposits. This iron-smelting was known as 'Iron Bloomeries'.

The ancient ironworks of Gairloch were all near burns so that the water could be used to drive the machinery.

Early in the 17th century, about 1605, Sir George Hay worked ironstone on the eastern shore of Loch Maree near Letterewe. The furnaces consumed over 100 acres of forest annually and a group of ruined houses marks the village of Furnace near and below Slioch. There were also other iron-furnaces at Talladale near Loch Maree Hotel, and near Poolewe.

Many of the workers came from Fife and remained in

Gairloch and district for several generations. Deposits of bog iron ore as well as charcoal deposits have been found in many places around the Gairloch parish.

Reverting to 'charm' or the *sian* again, there is another Gairloch belief which is worth recording if only to be read in lighter vein. It concerned one Duncan MacRae who lived near Poolewe and was 'gifted'.

He was a faithful follower of Bonnie Prince Charlie and, after Culloden, assisted in the Prince's escape, always keeping close to his master, using his 'charm' to dumbfound the government pursuers. Funds were often coming over from France to this man Duncan, to be handed over to his Prince at convenient times and places. A small chest of golden sovereigns was given over to him for concealment until there was an opportune moment to deliver it to the Prince in person.

Duncan and his men brought the chest of gold across from near Aultbea to Cove, and from there carried it up the hill to near Loch an Draing, not far from the lighthouse near Melvaig, and there they laid it on the ground. Ducan made use of the *sian* and the magic formula to make the chest invisible.

It is still believed in Gairloch by some that the gold is yet there, visible though, only (as in the previously reported 'Alastair of Charleston' case) once every seven years; and then only for a very brief moment of Time.

*   *   *

There is an up-to-date garage just near the hotel, under the genial management of Hamish (Anderson), and his assistants. These expert fellows are exceptionally obliging, and at times in the season you can see them toiling to all hours of the night, fixing up repairs to visitor's cars, or towing their cars in when they have been stranded or met with accidents. I often wonder how some of these cars ever get up here, for some ought surely to qualify for the Old Crocks rally, London to Brighton. There is a small Scottish Home Industries shop nearby.

I now take opportunity of inserting a map of this general area made a little larger in detail, than the main one given at the commencement of this Wester Ross region for the convenience of travellers.

From the hotel and a little further on, is the doctor's house, the County's Road Surveyor's office, one small public library and the nurse's house; then comes the Wild Cat shop with restaurant and petrol pumps. This is a fine building and serves a great need to visitors dropping in to pick up local souvenirs, coffee and

snacks. By the police station (near the public conveniences) the road turns to the left to Strath. The road going straight up the brae from the Wild Cat leads to Poolewe, Aultbea, Gruinard, Dundonnell, Braemore (meeting the main road from Garve) to Ullapool. The left turn-off (Strath and Melvaig) is narrow for about 100 yards and a real bottle-neck in the season. Widening and diversion is now being undertaken and the local county road men are making a fine job.

We are sadly in need of an Information Bureau, and with improvements being made at this junction opposite the Wild Cat, this would be an admirable spot to build a nice cedar-wood

E

structure, with a turn in and out for cars.   Strangers coming here
know 'YOU ARE HERE' (such as you come across on maps centrally
placed in many a town);   what they want to know is 'where to
go from here', what there is to see, where can they get accommodation, B. and B. places, and so forth.   Some one in charge
who is pleasant and able to answer the hundred and one questions
people put to them.   The Bureau should be on the telephone and
so be able to ring up various B. and B. houses to see if they have
any vacancies.   We don't want an old caravan temporarily fixed
up as a Bureau, with two or three rickety steps leading into it
through a narrow doorway, which some folk would find a
difficulty, but a proper dignified attractive structure.   There is no
recognised Information Office between Strathpeffer and Ullapool.
I have advocated this for years, but always there seems to be some
obstacles forthcoming from somebody.

Behind the Wild Cat is a most up-to-date Telephone
Exchange, and soon it will be automatic and one will be able to
ring up one's friends in Texas—nae bother!   It has under-water
cables to the islands, and to Iceland.   Carrying on we pass
Achtercairn School which has an excellent reputation having
produced many brilliant scholars, who have travelled far and
wide in making their mark felt.   Next we pass the village hall
—if we can call it such, for it is a very tin-pot affair which has
defaced the landscape for many a long year, probably 30 or 40
years.   It should be burnt or pulled down, and another hall built
elsewhere—and a decent one too—similar to the fine one built a
few years ago at Poolewe and which cost about £8000.

There are quite a few folk in this parish who look askance at
the very name 'village hall';   but I cannot see the reason, for it is
really an essential feature of a village.   In days gone by, we know
the Highlands bore a special trade-mark by the many CÉILIDH'S
(cayleys) they had . . . 'a meeting place for gossip and song' is
the meaning of the word.   In fact, surely, the whole history of the
Highlanders *revolved* around the ceilidh?   There is nothing nicer
in the real Highland life—and nothing wrong.

I know full well the meaning of a public hall in a town;
just a dancing, 'necking' affair, which with drink available leads
to a hall of iniquity.   There is no need for anyone to tell me
that; for I know.   But in Gairloch this could not apply.   The
hall—and I prefer to call it a *village* hall not a public hall—has

been there for donkey's years. It is a rusted iron building, moth-eaten and a disgrace. In fact if you chanced to have a wooden-leg, you'd run the risk of getting dry-rot in your system before you left! Such a hall for the community—and of course we must not neglect the young people—could and would, satisfy a number of things; meetings (political and others), crofting talks, women's institute meetings, agricultural meetings, badminton (nothing wrong with recreation; after all, 'The Battle of Waterloo was won on the playing fields of Eton.'), lectures on a host of subjects; and once a week the Highlands and Islands Film Guild, with decent films showing. There is no limit to its useful purpose. If the community and the young folk are denied this means of meeting in public, then what do they do? They go to a dance at Aultbea or elsewhere, which may at times be somewhat rowdy, and coming back, draw the car into a dark siding, get into the back seat—and to say the least chat with their girl friend! Not to erect a new hall in place of one that has been there since time immemorial, is just making worse, worser!!

To my mind, it is not creating a den of iniquity. I have travelled extensively in both Wester Ross and N-W Sutherland; and in all the villages there are village halls; and in these districts they are God fearing and law abiding people. Ardgay, Invershin, Lairg, Lochinver, Scourie, Kinlochbervie, Durness, Tongue and onwards. I ask the question, 'Are they all wrong?'

Always there is a black spot in our sunshine; it could be the shadow of ourselves. I would end by quoting Isaiah, chapter I, verse 18, 'Come now let us reason together'; and again (since we should appreciate and enjoy the beauties and amenities around us and provided for us) to quote 1st Timothy, chapter 6, verse 17 . . . 'richly to enjoy' (vide 'Dedication').

* * *

We now come to a beautiful recently constructed promenade (made by our own road men) which has enhanced the place no end. The Free Presbyterian Church is just at the beginning of the promenade and further on, a local fishmonger's very attractive shop where you can buy many varieties of *really* fresh fish almost just out of the water. Thence over a small bridge we come into the boundary of SRATH. There is an excellent Hand

Weaving shop just at the bridge which deals in all kinds of Highland Knitwear—the real product; no imitation stuff. Ties, socks, wool, 'fore-and-afts', pullovers, cardigans, tweeds, pottery (home made) and so on.

Some of the knitwear, is the work of local women and all of it very beautifully done. They make a profitable income to their meagre fare during the winter months and the beginning and continued rise of this home industry can be ascribed to the saying 'sweet are the uses of adversity'. During the years of the potato famine 1846–48, the people were in dire need; large sums were raised to help them and those in charge of Gairloch parish undertook to support all of them in February 1848 until the following harvest—the able-bodied men working on the roads; the women by knitting. An expert was obtained who supervised the women's work and it was not long before 'Gairloch stockings' obtained a ready market by reason of their superior quality. Other small Highland parishes followed suit; the Scottish Home Industries Association was formed to look after everything concerned and to bring the trade under a more business-like footing. And so it has continued to this very day. All the crofters those days owned sheep and these yielded wool which was teased, carded, spun and dyed at home from dyes gathered in nearby dykes, ditches and streams. One can see this art of wool being teased, spinning wheels being worked by foot and tartan rugs and scarfs being made by hand today in many parts, particularly in Skye, notably at Portnalong, not far from Talisker distillery on Loch Harport, west of Sligachan.

There is a popular belief in the south that all of us up in the Wild West here, wear plus fours or Harris tweed suits in order to keep us warm in these northern regions! It may well be that going upon the controversial theory of 'Continental Drift', started by one Alfred Wegener over sixty years ago, the north of Scotland may have been in the Arctic Circle 120 million years ago; but not so today. However, such tweed is mainly bought and worn by those who, having come to the Highlands, wish to have something savouring of a Highland garb to sport amongst the gayer places south. (I once had a *real* Harris tweed suit made me just before the Second World War by a local tailor of Badachro, which I simply could *not* wear out. It lasted me for years and years, and in the end I had to give it away!)

All genuine Harris tweed bears the 'Orb' trade mark, over which (in 1963) there was one of the longest and costliest actions in Scotland's legal history; known as the marathon Harris 'Orb' tweed case versus the competitive 'Shield' tweed mark. The case lasted fourteen weeks, and witnesses came over from the U.S.A., Denmark, the Hebrides and elsewhere to give evidence.

The question was 'What is Harris tweed?'

In July 1964 in the Court of Session, Edinburgh, judgement was given that the only genuine article is tweed processed entirely in the islands of the Outer Hebrides.

The 'Orb' is the trade mark of the Harris Tweed Association Ltd. of London—used by 15 producers; the 'Shield' being the emblem of the independent producers.

In November 1964, the appeal made by the 'Shield' was dismissed in 'Orb's' favour.

It was declared that some of the competitive processes and hand-weaving were not carried out in the Outer Hebrides; in fact some were not even carried out in Scotland, and the wool was not wholly Scottish. (By the way, it may not be commonly known that there is another 'Hebrides'—the New Hebrides, which are situate in the South Pacific Ocean.)

Originally the crofters of Harris made strong cloth for themselves from the fleece of their own sheep, and when it began to have imitators outside the islands, the people of Harris in 1909 secured their stamp from the Board of Trade, which guaranteed that Harris tweed was exclusively tweed hand-spun, hand-dyed, and hand-finished in the Outer Isles. As time went on, and with production so limited, mill-spun yarn became the answer to expansion; and in 1934 the stamp was granted to mill-spun cloth *provided* it was spun, dyed and finished in the Outer Isles, and woven by islanders in their own homes.

After the Court's decision it was a day of rejoicing for weavers, mill-workers and mill-owners in the Outer Hebrides; and many drams went down the hatch in celebration.

Talk about the 'Tangle o' the Isles'; this case was the 'Tangle o' the web'. So Harris tweed *is* Harris tweed, produced by the islanders.

Onwards past the Swedish-type wooden houses, we next catch sight of the one and only bakery—Mackenzie's bakery;

and *what* a fine bakery and shop it is. I know of a village up in Sutherland which had evidently determined to do a bit of 'trending', and the baker's shop became known as the 'bakeothèque'. So what about the 'bankorama', the 'groceria', and the 'fishtique'? Continuing, we pass Kowloon stores reminding me of my Hong Kong days and 'Yung Sang Wong's' general draperies. This shop is situated opposite the Millcroft Hotel, a small cosy place; and then we reach the square at SRATH, where you can park your car all day, all night or all the month for nothing. At the square, there is the ironmonger's shop, the Strath post office (a real port of call for visitors seeking accommodation, advice, etc.), the general groceries shop—MacIntyre's, now taken over by George Leask, of Shetland stock; and Angus the Court-tailor's shop. What more do you want? Oh! yes, there's the Coastguard/Excise Officer, Donald who lives near by—so we're all safe-guarded. His designation from 1969 is to be 'Water Revenue Officer'; though I much prefer the former title I have given him. I am sorry to say, Angus, is none too well, and the tailoring part of his business is more or less closed down; but David (of the Old Inn) Mackenzie has now taken over, and developing it as a drapery and boot and shoe stores. Angus the tailor—and his superb art—is sadly missed. He was for 36 years a most distinguished tailor in Knightsbridge, London, where he made dresses and uniforms for most of the Crowned heads of Europe and the Near East. To name but a few, the King of Norway, Prince Bernhardt of the Netherlands and Queen Juliana; King Peter of Jugo-Slavia; the late King George of Greece, and the late King of Albania; as well as our own late King George and most members of our Royal family; statesmen and their wives, too. Angus came to settle down here in the quiet of Gairloch six years ago. I wish him a speedy return to health, as we would deeply regret loss of our 'Royal connections'. Since writing these lines and going to press, I am grieved to say Angus passed away on 2nd February (1969). A large assembly attended the funeral at the F.P. Church on the 5th February.

Now, to turn to the ironmonger's shop—'Kenny Ironmonger'; where just in front of the door you can see, buried at road level, an old circular stone, where in olden days, cart-wheel iron tyres were heated, over a peat fire outside on the square, then carried across, put on the stone's rim, and shrunk to the right size by throwing water over it all. Undoubtedly, Kenny—who took over the old ironmonger's shop a few years ago from the late Simon MacIntosh (when in those days oil lamps, and gas mantles were the general form of illuminants), has the finest equipped ironmongering store to be found north of Dingwall to Cape Wrath, and even on to Thurso. He is most obliging, and his shop serves a vital need to the community. He is also the local Registrar of Births, Deaths and Marriages. He has anything from a needle to an elephant—so long as you don't ask for an Indian, African or Ceylon elephant! It is said elephants never forget; the reason being because nobody ever tells them anything!

The general stores in the square was owned for over 110 years by the MacIntyre family, Hecky, who was one of the figure-heads of the village and most respected. He died in December 1963.

He had given the general management of the shop over to his son Roddie, a few years earlier, because of failing health; and then when poor Roddie was involved in the boating tragedy on 5th June 1960, and was drowned, Hecky sold out to George Leask shortly before 1963. Here, again you can get most of everything in the grocery, papers, books, tobacco, cosmetics and such-like lines.

Further along is the butchers shop; clean, tidy and attractive, drawing queues in the summer. Just opposite is a fine shop displaying electrical goods of all description, owned by another local resident, Kenny. Everything from a fuse to a deep-freeze. Near here, has recently been erected several new Council houses of a fine substantial nature; and then across the bridge is the Old Folk's Home—Strathburn—a very beautiful place, opened by Sir John Stirling of Fairburn, then County Council Convener, on 12th May 1960. Sir John's daughter, Marjory, is married to Brigadier Mackenzie, the Laird of Gairloch.

The opening was quite a signal occasion for Gairloch, and colour was added to it by a notable piper—Alex MacRae, a member of the Duke of Atholl's Highland Army, who was Gairloch born and bred—who came up from Blair Atholl, where he has a business, specially to play his pipes at the luncheon and at the opening ceremony. The luncheon was given at the hotel to quite a large gathering of those who were closely connected with this new institution, and who had come a distance. When the

luncheon was ready Alex piped the guests from the lounge into
the dining-room playing 'The Mackenzie Highlanders', and
whilst the main course was being served, marched round the
tables playing a selection of marches; and before finishing stood
in a recess and played a Strathspey and Reel.

At the Home, after Sir John had declared its opening, Alex
played an appropriate slow march—a Gaelic melody called 'Mo
Dhachaidh' (my home), the translation into English of the commencing Gaelic words of the song being 'Sing cheerily, couthily,
canty and free; Oh this is the hour of sweet solace to me . . .'

One of the most poignant situations in the world today, is
surely that of elderly people who, through no fault of their own,
have become burdens to their relatives. It is a problem that
affects the lives of a very large number of folk. The country can
do with lots more of these Old Folk's Homes. Modern medicine
continues to increase the number of years old people can expect
to live; but when will we strike the solution of making those
extra years happy ones? Our population is getting older. Fifty
years ago, elderly people represented only 7 per cent of the
population; today they represent 18 per cent—more than double.
I am afraid we have little reason to be proud of our treatment of
the elderly, seeing to it they are happy in the spending of their
remaining days in peace and quiet comfort, but rather we should
hang our heads in shame. In other countries the elderly are
venerated. Here the fate of many is to be shoved around from
one son or daughter to the next, like a pawn in a game of chess.
One case in the South, of an old widowed lady living in a Council
house who was ordered to 'tidy up your garden or quit'; she
collapsed after trying to wield her spade. Those who, whether
they be individuals or Councils, are engaged in this work and
programme of looking after and catering for the old folk, are
always spoken of in a glib manner as doing a 'great work'.
Well, how about joining in the greatness?

Proceeding (with Gairloch's bay always on our left), there
are few houses or bungalows, and 'Skye View' where I live, is
the very last house. Nothing more for a mile and a quarter
until the Youth Hostel, CAIRN DEARG set in a magnificent spot,
overlooking the Minch and Skye. Then, Little Sands another
tiny village, with its lovely sandy beach, with desolate Longa
Island in the foreground.

Thereafter comes North Erradale—just a hamlet—with a good garage run by Norman and Ian Bain. Finally Melvaig, the end of the road, nine miles from the Wild Cat. Melvaig, a post office and quite a few houses, and from here one can carry on three miles to lonely Rudha Reidh (Rue Ray)—the lighthouse. On the way to Melvaig, and tucked away up on a hillside, is a B.B.C. transmitting station recently built, from which we can get V.H.F. and all radio services—and television. Reception is excellent.

The journey to Melvaig is somewhat twisty, brightened in many places by the views one gets of the Minch. Out of season you seldom pass anything or anybody on the road; unless it be a few sheep or Ian Bain driving the mail bus. There is one deep cave *en route*, into which, legend has it, a piper is said to have led a band of men into it in search of gold; and never returned. The sound of his pipes was heard in the neighbourhood for many a year after his disappearance. This kind of story is common in many parts of Europe—so similar to the 'Pied Piper of Hamelin'.

As we have reached the end of the road, we must retrace our wheel marks back to Strath, and then take the other road, near the Wild Cat, to Poolewe and Ullapool, and beyond.

*   *   *

There were in the old days, many famous pipers of Gairloch named Mackay. The most famous was one Rory, who had one son John, born in 1656 at Talladale (Loch Maree). Both these men lived to the ripe old age of one hundred years. John was struck blind by smallpox in his very early youth, and was later known as Iain Dall (Blind John, or the celebrated Blind Piper) and learnt most of his art from the Macrimmon School of Piping in Skye. He was piper to the first Baronet of Gairloch, Sir Kenneth Mackenzie; and when Sir Kenneth died, to his son, Sir Alexander, 2nd Baronet and ninth laird of Gairloch. He was both a bard (poet) as well as a piper. One of his songs is said to be still unsurpassed in the Gaelic language. Rory and John are buried in the same grave in the Gairloch old cemetery. The blind piper had one son, Angus, who became piper to the tenth laird of Gairloch. Angus also lived to be nigh on ninety years of age, and he had one son, also called John—grandson of Iain Dall, born in 1755—who on the death of his father, became the family piper to the then laird, Sir Hector Mackenzie of Gairloch. Young John lived at Slattadale (Loch Maree), married, had a large family, and later decided to emigrate to America. On his departure, there never was another piper to the lairds of Gairloch. Piper John made good in America and died there (*circa*) 1840. So ended the illustrious régime of 'the pipers of Gairloch'. The four named, all of whom lived to such advanced ages, were pipers to the laids of Gairloch for almost two hundred years; during which time there were eight lairds in Flowerdale.

Whilst on the subject of pipers and songs, it is very right to mention the name of William Ross, a very celebrated poet, universally known towards the end of the eighteenth century as 'The Gairloch Bard'. The Celtic inhabitants of the north-west Highlands have always been enthusiastic over *poetry* and *music*.

William Ross was born at Broadford in Skye in 1762. His mother was a native of Gairloch and daughter of the renowned blind piper and poet Iain Dall, just mentioned. His father built a small house on Aird the site of which, Leas-a-Rosaich, surrounded by rowan trees, can still be pointed out. It was the headquarters of the Ross family from which they came and went; and here it was that Ross died. He was educated in Forres and later joined his parents who had moved to Gairloch. His father was a pedlar and young William went along with his father in his journeyings through Lewis and the Western Isles, and so became acquainted with the Gaelic language in all its different dialects. At the age of 24 he was put in charge of the Gairloch parish school and was most successful in his work there and his reputation grew. He studied Latin and Greek and became quite a master of those difficult languages. He acted as precentor in the Gairloch church. From his youth upwards he was never a robust lad and he died in 1790 in Badachro near Aird farm at the early age of 28.

He was buried in the churchyard at Gairloch and it is recorded the whole population of the district were present to pay their last respects to a very clever man. He was of their race, their blood and bone. They knew and loved him well.

Many years later, in 1850, a handsome monument was erected over his grave through the efforts of Mr. George Ross, a clansman of his, who for many years was head keeper at Flowerdale House, Gairloch.

The monument bears inscriptions in both Gaelic and English and reads:

> In memory of *William Ross*, sometime schoolmaster of Gairloch, better known as the Gairloch bard, who died in 1790, aged 28 years, this monument is erected over his grave by a few of his countrymen and others headed by the amiable and accomplished proprietor of Gairloch, in testimony of their respect and admiration of his extraordinary genius and great native talent 1850.
> His name to future ages shall descend,
> While Gaelic poetry can claim a friend.

He was truly acknowledged as the foremost Gaelic scholar of his day, and his poetry, it is said, came from the heart.

It should be remembered that a song is composed under two conditions—the air or sound (Gaelic fonn) and the metre or measure. The air is the melody holding the words in a smoothly-flowing order; the metre is the number of syllables in the line. Both these elements occur, and must occur, in the same song.

In a tour Ross made to Stornoway he met one Marion Ross —mayhap a kinswoman of his own—and fell in love with her. The passion or infatuation was only on his part, not on hers. It is believed there was, however, a secret engagement and Marion invoked fire from heaven to consume her if ever she proved unfaithful.

Not long afterwards she married a sailor, a Captain Clough, and went to Liverpool, his port, residing there. But her thoughts constantly turned to her real lover, Ross; and it is thought that when her husband was away on long voyages she wrote to Gairloch suggesting that Ross should meet her. He journeyed as far as Stirling on this secret mission but there his better sense prevailed and he retraced his steps to Gairloch. He spent many nights in the open before reaching his father's cottage and broken in mind and body, took to his bed for the last time. When the unhappy Bard was breathing his last, his thoughts and soul went to far off Liverpool to make claims on Marion, the fulfilment of her promise to wed or the end which she had invoked heaven to send upon her. She was at that moment with the help of her maid dressing in white preparing to attend a ball. A knock was heard at the door and she turned white with fear. The maid

answered and told her that a tall young man in Highland dress
was waiting without. She heard her mistress whisper 'William
Ross'. Marion went to the door but there was no one to be
seen. She was holding a lighted candle in her hand, and that
very instant the flame was blown inward setting light to her
flimsy garments and she was burnt to death. The fate of the
hapless Marion had been fulfilled.

The monument—over 100 years old and exceedingly well
preserved—is in the form of a stone urn, with a flame on the
top—standing on a 15-inch square pillar; the whole being nearly
6 feet high, and is situate a little distance up on the right side of
the old graveyard after entering the iron gates.

Another great poet, author and piper was one John Mackenzie who collected and edited the work entitled, *Beauties of
Gaelic Poetry*, which contained many of the Gairloch Bard's Gaelic
love songs, unequalled for noble sentiments and tender passion
to the fair maid who had jilted him. Early in life Mackenzie
was apprenticed to a travelling carpenter, and during his travels
he carefully noted down all the Gaelic songs and stories he heard
and of their origin. At Gairloch he spent much time copying
William Ross's poems and then occupied himself to the com-
pletion of *The Beauties of Gaelic Poetry* which took him some
twelve years. It has all down the years been looked upon as a
standard masterpiece of work on Gaelic poetry. He also wrote
The History of Prince Charlie in Gaelic; and was the author of
the English-Gaelic part of MacAlpine's Dictionary.

He translated into Gaelic many religious works.

He died at Poolewe in 1848 whilst he was preparing a new
edition of the Gaelic Bible.

On a projecting rock outside the Gairloch churchyard there
stands a handsome monument, with the inscription:

> In memory of John Mackenzie, who composed and edited 'The
> Beauties of Gaelic Poetry' and also compiled, wrote, translated, or
> edited, under surpassing difficulties, about thirty other works.
> In grateful recognition of his valuable services to Celtic literature,
> this monument is erected by a number of his fellow countrymen,
> 1878.

Gairloch and district in its days has seen many worthy men
connected with poetry and music; for where there is poetry,

there is generally music to be found; and where there is poetry
and music, there is generally piety to be found. Gairloch parish
has been a religious parish since the days of St. Maelrubha came
to Loch Maree and built his first cell there on Isle Maree.

*   *   *

Gairloch and district—in fact the whole of Wester Ross and
north-west Sutherland—is generously endowed with spectacular
scenic beauty, as I have more than once said, but particularly
brilliant sunsets and impressive cloud formations. One thing we
do have to acknowledge about the weather is that it is very
variable, due to mountains. But it is seldom as bad as it can be
in some much more boosted tourist countries abroad; but it is
unpredictable. This we know, and should never attempt to deny
it. The Americans say, 'You have no climate here—just
weather!' or, 'You really don't have weather here—just samples!'
I am always amused at the B.B.C. weather reports for the north-
west, when they say we can expect, '*bright*' showers at intervals!
There is one drawback on the north-western coast in the
summer, when no wind is blowing; and that is midges. Of all
insect life, I think the tiny midge is the most obnoxious. They
occur in swarms on warm, calm evenings June–October. They
seem to abound at times and can inflict nasty bites and lumps on a
sensitive skin. There are lots of anti-midge skin lotions, but they
don't seem to be very effective. One good homely recipe is to
bathe the face and arms with a dilute solution of washing soda;
but even then . . .! Another is, to make a solution of a table-
spoonful of Epsom salts to a pint of warm water, and when cold
dab it on all exposed skin, even on top of the head, when out
without a hat. Of course you can escape them, by taking a
rowing boat out on the sea. There is another old wives' recipe,
and that is to put a sprig of mint behind both ears! The only
effective measure to my mind, is a smoke-screen; if you can
stand it! Yet I would point out, midges do not *seek* out tourists,
for they are not travellers, but stay close to their breeding grounds,
seldom straying more than a hundred yards. Even the swarms
which attack you are mostly harmless males, into which the
females only enter the fray when ready to mate! As I have said,
they cannot tolerate wind.

*   *   *

Only a hundred years ago up here, game and wild life seemed inexhaustible; grouse, partridge, golden plover, wild duck, rock pigeons, hares, wild geese, and ptarmigan. The area swarmed, not only with game but with predators, white-tailed and golden eagles, ospreys, polecats, pine martins, wild cats, otters, badgers, foxes and the like. This at the time so recent really, as Gaelic speaking laird, Osgood Mackenzie was busying himself with the making of what is now the world famous Inverewe Gardens— out of a scarp of Torridonian sandstone. Now, there is practically no game of any sort to speak of in any real number. Heather to a grouse is what water is to a fish; its essential environment; and grouse stocks fluctuate according to the nutrition of the moor, whose heather has to be selectively burned to provide the proper rotation of old and young plants for both food and shelter. It is not so simple a job as to just set alight to the moors, and leave it to burn as it chooses. The great Caledonian Forest of Scotland for thousands of years supported capercailzie, red and roe deer, wolves, beavers, bear, caribou, great elk by the thousand. Now—none. Today however Wester Ross is a favourite habitat of mountain goats. They are the most ancient stock in Britain today.

In one's wanderings around these parts, you very seldom come across a notice 'Trespassers will be prosecuted'. This stern threat will be familiar to many in England; but I would tell you there is *no* law of trespass in Scotland. It is true that under the common law of Scotland, simple trespass on the lands of another is of itself, neither a criminal nor a civil offence. The position south of the border (in Texas way!) differs in that simple trespass is *both* a criminal and a civil offence. In Scotland so far as the criminal law is concerned, trespass is an offence only in such cases as it is declared by statute to be such. This applies, for example, in the case of railway property (it would!), canal footpaths, forestry roads, etc. With us here (God's own country, you'll remember) it means nothing more than a person who intrudes on the lands of another, without that other's permission; and it does not involve or imply the commission of any legal offence. It is, in short, a popular term, not a legal one. So far as the civil law is concerned, the appropriate remedy for a proprietor who is aggrieved by an act of trespass, is an action of interdict against the trespasser. The court will not grant interdict unless satisfied that there is reasonable ground for anticipating that the trespass will be repeated by the same offender, and that the complainer has suffered some appreciable loss or inconvenience. What then can the landowner do, short of recourse to the courts? He may order the trespasser to leave, but unless the latter is engaged in the commission of an offence, there is little more he can do. The use of force is not permissible.

*   *   *

As I have repeatedly said throughout this book, the Highlanders are all of a generous, good-hearted nature. Nothing seems to bother them. In fact as Confucius would say, 'remember of all the things you wear today, your expression is the most important'. There is an old saying, 'you can take a man out of the Highlands, but you cannot take the Highlands out of the man'. In the Highlands, memories are long.

*   *   *

I now come to recounting details of *The Massacre of Gairloch*. Nobody has ever heard of this; it has not been recorded by historians, or any writers. Everyone will know of such important events as the battle of Killiecrankie, Prestonpans, Flodden, Bannockburn, the Massacre of Glencoe and other minor massacres enacted in various parts of the Highlands and Islands long years ago—but the Massacre of Gairloch? No. And so, as the tycoons of film producers would say, 'I now proudly present' the Massacre of Gairloch; but not 'in glorious technicolour' . . . for the very first time.

It was a dark and dreary night.

The date 21st August; the year 1968; the day a Wednesday; and the time 10 p.m.

It is unusual for that time of the year up here, to experience a dark and a dreary night; but the fact remains, and so it all lent itself to a massacre.

A lone driver in a small Vanden Plas car has just rounded the bend from the Wild Cat junction on the road to Strath, and had reduced speed into third gear down the brae passing the Achtercairn School, and came round the bend to the promenade, where the Free Presbyterian Church stands with its main gateway. Suddenly there loomed up against the windscreen of his car, two bright glaring eyes and then a 'bang' accompanied by a shattering of glass. The driver thought his end had come, especially as he hadn't a gun handy (and his bow and arrow were in the boot of the car). He stopped the car which was crawling along in low gear as I have said, and waited; then got out, holding up his hands to safeguard any further attempt on his life in this sudden raid. He could see no men or bandits around, but on looking down he saw a black cow lying just beside him; blood—'rivers of blood' pouring from the beast's body. A black cow on a black night on a black tar-macadamed road. No sooner had he stepped out of the car, villagers were running up; both men and women. Some of the latter were seen to waiver, and the fishmonger's wife nearby ran out with brandy. The Vet and the police sergeant were both on the scene before the poor driver could mop the sweat off his fevered brow.

A shot rang out; the animal had to be put humanely out of its pain and broken leg. 'Who is the man?' some of the onlookers were heard to mutter; 'Maybe he's joining up with the new butcher, getting some free Highland beef, the whiles,' others said. 'Butchery, indeed,' a thoughtful Highlander said, in a very sinister voice; 'another Cumberland.' 'He shouldn't be allowed on the road, or else there'll be no cattle left in the Highlands,' another chirped in. 'Another Clearances, eh Donald?' said Hector, slowly sucking at his pipe. 'Was he alone?' asks another red-head. 'Aye, Calum, of course he was alone, why else? for he wouldn't be wanting anybody to see what he was about; sure he was alone.' And so, comments continued to ebb and flow.

A gentle tap on the shoulder from the police sergeant, re-assured the driver, when hearing the law's words, 'away home, laddie, it's no fault o' yours ye ken'.

In defence, at the Sheriff Court in Dingwall, the driver said, that whilst regretting the death of a 3-year-old cow, the fact was that a black cow, on a black night, on a black road, should not be wandering quietly along unattended or unchaperoned. If it were, it ought to be wearing a 'fore-and-aft'. 'A fore-and-aft?' asked the Sheriff; 'Yes, m'lud,' said the barrister who had specially flown up from London, 'my client means the cow should have had one light on its forehead, and one on its behind; and also m'lud, if it had had a small bell on its head that tinkled as it went along—such as the cattle have in Switzerland—all this

would have prevented this sorry, and bloody, affair happening.'
His Lordship nodded (no! he had *not* gone to sleep!). 'Moreover,
my client tells me that since the massacre occurred just at the
Free Presbyterian Church, the cow might have belonged to the
Free Presbyterians, and . . .' but His Lordship ruled these com-
ments as irrelevant.

The driver was acquitted and exonerated from all blame; in
fact he was commended for driving so slowly and so cautiously,
or else a bigger massacre might well have resulted.

This, then, in conclusion is the true story as given me by an
eye-witness; and as I have said, is the first time ever that it has
been published. Oh! yes, I almost forgot to divulge the driver's
name. It was none other than Bee Jay himself!

*   *   *

We have come back to Strath square, which is generally
the hub of Gairloch during the summer season. I have mentioned
the need of an Information Bureau and a village hall. We sadly
need a public convenience building at Strath; and also one at
Badachro on the south side of the bay.

Before saying *adieu* to Gairloch, there are two sad matters I
must refer to; the one was of the 'tragedy of the loch', in which
four key-men of the village were drowned in the dawn of
Sunday 5th June 1960 in calm water off the Youth Hostel and
Longa island—the veterinary surgeon, the doctor, the leading
grocer Roddie MacIntyre, and the garage proprietor Angus.
All married, who between them left seven young children. But
for the hand of fate, two others, the butcher and a brother of
Roddie's might well have been drowned. It was a major calamity
to the village. As I have written fully about it in two previous
books, I will not go into details further; except to say there was
a Great Silence over the bay; a silence conscious to one's very
touch—even the waves lapping the shores of Gairloch and
Badachro, seemed to be lapping them with a gentle reverence on
the day of the mass funeral.

The other sad occurrences were the deaths of two pious,
prayerful ministers in 1966 and 1967. The first was the death
of the Rev. Duncan Morrison on Friday 7th January 1966, and
whose funeral was on the 11th January. The second was the
death of the Free Church minister, the Rev. Norman Macdonald

on Thursday 8th June 1967, and whose funeral was on the 10th
June.

The Rev. Duncan Morrison died at his daughter's home in
Strath. He was 81 years of age, and his death ended a lifetime's
work for the Free Church.

A native of Lewis, Mr. Morrison came to Gairloch fifty-four
years ago as an assistant to the late Rev. William Mackinnon.
He was ordained in 1931, and was inducted to Duirnish Free
Church in Skye—a charge he held for twenty-six years. In
1958, he retired, coming to live with his daughter as I have said,
and son-in-law. But he still carried on his active work for the
Church, standing in for other ministers on many occasions. His
wife had died some years before; he is survived by two daughters
and one son, a doctor. I often heard him preach in the Gairloch
Free Church; he was most eloquent and learned. Many times
I used to go into the post office house and have long talks with
him. The funeral service at the Free Kirk was most impressive.
There were about eight hundred people present, including
twenty-eight ministers from near and far, and close on a hundred
cars; reflecting the respect and affection in which he was held.
Of him it could be truly said, 'I love my Master, and I love His
service.' He was a student of the Word of God. 'He ploughed a
straight furrow,' an epitaph I once saw on a tombstone of a
ploughman-farmer. It is surely the coveted praise of any Christian
among us. Among those conducting the service were the Rev.
A. Macfarlane of Kilmuir (Skye), who led the prayer and Gaelic
praise; the Rev. Norman Morrison, Dunvegan; the Rev. John
Mackenzie, Leverburgh (Harris); and the Rev. Donald Gillies
(Lewis) who offered up a prayer and tribute at the graveside.

The second death which also came as a shock to all of us,
was of the Rev. Norman Macdonald, Free Church minister of
Gairloch for fourteen years from 1953. He was in his late 50's.
In 1928 he had emigrated to Canada where he became attached
to the Free Church. Returning home again he decided to study
for the ministry and in 1943 he was ordained and inducted to the
Free Church at Ullapool, where he stayed for ten years; and then
came to Gairloch. He was a most endearing man, and his
knowledge of the bible was extensive and precise. Dignity allied
to humility characterised his consistent walk and conversation.
With his death at such a comparatively young age—in the prime

of his life really—the Free Kirk in the Highlands and Islands lost
a well-known pastor.   The graces of the Christian life shone in
him, and he truly bore the marks of one who was in close fellowship with Christ.   His passing has left a blank amongst the Free
Kirk congregation, and at the time of writing these lines (early
1969), no new minister has so far succeeded him at Gairloch
Church.   The funeral service was conducted by the Rev. M.
MacLean, Lochcarron, assisted by the Rev. John Morrison of
Ness (Lewis), the Rev. John MacLeod, Shawbost (also Lewis) and
the Rev. John MacLeod evangelist.   The service at the graveside
was taken by the Rev. Donald Gillies, Crossbost, Lewis.   There
was a huge gathering in the church, the churchyard and roadside
packed with cars that had brought people from all over Ross-
shire, Skye and the Hebrides.   They came to pay their respects
and affection, just as they did a year and a half before, to the
Rev. Duncan Morrison.   Truly the righteous shall be in everlasting remembrance.   The Rev. Macdonald is survived by his
wife and son, now in college.

*   *   *

Further references to Gairloch and the village can be read in
Chapter 15—GENERALITIES—under the sub-heading 'A New
Face'.   I am sure most residents and well-wishers of Gairloch will
read of the Art Student's 'Plan' with astonishment, to put it
mildly.   One visitor writing me from Warwickshire used the
term 'horrific'.

*   *   *

As these lines go to press, the Gairloch Hotel Coy has started
to build a new self-service grill room between the County road
offices and the nurses' house, capable of serving meals for 160
people up to 11 o'clock at night.   A small 'dispense bar' and
lounge is also being provided.   Later on, a block of 20 double
bedrooms with private bathrooms is to be built; and when all is
completed, this extension will be a real boon to tourists.

CHAPTER 7

ONWARD TO ULLAPOOL

So far, I am sure we have seen a host of pearls since leaving Dingwall on the left arm of the Y to Wester Ross. Garve, Loch Maree and on to Gairloch. It is said that if Wester Ross had nothing more to offer than the beauty of Loch Maree it would still remain a beautiful county. And then as to Gairloch itself, the whole vista is a pearl—beaches, sands and mountains.

Taking the main road past the Wild Cat and over the hill and across the moors brings us to Poolewe, 6 miles distant. *En route* we pass Loch Tollie (Tollie meaning 'a place of holes'), and then a charming view of this—the western—end of Loch Maree, with Beinn Airidh Charr in the background, and which, on a bright sunny day, almost rivals the other view of Loch Maree from the top of Glen Docharty and before dropping down to Kinlochewe, you will remember. It was from somewhere near Loch Tollie that Horatio MacCulloch's great painting of Loch Maree was made.

There is a very nice, sheltered, secluded spot down the side road leading to Tollie Farm and, a little beyond, which brings you right down to the water's edge of the loch, pebbly, but very lovely and restful, little known to the ordinary visitor.

On the side of the main road to Poolewe, barely a mile from the Wild Cat junction, there is a big boulder on the right called 'The Shoestone' (Clach nam Bròg) which derives its name from the fact that in olden days the women walking over the hills barefooted on their way to church at Gairloch, carrying their shoes and stockings, rested at this boulder for a while and put on their footwear here so as to present a proper, neat and dignified appearance upon arriving at the Kirk; and on the return journey, off came their shoes and stockings again at this spot.

Nowadays, round this boulder seems to be a dumping ground for empty bottles, tins and so forth, thrown out by our lovers of nature. No matter how many litter bins are placed for tourists to conveniently dispose of their picnic meals, you will find litter thrown haphazardly. At Blair Castle entrance to its grounds in Blair Atholl, there is a big notice with the following words in bold lettering:

> Resemble not the slimey snail
> Which with its filth proclaims its trail;
> Let it be said where you have been,
> You leave the face of Nature clean.

There are many legends as we journey on at every tarn and rock. One tarn, into which the defeated warriors in local feuds were compelled to throw away their arms; a rock where two lads were killed and buried by their ruffian uncles, who brought the blood-stained shirts, to show they had done this foul deed, to the one who had enlisted their services in the murder; but a friend of the two youths stole the shirts, used them in evidence before the Crown and obtained just retribution; a cairn where coffins were laid down when the bearers needed refreshment; and the 'Field of Blood' where cattle used to be herded together and bled, as blood and oatmeal were the ingredients of 'black puddings' then, even as we know them today.

From Tollie Farm (side road) we drop down the steep Croft Brae to the short river Ewe, to Poolewe village, lying at the head of Loch Ewe—a big sea loch. The village has the usual post office, stores (2), and the office of the Clerk to the Gairloch District Council, the District Nurses' house, two hotels—both renowned fishing hotels—and a fine up-to-date village hall.

At the post office, our friend Alfred and his mail bus calls in to deliver the mails for that locality on his Wells-Fargo journey. And here again, everything works to plan.

Before going on to Aultbea and beyond, there is a most delightful run through the village, skirting the southern side of Loch Ewe, to Inverasdale, terminating at Cove, where you see relics of masonry work of dug-outs, and gun emplacements built during the Second World War period. The road, though narrow, is good. From the point at Cove, one looks across the boom to Aultbea.

The village of Inverasdale holds close association with the 'Stone of Destiny' (LIA À FÀIL) which was daringly removed from underneath the Coronation Chair in Westminster Abbey on

Christmas Day 1950. And why? Because one of the residents in that small village happened to be principally associated with the plot—namely Kay Matheson, who was then twenty-one years of age, who lives there—Miss K. B. Matheson, of Ach-da-Thearn-aidh. She teaches domestic science at Achtercairn School in Gairloch, not so far from where I live in Strath. She is still an ardent upholder of the Gaelic language, and is Convener to the Executive Council of AN COMUNN GAIDHEALACH, which deals with Gaelic youth; and it is in these hands that surely lie the future of Gaelic as a LIVING language, and the whole Gaelic culture and way of life. This exploit was fully and vividly described in *And It Came to Pass*, the author's first book, and so I do not propose to go into full details here again. The 'Stone of Destiny', was removed from SCONE to Westminster Abbey in 1297 by Edward the First, King of England. As a relic of her Westminster Abbey foray, she wears—on special occasions—a golden locket round her neck, an heirloom from her grand-mother; and inside is a fragment of the Stone of Destiny.

In my former book I said that six medals were to be fashioned (struck by an Edinburgh firm) for Celtic silver ornaments and jewellery for those who removed the Stone from the Abbey, sponsored by Scottish National Congress President, Mr. Mathew Somerville. But this did not come to pass. I had a letter from Mr. Somerville in July 1968 in which he said that Kay was the only one of the party, who was 100 per cent sincere in the handling of the Stone business; she was in fact the only ardent Nationalist and there was a lot of phoney background work beforehand. He tells me the Scottish *Daily Express* gave it the Editor's blessing and a contract for an exclusive story for the Sunday issue at the time. Mr. Somerville who lives in Clydebank, Dunbartonshire, undertook at the time to present the six persons involved with medals, and he proceeded to collect Scottish silver, and enlisted Mr. Walter Pritchard of the Glasgow School of Art to design them. But, as he tells me, how could we possibly present medals to those who had 'sold out'? And so the silver was returned to the donors. That was in 1950–51. Before all that and during the Suffragette troubles, a bid was made to destroy the Coronation Chair with a bomb. In 1934 Mr. David Kirkwood, M.P. was given leave to bring in a Bill to transfer the Stone to Holyrood Palace. Nothing came of it. In 1936 came the first 'Plot'. The Dean of Westminster revealed the projected attempt to take the Stone away, Scottish Nationalists being blamed. And in that year, the Wallace sword was stolen from the Wallace Monument, Stirling. Mr. Mathew Somerville was the leader of this group who removed the sword; and in the three years they had it in their possession, great care was taken of it. In 1939 a super burglar alarm was installed in the Abbey, and later an invisible ray alarm was introduced to guard the Chair and the Stone But for all that it was taken away on Christmas Day 1950 and brought back to Scotland. The whole story as Kay told me one evening in my home here in 1961 is most enthralling; not to say exciting.

A legend attached to the Stone says it was the stone which the patriarch Jacob used as a pillow at Bethel. An ancient Latin rhyme about it, is translated thus:

> Unless the fates shall faithless prove
> And prophets speak in vain;
> Where'er is found the sacred stone
> The Scottish race shall reign.

This prophecy is supposed to have been fulfilled when James VI of Scotland became James I of England. Another legend is that it was taken from the Holy Land to Spain, thence to Ireland and then to Scotland. The Stone was kept at SCONE (SKOON) near Perth and Scottish King's were seated on it at their Coronation.

When King Robert Bruce won back Scotland's independence from Edward III, he demanded back the Stone, for he knew of the superstition in Scotland that his land could never be prosperous until the Stone was returned, and in 1328, by the Treaty of Northampton, it was agreed that it should be sent back to Scotland with the other stately belongings that were taken by Edward I; but the bargain was never kept. As it was being conveyed through London the mob made so threatening a demonstration that its bearers were compelled to return it to Westminster Abbey.

Up till 1950, when it was removed, it only left the abbey once —when Cromwell as Lord Protector sat on it in the adjacent hall.

At the end of the 1950 exploit, it was decided to return the Stone to Arbroath Abbey (for it was there the original 'Declaration of Independence' was signed).

It was taken there by car by two of the male members of the plot and another keen outsider. The Stone was carried through the Abbey Gates, across what is now a carpet of green turf, placed in front of the High Altar and covered with the blue and white of the St. Andrew's Cross. As they turned away, the leader seemed to hear the voice of Scotland speak as clearly as it spoke in 1320 ... 'For so long as there shall be but one hundred of us remain alive we will never give consent to subject ourselves to the dominion of the English. For it is not glory; it is not riches, neither is it honour, but it is liberty alone that we fight and contend for, which no honest man will lose but with his life.'

Thus the Stone came to its resting place.

The prime mover of it all was one of Scotland's most fervent advocates of Home Rule; Dr. John MacCormick who died in Glasgow in October 1961, aged but 56 years. He was a lawyer by profession and one of the greatest orators Scotland has produced this century. He was knicknamed 'King John', and he might conceivably have become Prime Minister of Scotland; but in the end his various associates—his lieutenants—melted away. In short, he was a Wallace of the Word.

At the time of the incident, many letters appeared in the Press, and quite a few made up verses in connection with the affair. There was one, exceptionally good, under the title 'The Elusive Stone', that a young girl of thirteen studying at Inverness Royal Academy wrote, and she was awarded first prize, and was highly commended by all the teachers in the College. Her name 'Lesley Margaret', and her home was in Aberdeen. She is now in her early thirties, married and holds an important position in the field of education. I have purposedly omitted giving her surname. It is a privilege to reproduce the poem hereunder.

> 'Twas on a dark and windy night,
>   During the festive season,
> A band of people took to flight
>   For a very excellent reason;
> They'd stolen a stone, a famous stone,
> The ancient grey Stone of Scone.
>
> Away they dashed to the Scottish Border
>   With greatest possible speed,
> Evading attempts of law and order
>   Who tried their flight to impede;

For they'd filched a stone, an illustrious stone,
The ancient grey Stone of Scone.

Once safely over, they hid the plunder,
   Where it was, no one knew,
Official red tape was torn asunder
   As the Sassenachs looked for a clue;
For they'd lost a stone, a valuable stone,
The ancient grey Stone of Scone.

It was found at last in an age-old church,
   Where it was carefully placed,
Other news items were left in the lurch
   As 'tecs to the spot were raced;
For they'd found the stone, the historical stone,
The ancient grey Stone of Scone.

Now over it there's great controversy
   In countries far and near,
Loyal Scots believe it heresy
   For England to house this relic dear;
Both want the stone, the symbolical stone,
The ancient grey Stone of Scone.

The Stone of Destiny was also called the 'Fatale Marmor' from the notion inscribed on it, that wherever this stone is, the Scots shall be the dominant power; and the succession of the Stuarts is thought to be sufficient to justify the prophecy.

*   *   *

Leaving Poolewe village and rejoining the main road just at the post office, we head for Aultbea. Just along the road and beyond the village hall, the National Trust has built a new caravan-camping site with all modern conveniences (including clothes washing machines), and surrounded it by attractive open baffle boards and named it 'The Stage House'; and if there were a few horses tethered to the boards, it would certainly resemble the Wild West. There is a petrol station nearby. Next is Inverewe Gardens, complete with restaurant; and Inverewe white house looking majestically out over Loch Ewe. These sub-tropical gardens draw thousands of visitors each summer. During 1968, 105,700 went through the turnstiles, and in time it will be Inverqueue they'll be calling it! There is ample car parking accommodation outside the gardens.

INVEREWE, the Highland Garden famed for its rare plants and superb background of loch and mountain; situated at Poolewe, Wester Ross, 85 miles from Inverness, 36 from Achnasheen, and 7 from Gairloch. Open weekdays 10 a.m.–dusk; Sundays 2 p.m.–dusk.

So reads, in generally accepted terms, the references one sees in many places as to these sub-tropical gardens.

Briefly, the famous Inverewe Gardens and Estate situated on the Inverewe peninsula—so aptly described by its Gaelic name Àm Ploc Ard, the high lump, and a mass of red Torridonian sandstone—were commenced by Mr. Osgood Mackenzie in 1862, just over 100 years ago. The big white house itself was built in 1865.

At that time the ground was a bare promontory on which were growing only stunted willows. With the exception of the thin low line of the north end of Lewis, 40 miles away, there was nothing between its top and Labrador, and it was continually soused with salt spray. Mr. Mackenzie planted trees and waited for 20 years. He cut clearings and to their shelter carried earth and peat to make these gardens. He filled them with rare and lovely things; trees, shrubs and plants from China, Tasmania, Tibet, Central America, Chile, South Africa, New Zealand, the Himalayas, Australia and Japan. And today it is a paradise, a Garden of Eden. His daughter, Mrs. Mairi Sawyer, carried on her father's work until she died in 1953, shortly after formally handing over the Gardens the year before to the National Trust for Scotland, with an endowment for its upkeep. (It was only in 1950 that this N.T. for Scotland set up a Scottish Gardens Committee to act as an advisory body to the Trust and to guide policy concerning the administration of gardens connected with properties owned by the Trust.)

In respect of Inverewe the Trust is deeply indebted to the Pilgrim Trust who made a grant for the maintenance and development of the property, and to a Life Member of the Trust who contributes a generous sum annually from the income of a private charitable trust. By this combined effort the Trust is now in a position to ensure the preservation of the gardens in the years to come.

Mr. Osgood Mackenzie believed that the proximity of the Gulf Stream would provide the warmth for a garden at Inverewe and would be virtually free from frost.

There are exotic plants by the hundreds, and its charm lies in its naturalness and true magnificence of its setting.

As I have said in 1968 over 105,000 visitors paid to see these gardens, enjoying its quiet beauty; sometimes as many as 600 or 700 visited it daily. All this could not have been accomplished without the most careful planning and it will for all time remain a monument and tribute to the enterprise and forethought of its original owner, who died in 1922.

In 1954, Dr. J. Macqueen Cowan, C.B.E., V.M.H., F.L.S., F.R.S.E. retired from the office of Assistant Regius Keeper of the Royal Botanic Garden, Edinburgh, and took up residence at Inverewe House to look after the gardens for the Trust, and when he died in 1960, his widow, Mrs. Cowan, carried on her husband's work. The centenary of the gardens was held on 7 April 1962, and shortly afterwards Mrs. Cowan relinguished charge.

Early in 1963 Miss Alice Maconochie, who had been general organiser of Scotland's Gardens Scheme since 1954, was appointed the National Trust's representative. She and her mother, Lady Maconochie, reside in the big white house. In the New Year Honours List, January 1969, Miss Maconochie was awarded the M.B.E.

The question is often asked, 'What is the best time to see Inverewe?' Conditions vary from year to year, and so no definite answer can be given; but there is plenty of interest to be seen at every season.

In a good rhododendron year the display of colour reaches its height *late April–early May*. The early rhododendrons flower in *February* and *March*, and towards the *end of March* daffodils are coming into bloom.

Azaleas enhance the coloured glory towards the *end of May*.

The Rock Garden is at its best *late May–early June*, apart from a host of other plants flowering throughout the whole season.

By the *middle of June* most rhododendrons have finished flowering.

All through *June* and *July*, colour is to be seen in the massed plantings of primulas and meconopsis.

The herbaceous border is at its best in *July* and *August*.

Hydrangeas begin to flower in *August* continuing through *September*, *October*, *November* and even into *December*.

In *September* heaths and heathers are at their best; and in

October and early *November* the leaves of maples and other trees and shrubs have turned to yellow, red or russet brown. Even in *December, January* and *February* a few plants will always be found in flower.

Inverewe is a 'must' for everyone who comes to Gairloch. It is an amazing accomplishment, an unknown quantity quite unbelievable in the far, far north of Wester Ross. Eucalyptus trees over 90 feet high, and a Eucryphia with a spread of over 80 feet gives some idea of this isolated Paradise, or as another book terms it, an 'oasis of the North'.

Just before reaching the garden entrance gate, you pass on the seaward side a carefully made conical cairn to which a plaque has been fixed with the following inscription cast in bold lettering:

> In memory of Alexander Cameron
> The Tournaig Bard, 1848–1933
> Who lived all his long, useful and highly respected life on
> the shores of Loch Ewe and whose Gaelic poems and songs
> earned for him a wide and an honoured reputation
> throughout the North.

Here follows another eulogy to his memory in Gaelic. (*Tournaig* is a large house with a croft or two around, a mile out from Inverewe on the Aultbea road.)

As I have said the gardens are a veritable tribute to those who undertook such a task. It clearly demonstrates that the labour put into any worthy conception is never wasted; and after a thorough tour of these gardens you cannot but come away, closing the gates, thinking of those words written on Wren's tomb in St. Paul's Cathedral:

> SI MONUMENTUM REQUIRIS CIRCUMSPICE
> 'if you seek his monument, look around'

Such words are so appropriate to Osgood Mackenzie and his daughter, who carried on her father's wealth of fortitude.

From Inverewe, the road rises, sometimes quite high looking down on to Loch Ewe. There is another grand view-point with car park recently made on this route. Coasting and cruising along at a gentle pace we drop down the hill to AULTBEA (Alt-bay), where you see a pier newly built (for a NATO base here); and as you turn left into the village, many hidden fuel tanks have been built into the hillside. There is an excellent hotel—a fishing one, again; a few shops (and a grill room establishment) and of course the village hall, which they tell me has the finest dance floor in the Highlands; people come from Strathpeffer and Dingwall to join in the fun. Aultbea was a great naval base in the two wars, and there is still naval personnel living there, since the boom can still operate. There is a pretty little run down to MELLON CHARLES. Mellon means 'small hill' and Bonnie Prince Charlie is said to have sailed from here on his way to hide in South Uist.

We carry on to LAIDE, only another few miles across the peninsula—or neck of land—which again is a tiny hamlet at the southern part of GRUINARD BAY, with Gruinard island facing, and the Summer Isles afar off. There are eight small islands which make up what is known as the Summer Isles. The whole —on a fine day—provides an enchanting panorama. No wonder, in all the coastal regions we have travelled, both in Wester Ross and north-west Sutherland, this whole area has been called by experts as having the finest coastal scenery in Europe. These Summer Isles were the scenes of much smuggling in olden days.

There is a lovely little sandy beach and bay a little over two miles north of Laide named Mellon Udrigle; a nice cooling name too! On the way you pass Loch na Beiste which long years ago was haunted and inhabited by a monster (the devil) and no walker would ever venture past this evil loch. In order to allay the fears which this legendary beast had upon the local folk, and which the local Free Presbyterian minister failed to exorcise, it was decided to drain the loch. This, however, was found to be too formidable a task, so they resorted to killing the water Kelpie by emptying barrels of lime into the loch; and nothing further was heard of this beastie, only the name of the loch reminds us now of this legend.

Still another piece of legend which is recorded as taking place as late as 1826, and connected with Mellon Udrigle.

It was communion week, miles distant at Clachan church, Loch Broom. All the men-folk of Mellon Udrigle were there, but it was too much of a journey for their women-folk to undertake. These latter witnessed a remarkable sight. The whole sea near Priest Island, situated almost in the middle of Loch Broom, appeared to be filled with warships, and everyone was greatly excited.

They saw the galleys being filled with soldiers and arms and were rowing to the shore as fast as their oars could bring them. One of the women left the crowd and made for her house to bury her jewels and money in the sand out of harm's way. The young girls were told by their elders to take to the hills, to Greenstone Point—which is the tip of the peninsula—as the Redcoats' reputation was very questionable regarding women.

For a long time everyone watched the galleys pulling shorewards, but strange to relate no boat reached the shore and no soldier landed. It was undoubtedly a vision corroborated by hundreds of witnesses; possibly it was a mirage that accounted for this phenomenon.

In 1914, eighty-eight years later, the Grand Fleet under Lord Jellicoe at the outbreak of the First World War, used this and other nearby bays and lochs for his bases. Possibly what the inhabitants of Mellon Udrigle saw in 1826 was the forerunner of things to come?

Priest Island, one of the Summer Isles aforementioned, is reported to have got its name in a peculiar manner. An Excise officer had been sent to investigate smuggling which was believed to be taking place near Laide. To avoid and throw off detection, he disguised himself as a priest and asked to be ferried across Loch Broom to Achiltibuie; but the boatman, being suspicious, left him on Eilean a' Churich (this island under review) instead, and thereafter returned to the mainland to market the brew. When the illicit spirit had been safely disposed of, the boatman returned to the island to collect the angry 'priest', and that is how this island was called Priest Island, or Cleric Island, to this day.

Near by on the shore of Laide district, is the ruined Chapel of Sand of Udrigle, with the tide gently lapping at its walls. This Chapel is reputed to be one of the earliest Christian churches on the west coast, erected by St. Columba of Iona fame. There now remains only the four walls. The evening sun, streaming through the empty shells of windows alights on two graves: John Maclaren and Andrew Urquhart, both of Aultbea, who after years of war service, are laid to rest in the shadow of that little isolated church.

As to the name Udrigle, it is thought it is the little hill of Udrigill, one of the many Viking warriors who ruled the roost in these parts until the battle of Largs, 700 years ago.

Reluctantly you will leave Laide (and incidentally the Council

have made a fine view-point shortly before coming to Laide)
and soon pass through two little croft villages, known as FIRST
COAST and SECOND COAST, *Bad an T'Sluig* and *An T'Oirthir
Dunn*, to quote the Gaelic; strange names, but this comes of the
bygone days when there existed the custom of numbering the
compass from the sun's position, viz. 1st, East; 2nd West; 3rd
North; and 4th, South. This part of the journey is called the
Gaza Strip, for there always seems to be a battle going on 'mongst
the dwellers there!

From here, we soon reach Gruinard Hill (Cabeg Hill) which
has now been greatly widened, affording easy passage, and there
we view the wonderful beach of white sand and blue water
which on a warm sunny day resembles a tropical lagoon. Here
you verily see a 'Pearl'. After getting down the hill and rounding
the bay near Gruinard House, you see a War Department warning
notice in respect of the little island just off-shore—Gruinard
Island—bearing the words to keep away from landing on it, as it is
'Contaminated'. It was used for experiments during the last
war, and for all these years, secrecy has surrounded this lovely
island, which is out-of-bounds to the public. Evidently it was the
place where Britain was to find an answer to Hitler's germ
warfare; for the island was contaminated with anthrax, a disease
which is fatal among farm animals, and has even claimed human
victims. Government officials say the island will not be clear of
these germs for at least 100 years. It was, as I have said, during
the Second World War, secret service agents reported that both
the Germans and the Japanese were experimenting in germ
warfare. Gruinard island was chosen for our experiments, and
anthrax the germ.

Further along via Little Loch Broom we arrive at Dundonnell
with An Teallach ('The Forge') (3483 feet) towering in the
distance. An eminent geologist left on record, nearly 100 years
ago, that Dundonnell was unsurpassed as a field for geological
research. Quantities of rose quartz, moss agate, topaz and
amethyst quartz can be found in this region; and when duly cut
and polished by lapidaries, they appear beautiful.

After Dundonnell we leave the sea, and the road we travel is
one of the several destitution roads in the Highlands which were
built to provide relief during the famine in 1851; the Gairloch-
Loch Maree road as previously stated was one of the first schemes

to be really effective as a measure to provide work, food and money for the practically starving Highlanders. The Dundonnell section to Braemore (at which junction we meet the road from Garve-Ullapool) was achieved through the efforts of Mr. Hugh Mackenzie of Dundonnell, but great difficulty was experienced going through peat-bogs, deep gorges and the like, and the track is today still known as Destitution Road. Dundonnell is a popular climbing centre to which climbers come from all parts of Britain.

At Braemore junction, where there was a prisoner of war camp in the First World War, turning left we commence the road up by Loch Broom itself, to Ullapool. A footpath near Braemore Lodge leads to a wooded gorge (now belonging to the National Trust) where you look down 300 feet to the Falls of Measach, also known as the Corrieshalloch Falls ('the dirty corrie or hollow'); a most remarkable defile, the water tumbling over like the graceful drapery of a Shetland shawl. The differing colours of the rocky walls, combining with the silver of the cascade and being enveloped in the wooded canyon and chasm below is a spectacle you cannot afford to miss—awe-inspiring in its depth. The extensive Lael deer forest that one passes *en route* here adds a softer note to this wild country. From 1865–1916 the whole of this valley was thickly wooded with larch and spruce, but much was cut during the 1914–18 war: and has now been reafforested.

Close to Braemore House, are four large stones placed, it is said, to mark the 'leap of Rory'. Rory was born nearby in Strathnacalg, and when as a child he was sent by his parents to keep the bull from the croft, he struck the animal such a blow that it fell dead. Later on in life he became mixed up in smuggling and was outlawed, finding himself eventually confined in Edinburgh Castle. At this time there happened to be an English outlaw at Perth, and someone was needed to give him a sound thrashing. The Governor of Perth jail, hearing of Rory's strength, got in touch with Edinburgh. Rory was granted freedom and a sum of money if he would beat up this Englishman. The encounter took place in Holyrood Palace of all places! Rory hit his adversary over the heart with a terrific blow, and the Englishman fell dead. Rory was then a free man, and made for home. He first caught sight of Loch Broom, a spot to the north of Braemore House, whereupon he gave three terrific leaps of joy which are marked by these stones.

A little over 12 miles further along Loch Broom ('Loch of Showers') we are in Ullapool standing at the entrance to Greater Loch Broom with, let us hope, the striking view of the fishing fleet in the bay. This 12 miles of road is very beautiful, being flanked, for the most part by masses of rhododendron bushes on each side.

The beauty and splendour of Wester Ross is still to be seen in this village of white-washed cottages and countryside. It is the largest village north of Gairloch, and out to sea like a fleet at anchor lie the Summer Isles, already named, and a sunset over these islands can be impressed on one's mind for many a year.

Ullapool, once entirely a fishing village, is first mentioned in the Fishing Acts of 1587, but fishing did not really flourish until the late 1700's. In 1788 the British Fishery Society proceeded to lay out and build Ullapool village as one of their chief stations. They erected a pier and large stores and the village in those days was presided over by a Provost, John Mackenzie. In 1847 it was all sold to James Matheson of Lewis for just over £5000; and the fishing flourished for many years bringing many benefits to the inhabitants. Ice was an unknown quantity in this area in those days, so boiler houses were built and the fish partially cooked to preserve it for transport. They were called 'boil houses'.

Herring fishing during the winter months then brought prosperity to Ullapool. In its train came gutters, packers and curers, all requiring accommodation taxing the resources of the village to the utmost.

It was recently thought Ullapool would become quite a busy village in that there was a proposal to operate a big ferry service, capable of taking 600 passengers and 70 cars at a time across the Minch to Stornoway, a trip of only three hours, which would cut out the long journey by the *Loch Seaforth*, which daily plies from Kyle to Stornoway, and the inconvenience of having to book so much in advance for your car, for at the most that vessel can only take about six cars at a time; an insignificant number really. Unfortunately at the last moment, this most useful service, sponsored by Stornoway business men, fell through. No doubt as time goes on, MacBrayne's or someone else may come to the rescue in this very necessary ferry service.

F

There are two big hotels in Ullapool. The Royal as you enter this wee fishing village suffered a disastrous fire a few years ago and just the shell remained; it looked a sort of battlement of Elsinore effect, but it has now been entirely rebuilt. Without doubt, the design, approach, décor and the personal attention given you is beyond compare. And the food leaves you with no doubt that the management and his chef are all out to give you the best. The other large one is the Caledonian Hotel, centrally situated and for years has held a high reputation. Both are well patronised and always full-up in the summer. There are many other smaller hotels, and the list of B. and B. houses is as big as your arm.

Ullapool is a very progressive village, and the folk there are always clammering for more capital and grants from the government to help them to continue developing—for Ullapool 'thinks big'. The very mention of the Board of Trade—the B.O.T.—is the body that brings the flush of annoyance to the cheek of enterprise in Ullapool. The Ullapoolites may be in the Scottish Wild West, but they have big plans. The ferry across to Stornoway, as I have just cited, would be the greatest boon to everyone concerned. It is such a convenient and easy crossing, and should have been in operation years ago. Ullapool runs constant cruises down Loch Broom in small cabin-cruiser boats, and a ferry across the loch to Aultnaharrie; there are plenty of small boats for hire, but never on the Sabbath.

Before leaving Ullapool, I would recount the story of an Ullapool worthy long ago who was trudging one wintry day all the way to Laide. In order to remove a lump of snow from the sole of his boot, he kicked his foot against a boulder which became dislodged and started to roll down the steep hillside near Dundonnell. As it gathered speed it collected snow to such an extent that an exceedingly large snowball—an outsize really!—landed on the shore of Little Loch Broom. Some weeks later, when the snow melted, two fine stags and a hare were found lying dead beside the stone, caught in the boulder's rapid descent. Strange the Highlanders with their legendary flair and taste have not called that boulder by some fairy name, but just left it lying by the roadside, unnamed and unsung?

Another traditional story connected with the sea and Loch Broom is concerning one Mackenzie, a native of Gairloch, who lived in Ullapool. He was known in the Gaelic as Murdo the son of Murdo (MURCHADH MACMHURACHAIDH); handsome and tall. He had a fishing boat and spent his time going round the villages with his herring. One day he put into the island of Luing, south of Oban, near Loch Melfort. Going ashore that night he found there was a fashionable ball in progress, and the daughter of Lord Breadalbane was there. She saw this handsome fellow, and fell in love with him at once. He took her off in his boat, and they were married when they arrived back at Ullapool.

In those days no boat had any name or number, and Lord Breadalbane offered much money to anyone who could find his daughter. When Murdo heard that money was forthcoming he dressed himself up, and visited the lord at Taymouth Castle, near Aberfeldy in Perthshire. At the interview, Breadalbane said: 'you'll get the reward if you tell me where my daughter is'. Murdo replied 'When I get the money I will tell you', and he got the money and then said 'if I get another £300 I will tell you where the man is who stole her'. He got his £300, whereupon Murdo, holding out his hand, said 'there is the hand that stole her from the Isle of Luing!' Lord Breadalbane was so amazed at his courage that he accepted him as his son-in-law, and gave his daughter a substantial dowry. Prior to all this, and at the time Breadalbane knew his daughter had eloped in a fishing smack, he went to the King and a law was duly made that all boats should have their name on them; and that is how such boats are named and numbered to this very day.

A few miles south of Braemore and off the wayside is Loch-a-Bhraoin, a fresh-water loch 4 miles long. Here are the graves of Lochaber men who had been cattle-raiding in the strath; yes, these Highlanders were aggressors, even as there are aggressors today. They were followed by an Ullapool man in the guise of a beggar. When the raiders had supped well and were sound asleep, he snatched a sword which he had hidden under his rags and slew them all but one, the sentry, whom he spared so that he might tell the tale when he got back home to Lochaber.

*   *   *

Ullapool was one of the chief ports from which the ships carrying emigrants from the Highlands sailed; at first to America and Canada, and then to Australia and New Zealand. Between 1763 and 1775, twenty thousand emigrants are estimated to have left the western coast for the colonies. Checked by the American Revolution and War of Independence, the famine of 1783 stimulated the numbers again; but the years of the great emigration were 1831–32, when over 120,000 people left the Highlands. If you pause to think, this is a stupendous number, to say the least. The great potato famine of 1846, when the entire west coast crop failed, also stimulated this exodus. Hard—very hard—days.

Upon leaving Ullapool on Loch Broom (this loch is in three parts; Loch Broom proper 15 miles long, Little Loch Broom about half that length, and Gruinard Bay, a wide inlet some six miles across by seven miles long) and taking the main road northwards, the journey on a very good road, passes through rugged country skirting the shores of Loch Kanaird and Strath Kanaird, there lies the sacred St. Martin's Isle which you can see to advantage from the wee village of Ardmair. At one time St. Columba ministered on this small isle where he left an impression of peace and sanctity. As to its name, there exists doubt whether it was called after the famous Saint Martin of Iona, or from the actual cleric who built his cell upon the isle, and who had been banished as a student from Iona, for his general manner appeared to be distasteful to St. Columba; and he was debarred from Iona until he had given proof of changing his mode of life. It is thought he first went to one of the other eight Summer Isles—to Priest's Isle. Howbeit, St. Martin died on St. Martin's Isle and over his grave there is a large stone on which the cross is seen covered with hieroglyphics. The ruins of his chapel are at the west corner of the isle; close by are the graves of his followers.

Continuing a little further on this main road, we come to a turn-off on the left, clearly signposted to ACHILTIBUIE, where one obtains an open panoramic view westwards, seeing Ben More Coigach (2438 feet)—a wall of sheer rock and scree. If we had not taken this turn, we would have gone further crossing the Sutherland border at Knockan and Elphin—the villages I have mentioned earlier on; and of course further, we would have come to the junction of the Lairg and Lochinver road, at Ledmore. Travelling now to Achiltibuie by one loch after another—the first one being Loch Lurgainn (the loch of the legs as you will remember from the legend given before)—you pass a road to the right which takes you by the twisting narrow shore road to LOCHINVER, but carrying forward you come down into the long village of Achiltibuie (said to mean the 'field of the yellow flowers' in Gaelic) having skirted Lochs Osgaig and Vatachan. Achiltibuie is charmingly situated on Badentarbet Bay in which lie the delightful Summer Isles.

You may ask why the Summer Isles should have that name? Somebody once said it was because the sun was often shining on them when it wasn't shining anywhere else.

The island immediately facing Achiltibuie is named Tanera Mor; further out to sea is a small island Tanera Beg. A little south of the larger Tanera is Horse Island, renamed Elizabeth Island by the locals after the Queen's visit to their little township four or five years ago.

There is a very nice little hotel, The Summer Isles Hotel, towards the end of the village, set right facing the bay and consequently has an unrivalled view. A little further along from the hotel—about four miles—is the small village of Culnacraig from where you can look up Loch Broom; and from this village an easy ascent of Ben More Coigach can be made; a splendid viewpoint resulting. All in all, Achiltibuie is a dream of a place; perhaps I should have said a pearl set amongst pearls.

* * *

This now completes the why's (and the wherefore's) of the Y journey promised you at the start of this book. I hope I have been able to adequately portray everything, and to have kept your interests alive. There is not the slightest doubt, but that both Wester Ross and the north-west of Sutherland have the greatest scenic spots in the whole of Britain. 'Pearls' without number. I have not exaggerated in any degree. Why should I? I am not a member of the Scottish Tourist Board! In these parts we have—at the risk of repetition—the *finest coastline in Europe*. When you visit up here—the Wild West—you have just to become accustomed to the idea that you have no sooner seen one surprisingly beautiful place than you'll see another. Adjectives and adverbs begin to lose their meaning. Have I made myself perfectly clear? Pearls . . . strings of pearls. And you, readers, who should ever take these steps into the Highlands, will I am sure, come and thank me for bringing to light all the beauty, and the QUIET, which is on our doorstep—all for the taking.

Verily, all roads up here lead to beauty. It is said 'there is never enough Time in life for friendships, *but* there is plenty of Time to gaze upon beauty in the Highlands'. I could have titled this book as 'CADUCEUS of the North-West'; a Greek word, for a wand carried by heralds in ancient Greece and Rome, for proclaiming Beauty and Love and Life; it is, at the same time, a symbol for the medical profession.

The poets and bards speak and sing of the Highlands, as the land of the mountains, the glens, the lochsides, and the heather. Americans term the lure of Scotland, as 'magic'—and this magic draws people to the north-west in ever-increasing numbers, year by year . . . for a personal paradise always awaits them. This so-called magic is certainly not a promise of unending sunshine, for the Scottish weather (except for 1955 and 1968) is as unpredictable as a woman's mind—and as surprising! Someone once said the north-west has more scenery than sunshine. It is not the bright lights of a Blackpool-style vacation, or the caress of a Mediterranean sea at midnight. People love Scotland simply because it is unique. This is not an over-statement. Motorists, caravaners and the like, can find their own particular pleasures here; and it beckons them, young and old, with its incomparable safe beaches 'mongst little fishing villages.

Throughout the pages of this book, I have always referred to 'Lochs'. There is only one notable *lake* in Scotland; the Lake of Menteith; but I believe there are two other small waters, known as 'Lakes' viz. Raith Lake in Fife, Pressencennen Lake and Spot Lake in East Lothian.

The lake was originally known as the LOCH OF INCHMAHOME, after the largest of its three islands. Menteith is a corruption of the original Monteith (the second letter being an o instead of e); the Mounth or Watershed of the River Teith, and is situate a little south of Callander. In the gazetteer in 1842, it is described as the LOCH of Monteith; but forty years later, it is named LAKE. This was the period of depressed National pride when England considered herself to be above reproach and Scotland a handicap. Going back still further older documents (of 1485 and 1493) the 'Lake' is given in Latin as LACUS DE INCHMAHOMOK.

One story I know of is that in the 14th century Sir John

Menteith betrayed William Wallace to the English, so the local people cast a slur upon the name Menteith, by calling the loch a lake. A large number of people seem to think the Lake of Menteith is the one mentioned by Sir Walter Scott in the *Lady of the Lake*; but that is incorrect. It was Loch Katrine that was inferred, and the lady was Ellen, daughter of the outlawed Douglas. Douglas, Roderick Dhu and her sweetheart, Malcolm Graeme, were imprisoned in Stirling Castle.

*   *   *

To close this chapter on a less scholastic pedestal, I would tell you of what happened at one of the Western Isles steamers berthed in Glasgow Docks in the years when MacBrayne's starting port was at the Broomielaw, Glasgow. The man on watch saw what he took to be the shadowy figure of a young girl with a bundle under her arm standing near the gangway. Thinking she was an Islander sending a parcel back home, he went round the deck house to take the parcel from her. But when he reached the spot, there was no one there to be seen. Puzzled, he told his mates next morning, who chaffed him by saying he had had too much to drink that night! But in the afternoon the laugh was on them, when the coffin of a young Island girl killed in a street accident, was laid on the exact spot where he had seen the figure the night before.

Adverting to Inverewe Gardens, I mentioned the Gulf Stream and its beneficial warmth; but strictly speaking the Gulf Stream itself does not come near Britain and the north-west coast really. It is the extension of it, known as the North Atlantic Drift which we experience.

CHAPTER 8

ALBA GU BRAGH

'SCOTLAND FOR EVER!'
As you may imagine, this chapter is devoted to Scottish gaeldom whose stronghold of course is in the Highlands, for gaeldom (*gaidhealtachd*) and the Highlands were originally synonymous; and today Ross-shire claims the highest percentage of Gaelic speakers of all the counties.

The Gael's contribution is a valuable one; his language, song poetry and story, enhance the arts of the world, and should it ever die, it will be a loss to civilisation. In general terms as I have said, the Gaelic-speaking communities (one of the oldest remaining cultures in Europe, possessing the same roots as the Irish Gaels) are almost entirely confined to the islands and the districts along the north-west mainland coast. Gaelic may be giving ground but it is still as full of life up in real Highland territory as a flowering hawthorn tree; and of course at the Mods (a yearly festival of Gaelic music, song, dance, oral competitions and so forth) Gaeldom runs riot. In 1800 one Scotsman in five spoke the Gaelic. In 1860 the ratio was one in ten. Today it will be about one in a hundred. The vocabulary of Gaelic is much greater, and less defiled, than most; it is not a mongrel language. It is a clear-cut, pedigreed language, with a subtle gradation of meaning in the words it employs. In the Gaelic alphabet there are only 18 characters; 5 vowels, 12 consonants, and one 'h'—the sign of a breathing or aspiration only. There is no indefinite article (nor is there in Greek or Latin) and there are only two accents, grave and acute. Some words are spelt the same, but the accent and pronunciation gives them a different meaning. The Gaelic *verb* always precedes the noun or pronoun and is *not* declined; it is the same for all persons and numbers; so different from the English verb in form and structure. Gaelic is therefore a very different make-up to other foreign tongues we hear.

On one very pleasant day I spent with a family near Kinlochbervie not so long ago, I was given an unusual paper napkin which had small illustrated squares of Gaelic words with the English rendering; and think it will be helpful to strangers if I record them:

BEAN, woman	TEINE, fire	BALACH, boy
BATA, boat	MUC, pig	BROGAN, shoes
CU, dog	TRI, three	EUN, bird
ABHAINN, river	CEITHIR, four	NAOI, nine
TIGH, house	CLACH, stone	DEICH, ten
CNOC, hill	CEANN, head	CRAOBH, tree
CAORA, sheep	CAT, cat	LAMN, hand
CAILEAG, girl	GRIAN, sun	FAINNE, ring
IUCHAIR, key	COIG, five	EACH, horse
DUINE, man	SIA, six	TASDAN, shilling
EAGLAIS, church	ARAN, bread	COIRE, kettle
AON, one	IM, butter	CEOL, music
DA, two	CEARC, hen	SGIAN, knife
MUIR, sea	BAINNE, milk	LEABHAR, book
UBH, egg	SGILLIN, penny	RATHAD, road
SGOIL, school	BO, cow	CLAG, bell
CAISE, cheese	LEABAIDH, bed	DORUS, door
GLEANN, glen	IASG, fish	TUNNAG, duck
BORD, table	SEACHD, seven	PIOBMHOR, bagpipes
CATHAIR, chair	OCHD, eight	PEANN, pen
GEALACH, moon	CASAN, feet	FEUSAG, beard
CLARSACH, harp		

Gaelic now seems to be the fading language of the home, of the fisherman and of the modern croft; certainly not the language of industry as we know it today. Up in Ross-shire where I live and have my being, the Gaelic tongue is widely spoken in its soft native sibilancy. It is a great bulwark in the preservation of the traditional loyalties and the simplicity of their natural life. In this age we live in, the old forms of warmth, grace, charm and the very poetry of life itself seem to be slipping from our grasp. More's the pity. To the young in heart one should urge 'forsake not the Gaelic' . . . NA TREIG À GHÀIDHLIG. They say Gaelic is the language of Love, and that it was first spoken in the Garden of Eden. I wonder?

This is a land of crofts and crofters. There are seven crofting counties in Scotland—Argyll, Inverness-shire, Ross and Cromarty, Sutherland, Caithness, Orkney and Zetland—and they involve a wide variety of ground from the rich soil in the east to the peat and bare rocks of the west. In all, there are about 25,000 crofts. You may say a croft is a wee bit of land, and that crofting is a special way of life; but farming is a way of making money. A croft may be a little arable land at the best, probably three or four acres. It is not worth much; just a few pounds a year as rent to the landowner. Security and a home, but not a great deal of wordly money. In effect it is a way of staying on the land.

Some of the houses on a small croft in out-of-the-way districts, are no more than a 'But an' Ben'. The word *But* denotes the front of the house, known as the kitchen. If you were 'gawn ben the hoose' it meant you were away to the back o' the house, or the parlour. So that a *But an' Ben* simply consists of one room and a kitchen.

Highland history really began on the west coast, *Dalriada*. It was an ancient kingdom founded early in the 6th century in what is now Southern Argyll, by a group of Irish invaders, called Scots. The old Kingdom of Dalriada lay on the long peninsula of Kintyre from which it was only separated from Ireland by twelve miles of sea. Long, long ago, men of the Irish shore crossed over to Kintyre. One such wave about A.D. 500 brought the Christian Scots from Scotia, as the Romans called Ireland. There were other races on the mainland then. Celtic Picts in the Highlands. The Romans arriving in A.D. 80 managed to subdue the Britons, but never the Highland tribes; and by the time the Irish Scots came, Rome had fallen, and her armies had withdrawn. The Scots then created their new Kingdom of Dalriada. The Picts valued that part of the country, and for a time Celt fought Celt. Then, in A.D. 563 the tribal warfare abated by the coming of St. Columba from Ireland, followed by other saints. The Picts then became Christian. As Norse attacks in the northern parts and islands weakened them, they turned more and more to their real Scots kin, and co-religionists. In A.D. 843 Kenneth MacAlpin, half Scot and half Celt, merged the Celtic moieties and became the first King of Gaelic Alba (Scotland).

Although Gaelic is fading, and that a generation ago youngsters —and old folk too—were punished for speaking the language, today it is being taught with renewed vigour. It was the English (the oh! so bad, English!) who tried to kill the Gaelic language, but it was Calvinism that tried to kill the Gaelic culture. The reformed kirk was puritanical—it wanted to ban music and story telling and dancing—and that amongst a people with some of the finest literary and musical traditions in the world, even though they were not written down. However, nowadays, the church is becoming more tolerant and there are still songs to be heard, and pipers playing.

Gaelic place-names are always intriguing, not to say tongue-twisters to strangers. If they begin with *inver* or *aber*, this means they are at the mouth of a stream. If they start with *strath*, they are in a valley. If *bad*, in a grove, and *kin* or *ceann*—meaning 'head'—at the upper reach of whatever it may be. *Kil* refers to a monk's cell of medieval days. Most Scottish mountains are prefixed by the Gaelic *Beinn*, meaning peak or mountain, and frequently Anglicised as *Ben*. Yes, many of the place-names up north sound strange music to the Anglo-Saxon tongue. To many from America they will look upon such peculiar sounding names as urging the clansmen into battle staunchly following their chief and a piper playing stirring strains of war. Today these old type warriors have faded out, and only those whose love for the land and the way of life outweighs the wish for wealth, remain to till the soil. In the days of the Clearances, the Highland spirit proclaimed an independence born of solitude in the wilderness and wildness of the vast moorland reaches in the north-west.

Going back through the years when one believed in water kelpies, elfs and so forth, legend has it of a north-bound stranger who was crossing the vast country up hills and mountains, down hills and mountains, through rain and warm sun, through the glens and trampling the heather; the morning on his right hand, the evening on his left hand. One night when he came to the edge of the Great Glen, a grey crow flew on to his shoulder.

'Have you reached where you are going?' she asked. 'No,' said the voyager, 'I'm bound for the top of the kingdom, and the two sides of it. If I go up by the hills, I'll come down by the valleys; if I follow the rivers, I'll walk by the ocean, and if I am high on the moorlands, then the lochs will be below. I'm going wherever the wind blows and the water flows until I reach the *Kingdom of Gaeldom*, and gaze and drink it all in.' 'You'd best take up your travel in earnest,' she said, 'for the kingdom stretches far, far, before you.'

If legend tells us she was with him then, she flew off into the wind and Scotch mist; and the traveller tramped along till he reached the promised land, threading his way past shaggy contented Highland cattle wandering in search of fodder, through bracken, heather awash with purple and for all the world looking like a carpet of spilt claret; glens, lochs and lochans—to the 'tartan dawn'—a new Kingdom, a new way of Life.

I have previously mentioned the Scandinavian (Norse) attacks and occupation in the north and the islands; the roving Vikings came along skimming the sea in their sharp-prowed ships, foraging and worrying the Gaels. The year 1968 saw the commemoration of the 500th Anniversary of the 'pledging' of the Orkney and Shetland islands to Scotland. The agreement by which these former Norwegian islands—the last group of islands off the Scottish coast to belong to a foreign power—were handed over to Scotland was somewhat peculiar.

It was the year 1468, and King James III of Scotland was betrothed to the Danish princess, Margaret, daughter of King Christian I of Denmark and Norway. This was to solve a number of political differences between Scotland and Scandinavia. The fly in the ointment was, what dowry could go along with the marriage? It needed to be a sizeable one. The Scottish ambassadors embarked for Denmark and thought that 60,000 florins of the Rhine (some £25,000 in English money then) was fair and reasonable. King Christian agreed readily and proudly, for he did not want his daughter to go empty-handed to her new kingdom. But where was the money to come from? There was nothing like that sum in the royal mint. So in the end King Christian 'pawned' his royal rights in the Orkney islands for 50,000 florins, without consulting his other kingdom, Norway; but of course he meant to redeem them. However times were bad and next year, for 8,000 florins, Shetland too was pledged. In all, King Christian could only summon up 2000 florins in cash; and although several efforts at redemption were made on Denmark's part, both set of islands then remained Scottish, and since that date they have remained and been treated administratively like the rest of Scotland. Surely the oddest case of the mortgaged islands?

And the thistle as Scotland's national emblem, came about during the era of these Norse invasions. The tradition is that around 980 A.D. a Danish force landing on the north-west, were trying to creep up on the Gaels soldiers under cover of darkness. To make as little noise as possible they were marching barefoot. But just as they were nearing the Scottish clansmen a Danish soldier stepped on a thistle. His cry was heard by the Scots who were thus warned, and as a result completely defeated their enemy. Hence the thistle was given a sacred place in Scottish history.

The Gaels who colonised Dalriada (Southern Argyll) long, long ago and who were known as 'The Scots', were the first Scots, and thus the Highlanders as we know them today can assuredly be termed the most Scottish of all Scots; and Gaelic identifies the Gael.

Definitely life in those olden days was hard and demanding, but even so the poorest of the poor were part of the general society then existing; wearing the same costumes and speaking the same language as their superiors, and they all joined in with the story-telling, poetry, songs and dancing. In short they enjoyed the same culture. There was no hard and fast line between gentry and peasantry in the Highlands then. This, in essence, was the Clan system; there was merely service and duty—labour, contributions in money and kind, and military obligement. Just cattle, sheep and goats, fish, game and crops; and above all love. They would say in the Gaelic 'CHA'N EIL BACADH TEANGAIDH AIR GAOL' meaning 'love knows no language barrier'.

After Culloden, 16th April 1746, when the savage fighters of the glens died, and their way of life died with them—for so it seemed—the power of the chiefs was taken away, but the land was left; but to secure bigger income they caused wholesale eviction of their people to make way for sheep farmers from the borders. Those of the dispossessed who could, emigrated; but

the greater part drifted and crowded the rocky coast line in the
north-west and suffered untold poverty, living a life of des-
pondency. The 'Clearance days' which eventually eased in
1886 on the passing of the Crofters' Act, following the Napier
Commission's report of 1883, that security of tenure and fair
rents came to be established—exactly one hundred and forty
years after 'Charlie's year'. Surely in all Highland and Gaeldom
history there is no more poignant date or any past event so clear
in the Gaels' memory as Culloden. It was the Highlander's
hopeless battle for independence. Bonnie Prince Charlies' clansmen stood no chance against King George II's far larger forces
and with far superior modern fire-power, in so unprotected a
spot. This disaster saddened all Highlander's hearts and they
were inclined to believe as Kipling wrote long after 'Lo, all
our pomp of yesterday is one with Nineveh and Tyre', when
they dispersed and disbanded. It was to them the end of Gaeldom.
But they were wrong.

The Kingdom of Gaeldom; the 'Tartan dawn'.

And here is an old Gaelic blessing; 'may the roads rise with
you, and the wind be always at your back; and may the Lord
hold you in the hollow of His hand'. And they also say, where
there is hatred—let me sow love; where there is injury—
pardon; where there is doubt—faith; where there is despair—
hope; where there is darkness—light; and where there is
sadness—joy.

There is a thousand year old, yes and more, version from the
Sanskrit, the ancient language (now obsolete as a spoken language)
of Hindustan, embodying the philosophy of the Brahman's,
which can well apply to this 'Dawn' our voyager was seeking
in those far off days; and I give a rough translation from this
Salutation of the Dawn:

> The glory of action, the bliss of growth, the splendour of
> beauty. For yesterday is but a dream and tomorrow is only a
> vision. But today well lived, makes every yesterday a dream of
> happiness; and every tomorrow a vision of hope. Look well then
> to this day of Dawn.

CHAPTER 9

CROFTING AND THE CLEARANCES

As mentioned before, Sutherland and Ross-shire are two of the seven crofting counties in Scotland. A croft is in essence a small plot of land adjoining a wee dwelling house; an agricultural small holding in fact, ranging from a few acres to around 50 or 75 acres for the largest. It is on the west side that one finds the greater number of these small crofts; but although there are comparatively speaking few crofters in Scotland they occupy nearly two million acres—over a tenth of the land area. Another interesting feature is that one acre in ten of the land surface of Scotland is covered with peat. In Lewis the ratio is even eight acres to ten. The crofter and his way of life means many things to many people. To the crofter of the olden type it is the reason for an existence which brings together the spiritual and material things of this world hardly found elsewhere in Britain.

For many years now the crofters have seemed to have had lots of troubles of their own. It is said crofters are making as good use of their land as the men on the bigger upland farms; but to make a living on present day standards from crofting alone is most difficult, and the economists say the reason is the majority of crofts are too small; their resources are far too limited to give an adequate volume of output.

The Crofters' Commission as we know it today, was set up in 1955. In August 1961 a new Crofters' Act came into being in which provisions were made for sub-letting, but which would not affect the crofters' tenure in any way. The main change provided in the Act was to get more crofting land under cultivation by re-organising the township or village and sub-letting crofts to create bigger holdings.

The crofter has a statutory right to engage in non-agricultural activities on his croft, provided the agricultural value of the holding is not impaired, but this is a much less valuable right than it appears to be. Because of the peculiarities of crofting tenure, the crofter cannot use his buildings as security for a loan except when borrowing from the Secretary of State, or the Highland Development Board. He is thus restricted in the amount of capital he can raise and, despite his statutory right, if he wishes to develop he must generally go to his landlord for a more secure title to the land he wishes to develop; and his landlord may be found unwilling to oblige. In spite of his tenancy of the land and his statutory right to develop, he is little better placed even in regard to a site than any other developer coming in. Which is very unfair. The limitation on his ability to borrow restricts the expansion of his agricultural as well as his non-agricultural activities. Even should his landlord agree to sell him the holding he does not become an owner-occupier in the ordinary sense of the term. He is legally the landlord of a vacant croft and may be called upon to relet the holding. So where is he?

A small croft occupied by a man in full-time employment may be regarded as hobby farming. In a high cost area like the Highlands many people, even given full employment, require the supplement of a small croft to maintain a reasonable standard of living. The crofter's resilience despite many difficulties is shown in many ways. With grants for land improvement offered by the Commission, crofters have now converted some 30,000 acres of inferior hill land into good pasture—even arable. More than 20,000 acres of common grazing land have been apportioned to individual crofters to enable this improvement work to proceed. Of course only a minority of crofters have participated in these various developments; but this is not surprising considering the age level of the population. The initiative is to a certain extent concealed by the general run-down, but it is never the accepted view that crofters are slow to change or lacking in initiative. It is opportunity which has been lacking, not enterprise. Be what it may, the traditional crofter *is* a part-time agriculturalist who looks to other ways and means to increasing his modest income.

When land is abstracted from crofting for development purposes, the crofter receives compensation to cover his agricultural loss, but he does not share in the increased value of the land resulting from the change in use. He has no incentive therefore to welcome or even to acquiesce in development. This problem is often brushed aside by saying 'if employment is provided, the crofters will benefit'. This half-truth ignores the fact that it is not necessarily the crofters who lose land who will receive employment, and crofters cannot reasonably be expected to take a more enlightened and less self-centred view of changes which affect their interests than other classes in the community.

In an area where crofting subjects and owner-occupied subjects exist side by side it is much easier from the financial point of view for the owner-occupier to acquire the croft, than for the crofter to acquire the owner-occupied subject, with the result that when amalgamations are taking place the croft is always vulnerable. So one can say what one likes, but there are many snags in a crofter's existence.

The crofter has all the virtues of a generous man—a sense of humour, a sense of companionship, a sense of occasion. He is a man, following a time-honoured occupation, that must not be forgotten. If he is, albeit Commissions, Acts and so forth come and go, then heaven help the Highlands. Governments come and go, dictators rise and fall; people are born and die, machines wear out—but crofting and farming go on for ever. What a change it would be for visitors coming up from the reek and grime of the ugly cities, to watch all that is going on and cheer it on its wholesome way; revelling in the goodness and purity of Highland air, and realising what happiness in good living really means. Then, and then only, will you breathe in the atmosphere that evokes what the Gaels call 'the wave in the heart and the dream in the eye'. You will go away, and when back home and thinking of your travels in the jungle north, the words 'they are a people living in a world apart' will unconsciously flow from your lips. 'Never a dull moment' could well be inscribed as a motto over the doorway of a crofter's house; and any girl thinking of marrying a young crofter should appreciate this before letting the wedding ring slip gently on her finger. Which is the cue bringing me to a few significant lines as to a crofter's wooing. 'The moon has risen with nothing in orbit round it. Corn rustles surreptitiously, and the stench of the byre is drowned by night-scented stock. The young crofter puts his arm round his lassie's waist. Before speiring her, a question remains to be cleared up. 'Lassie,' he asks, 'dae you swite?'

The seasons come and go; but a crofter is hard at it all twelve months of the year. Except perhaps those who are not of a bothering kind; as one I knew who couldn't be bothered spreading out the rat poison himself, so he just opened the tin saying to himself 'the rats can come along and read the directions for themselves!'

In March the days have lengthened; the larch and the birch begin to herald spring; and towards the end of May nature has begun its revival. The cuckoo pays us its annual visit from across the ocean; and we get bored with its constant song; the bluebells of Scotland burst into bloom. The earth, surely, seems to receive instructions from Heaven to reclothe all Nature. In the spring-time, a young man's fancy turns to love, 'tis said. But as to a crofter, he has work on his hands; he is far too busy to be think-ing of love. At the beginning of March he starts to turn over his land with the foot-plough—the *cas-chrom*—quite a tricky, Old Testament type of primitive implement to handle. By the middle of April most of his spring work is done and then the peats have to be cut—here again with a special primitive cutting tool (a turfing spade CABAR LAR)—stripping the sods from the heather thus exposing the peat proper—and the peat knife, a tool to cut the sods into shape and to throw them on to the bank to dry. When partially dried they are put on end in small stacks, thereby letting the wind and sun thoroughly dry them out. They are then ready to be carted home for the winter's fire. *Peat*, the very name gives one the real smell o' the mystic isles and the north-west Highlands. It is the real crofter's main fuel.

Early on in the year, say February to March or April, the heather needs burning in order to produce more and better crop for sheep, grouse and such-like. After four years, heather gets coarse, and needs pruning as we would a bush or tree; and pruning in this case means burning. Vivid fires are to be seen on the hillsides during this period, and much care is needed to keep the 'burning bush' under control. It appears to be a real scorched-earth policy, but new growth quickly comes along, and all is well with man and beast.

At this time there will be fences to be seen to, crops reaped, potatoes lifted, out-houses repaired, drains sorted; and so it goes on.

The sheep, of course, have to be cared for, and continually rounded up by the crofter and his faithful collie. Some of these dogs seem to have a veritable hypnotic influence on sheep, getting them to do exactly what their master requires of them; and a crofter with only a few sheep is really helpless without his sheep dog. They are lovely animals, sensing one's mood like a loving, dutiful wife. It may be said sheep do not sit about the hillside at random. Experts tell us they have a social behaviour of their own. Each sheep has its own patches of vegetation— known as 'rakes'—over which it moves in regular daily fashion. So they are not as dumb as we would make them out to be; except when they're on the roadway, and particularly so with their lambs, when you and your car need to exercise every caution to avoid running over them. Many, poor things, are killed each year by careless motorists. The 1964 hit-tune 'There'll never be another you (ewe)', is often occurring up north.

Sometimes one comes across a sheep lying on its back, its four legs sticking up, and probably dead, for once it gets on its back it is unable to right itself—and so it lies and dies; the other flock paying no heed to it. If there had been a goat around it would probably have 'boxed' it into the upright position, for goats are usually good 'boxers'. So here is an instance where it is not always wise to separate the sheep from the goats.

Yes, they have a hard life, turning their modest land into as rich and as productive a unit as is possible; small though it may be, but interest keeps them smiling. Even the most menial task in life can be an interesting one, if you give your whole energy to it and find delight in doing so. Jokingly they will tell you that as they work so hard all the year round, they become eligible for their old age pension when they reach forty-five years of age! Faith in all things is the answer, when you look under the surface. The Highlander has full faith in his country, for he knows he cannot compromise with its mountains, its lochs and its glens. Not forgetting the shaggy Highland cattle (that look so awesome, yet are so docile) that roam about, and which plod through the moors and the bogs in all weathers 'neath the misty landscape. No Highlander, deep down, ever wishes to leave his native homeland. Nowadays of course there are far more mechanical devices at hand to help him in his toil; at the same time one misses the hiss of the old-fashioned scythe.

After seeing crofts set amidst the Highland background so different from elsewhere, the visitor will say to himself there's nothing like an outdoor life and an outdoor holiday, and so the following year you'll be persuaded to holiday in the Highlands in a tent, and find yourself bringing everything with you, bar the kitchen sink. Getting close to nature, your wife, self and family will say. You come, and you set up camp in a quiet spot off the beaten track, amongst the bracken and birch and near a babbling brook, looking forward to having a wonderful time—dog included! You forget that wasps, midges, cows and sheep come out any time in the twenty-four hours; and if it be hot the wasps wear their best striped football jerseys! You open a jar of jam just to satisfy them; you open another jar and this curriculum goes on daily as a means of peace and as a burnt offering. And in the end you will probably take home a dozen full jars of wasps—not jam! The cows will pass the tent at daybreak and at sunset and take a fancy to leaning against the tent poles threatening a collapse of your home from home, and drop their visiting cards with a 'splosh', instead of ringing the door bell. The midges are scared away by lighting the primus stove and making it belch forth smoke and smell, and in the morning you will all look like the Black and White minstrel show on TV. Then earwigs suddenly claim a Scottish relationship and pay no heed as to when its bedtime. If you think you'll land a trout for breakfast you'll probably find it is either too sunny or too windy and the dear little morsel is not interested in your amateurish handling of the fly; and so you come back shouting out to your wife to open a tin of sardines. The dog barks all day long at something he fancies is in the undergrowth and the children get blistered feet and jelly-fish stings. But who cares. You return home with a healthy tan and peaty perfume which Coty's have so far not discovered! Next year you think you may try a B. and B. place instead of a tent, thinking that at the worst you won't have ants in your pants all the time.

*   *   *

Whilst, as I have written, I have a very high regard for the crofter and his work, you will find some—especially so-called economists—who disagree strongly on crofting views. You will always come across some high heid yins or subordinates in government offices far removed from the crofting land, who like to strike a note of discontent. I have seen it reported by some saying that crofting has very little to do with serious economic problems but that it has proved administratively convenient for governments to suppose it has; that the Crofters' Commission has ceased to have any meaning and should be disbanded. I have been told this in all seriousness in many quarters up in Sutherland, and that the land should be taken from those who won't use it and given to the young and enterprising; that the Highlander should cease to regard himself as a member of a chosen race to whom normal economic laws do not apply. They go on to say it is not the possession of the land that is important; it is how the land is being used. Like the poor, it would seem the crofting problem is with us always!

In the census of 1861—over a hundred years ago—the islands of Scotland numbered nearly 800, an island being defined as any piece of land surrounded by water which would support one or more sheep and one man, or one man and his wife. Today many of the tiny so-called islands, have been left to look after themselves, barren in relation to sheep and humans, standing as lonely sentinels as in the days of the Vikings who came seeking and plundering.

I will say this, however, that the County Councils or the local councils should put a ban on the use of corrugated iron as an outside building material and so free us from seeing such a lot of rusted sheeting about—even though it is painted, for the rough elements we experience at times can soon uncover the paint and rust again starts. And petrol filling stations could be made more attractive, blending more into the landscape, and new dwellings going up need better planning ideas incorporated; again to enhance and not detract from the scenic surroundings. For scenery is money and you don't want to whittle down or throw away this precious capital—this precious pearl.

Yes, it must be admitted crofting has had a turbulent history; one long struggle in face of the repressive and indifferent attitudes of early governments, from the persecution of the patriarchal clan system, which gave the Gaels their leaders, to the times of Jacobite rebellion and the firing of townships, cottages

and crops by government troops; and then the disastrous replace-
ment of people by sheep—the Clearances—which even today is
still bitterly termed barefaced stealing. All this, so that a degenerate lord might boast his sheep. Then the sheep went too.
One may well ask why the Highlanders did not offer more
resistance to the inhumanity of these clearances? One factor
was their God-fearing nature, for many of their ministers told
them it was the Will of God. And another cause was the young
active males were away at the Napoleonic wars, fighting for the
very people and government that were clearing them away. And
when they returned they found their homes and people gone.
It was too late; the damage had been done. And so I now come
to record a few pages of this most distressing period of Highland
history.

The Clearances

The late 18th century saw the start (it was the year 1780)
of this brutal period of enforced Highland emigration. People
were evicted, as I have said already, to make way for the new
economies of sheep and deer. The inland crofter, fearful of
further retribution, moved westwards towards the sunset and
even further. The Highlands never recovered from the battle of
Culloden, 16th April 1746, nor did Scotland's quasi-independence
of the English. The glens were occupied, the clan system
destroyed, and for years the whole country seethed with suspicion
and bitterness. There was a complete decline of the Highlands
in every aspect of life in the area. The Highlanders then received
a deep-seated knowledge of defeat, and this together with the
subsequent Clearances gave a widespread belief that the prolonged occupation of land—from whatever source—gave a right
to a 'kindness', a right of permanent occupation of it.

However, despite Culloden, families as happy as they reasonably could be, dotted the straths and wee hamlets and smoke
from many hearths rose in the air; *que sera, sera*, 'whatever will
be, will be' was their pious hope. Then wreckers came along
to tear down their homes and to set fire to them. It started in
1780 when the first families to be ordered out sadly picked up
their belongings, left the land and homes they loved, and trekked
towards the barren coast. They tramped and carried all their
meagre belongings miles and miles on their backs just like snails

as I have said earlier in this book. It ended seventy-four years
later, in 1854 (just over a hundred years from now) with a frenzy
of barbarity when the women of Strathcarron were savaged like
hunted beasts by Scots policemen. It was all done in the name of
progress and sheep. Landlords like the southern Marquis of
Stafford found that sheep paid better than people—and so they
had to go. The people had no rights and the law upheld the
landlords. As previously indicated the God-fearing Highlanders
turned to their Kirk for spiritual succour. But the ministers railed
at their wickedness, declaring it was God's Will. Little comfort
this? Huddling in primitive shelters on the cliffs and rocky
coast line of the north-west, or packed miserably in the holds of
disease-ridden emigrant ships, these utterly wretched and dejected
men, women and children found life, at the best, empty, or at
worst they died. Just that, and no more.

In all this sad affair, the name of Patrick Sellar stands out in
bold relief. He was the factor to the Duke of Sutherland at
Dunrobin Castle, and he looked upon the district of Strathnaver
to become a great sheep farmer and make a fortune. STRATH-
NAVER was a Celtic country and few of its inhabitants understood
any language except Gaelic. Actually the agent the Sutherland's
chose to transform their northern estates was William Young
(from Morayshire) who had put forward a Plan for Development.
He was appointed commissioner of the estate to supervise this
improvement (of clearing the land of inhabitants, except on
coastal strips, and giving it over to sheep), but Patrick Sellar who
joined him (also from Morayshire) acted as legal agent and
accountant, though he was really the factor and full agent with
unlimited powers and was the moving spirit. The partnership
began in 1810 and prospered so much, that Sellars was himself
able to bid in 1813 for the huge sheep farm in the district between
Loch Naver and Badenloch. William Young resigned from his
position the year of Sellar's trial in 1816, when Sellar appeared
before the Circuit Court at Inverness, charged with culpable
homicide, and with 'wickedly and maliciously setting on fire and
burning'. Sellar was the man who personally supervised the
burning of Strathnaver. There was a jury of fifteen men, eight
of them being landed proprietors! Nine witnesses were called
for the defence. These were sheriff-officers and servants who
had accompanied Sellar to Strathnaver and they would have been

stupid not to realise that they were on trial too. Sellar was acquitted on 23rd April 1816.

A brief summary of these Clearance happenings over the northern areas, may be recorded as follows: 1792 Strath Oykell, where men gathered in their great bid to drive sheep from their lands. 1812 Assynt Hills, where wide areas were cleared for sheep, the inhabitants fled to the coast, where there was no shelter for them. 1814–19 Kildonan Glen was twice savaged by the burners. 1846, Wick where the soldiers fired on hunger rioters as they tried to stop grain ships sailing for the South. 1849 in North Uist, angry women halt a regiment of police sent by boat from Inverness to serve eviction notices. 1853 in Skye, sixteen families forced to live in holes in the ground after townships of Suishnish and Boreraig razed. And the emigration ports were at Thurso, North Uist, South Uist, Fort William, Greenoch and Campbeltown. Can any such reading be more gruesome?

With sheep, Highland overlords found that wool gave better returns than paltry rents. Some of the clansmen in the north joined forces to drive every Lowland shepherd, his dogs and his flock southward to the Beauly Firth and onwards into Inverness. But it was hopeless. And all such attempts, including mobbing, rioting and deforcing sheriff officers, were ruthlessly punished by the courts. In this way flames of resistance were extinguished. Homes were burnt, people wept—but the Duke of Sutherland said nothing. George Granville, first Duke of Sutherland, born 1758, died 1833, and a statue was erected on a prominent hillside near Dunrobin, by his tenantry and friends 'of loved, revered and cherished memory'. Every tenant of that day was invited to subscribe to the cost of erecting this great statue, seen for miles distant. And yet the cries of the old, infirm and paralysed women never ceased to be heard. At nearby Kildonan, all but three families, out of two thousand people were burned out of their homes. Loved? revered? cherished? What a mockery. It is a red sandstone statue high above the top of Ben Bhraggie which rises 1300 feet above the waters of the Dornoch Firth; the 'most noble George Granville Leveson-Gower, second Marquis of Stafford' and for the last six months of his life, the first Duke of Sutherland. The back of the statue is to the glens he emptied for Lowland graziers and their sheep; and it faces the sea to which he committed 5000 people as emigrants. It is said, because he was an Englishman and knew no Gaelic, he did not hear the bitter protests and the agonising tales among his people. Yet it was all done in both his and his wife's name, under their authority and to their knowledge and certainly with their sanction. Can one add more, except to say they cannot be held blameless? Lady Stafford, the Duke's wife was known as 'the Great Lady of Sutherland'. She had inherited her family's contempt for the manners and customs of the Highland people. And yet her home and estate was essentially Highland. She married in 1785, and almost the whole of Sutherland became her husband's when she married; and with his father's estates he became the richest landowner in Britain. And yet, why should they sink to such abysmal, terrible human depths? Echo can only answer 'why?' Their people walked to the barren coast, where the villages in which they were told were there for them to live in, had not even been built. And so they were expected to exist. The only port of haven on the coast, seemed to be the Port of Eternity.

In respect of emigration, the 500 families who were shipped to Carolina in a vessel of only 300 tons, were cooped up like animals with only two square feet of room for each person. Twenty-three of them died. In 1831, 60,000 left for Canada; the following year another 70,000 left. In 1853, thirty emigrant ships left Scotland; of the many thousands aboard more than a third went down with cholera, and some two thousand died *en route*. Distress and destitution personified beyond all human imagination. Men and women throughout the land wept without restraint. In one ship boarded at Ullapool, Loch Broom, it was so rotten that the emigrants were able to pick away its timber with their nails, eating the powdered dust. All these unhappily placed folk left Scotland—their cherished home saying 'we shall return no more'. Emigration 'midst filth, foul air, darkness, fever, dysentery and cholera; and for most passengers, semi-starvation. The stench and horror of these happenings gives me a nauseating feeling as I write of them.

In Strathcarron in 1854, women were brutally maimed in truncheon attacks by police, as they defended their homes, and just at that time war was declared on Tsar Nicholas I of Russia. Britain was far more concerned as to the Crimea, and how many Russians were being killed by the Black Watch. But in the

Highlands, people lost their memory, their reason and their all. The fact that a woman might be pregnant had no bearing on eviction orders. It was the word 'Improvement' that was paramount; the economic argument was unanswerable. Land which had produced 2*d*. an acre under cattle, yielded two shillings under sheep; so how could there be any argument?

Patrick Sellar did not remain long in control, and in the end he died the death he richly deserved in 1851. His place was taken over in 1855 by one James Loch, from Bloomsbury, London, whose father at that time had written a book in eulogistic terms on the improvements being carried out on the Estate of Sutherland. Improvement, was on everyone's lips and in his book Loch defined its cause . . . 'to emancipate the lower orders from slavery has been the unceasing object of the Highland Proprietors'; and for his father's sake he became General Agent of the Sutherland Estate.

The stark lesson of the Clearances may be judged by a recent census for Sutherland; its population has barely a mere seven persons to each of the 2028 square miles.

One effect of the Clearances on Gaelic life was that more than anything else the clearing for sheep broke the old ties of affection between the people who owned, and those who lived on the land. It has left an enduring feeling of bitterness that is part of the mental heritage of present day people. There is no escaping this feeling. The psychological consequences after Culloden, aggravated by the Clearances is well documented in the evidence presented to the Crofters' Commission in 1884, but few of the many ramifications of the complex problems involved have been worked out. This report plus that of the Napier Commission set up by Prime Minister Gladstone in March 1883 was the trumpet which demolished the walls of Jericho that landlordism had thrown around Westminster. In 1886 the Bill was enacted which gave to the people of the Highlands and Islands protection in the lands they occupied as statutory tenants. The power of the factor based on the threat of instant eviction was destroyed. Exactly fifty years after Patrick Sellar had been acquitted at Inverness.

All this sordid business is fittingly and simply summed up by crofters in the far north by these words . . . 'There was neither sin nor sorrow in the world for us, but the Clearances came upon us with such suddenness, destroying all, turning our gladness into bitterness, our blessings (of which we had many) into blasphemy, and our Christianity into mockery' . . . What sadness must have been experienced; what glens of weeping. I feel none of us reading these details cannot but be filled with abhorence and repugnance—and pity.

*   *   *

I would now like to tell you of the church at Croick, which has sad and terrible memories of the Clearances.

The hamlet of Croick is approached from the small village of Ardgay which is just on the border of Sutherland before you cross over the large bridge taking you to Bonar Bridge. From Ardgay you continue up the narrow, level Strathcarron road (left) running south of the river Carron—not the road going to Culrain—for some 12 miles. It is a lovely run through the quiet glen, a lonely road in fact, its emptiness relieved only by one or two shooting lodges, and a farm here and there; and the road ends at Croick, from whence stretches Strath Cuileannach with the pretty slow-flowing river running between it and another strath, Strath Chuileannaich. All is very restful. There is the Amat forest nearby and Glencalvie . . . though nothing but track paths to these spots.

I paid a visit to Croick Church in the autumn of 1968, its adjacent manse is now a keeper's house, its only neighbour a small sheep farm. Although the church and its grounds are well tended, there is a forlorn air surrounding everything, and one asks the question, where are the people and the houses to justify it being in this remote spot? Croick Church was built in 1827 and was then a centre of worship attended by a congregation of over 200 from the little communities nearby. Nothing remains now save a few old tracks through the heather to the hills; and only stones marking where the houses once stood bear evidence of the Clearances and subsequent depopulation. However a service is conducted every Sabbath morning by the minister from the parish of Kincardine, a mile or so south of Ardgay; and every year on the last Sabbath of July, a Communion service is held.

Inside, the church is plain, very plain and well preserved. One's interest is centred on the east window where a few words and names have been scratched on the diamond panes, vividly

reminding you of the story behind the depopulation, the out-
come of the Clearances and of 'Improvements' of the last
century. It is recorded the landlord of the day, Major Robertson
of Kindeace, puts the blame for the clearances in this area on the
initiative of his factor, James Gillanders, who lived at Tain. The
object of his policy of improvement was Glen Calvie, which lies
near Croick and which to some degree had suffered a few years
earlier. In 1843 the people of Glen Calvie reduced in numbers to
no more than seventy by the earlier 'alterations' were described
as a happy self-contained community. Although the glen was
poor and rocky it was rented at £55, considered an exorbitant
figure; yet the people found the money and paid. They could
trace their tenancies back 500 years.

In 1843 Gillanders began his scheme to turn the glen into one
big sheep farm claiming even higher rents; and he served
summonses of removal. Anticipating this, and on watch outside
the boundary, the women of the glen intercepted the constables
and seizing the wrist of the man holding the writs, they applied
live coals to the papers until they were destroyed, so proving they
had neither been seen nor handled in the glen. Next year Gillanders invited the chief tenants to Tain for a friendly discussion.
Instead he placed the formal notices to quit in their hands. Crafty
Gillanders. The law then took its course. Stunned and be-
wildered the people began to hunt for alternative holdings, but
only six families, it is said, could find a place. The others were
evicted by force, their homes ruined and looted, and whilst their
menfolk were searching for new plots, the women, children, and
infants were allowed to shelter in Croick churchyard exposed to
the elements, and praying that death would come so they could
join their forefathers beneath the turf. They were not allowed to
shelter *inside* the church, although the minister did all he could to
ease their sufferings. The reason for this was, in those days, that
it would have been regarded as desecration of a holy place.

As the people passed the agonising days among the tombstones,
some of them scratched idly on the panes of the east window,
leaving their own memorial for posterity to see. I have seen these
writings, all in the unhurried copperplate style, which today is a
thing of the past. Over a hundred years ago and still their living
record. I could plainly read the names—'C. Chalmers'; 'John
Ross, Shepherd, Parish Ardgay'; and others. And in another

pane 'Glen Calvie people was in churchyard here May 24, 1845'; and the words 'Church officer' appears under the name 'Ann McAlister', but I doubt very much if these two markings relate to one another, for it would not have been possible for a woman to be acceptable as a church officer. There were many other scratchings and names which I could not make out plainly.

After gazing on this window, one goes away in deep thought. I took off my hat and bowed in reverence to a lost people—and left. Where the people went to, if they swelled the emigration queues to the Colonies, no one seems to know. Maybe they got no further than the next churchyard, and lie buried there?

When Gillanders died, he was buried near the side gate of the churchyard. I looked for it, but could not see it, for generations afterwards the memory of his cruelty and deceit was kept alive by the casting of stones and refuse on his grave until it became a weed-grown mound. His soul is not there now of course; it will most likely be in Hell and tormented for his evil. This then, gives readers some idea of the Clearances. It is a sorry chapter. My sketch at the top of the next chapter (The Kirk), is that of Croick Church.

In the Kinlochbervie district there is a small hamlet Ardmore on the coast a mile or so after leaving Rhiconich, approached by a 3-mile stretch of rough road. A large number of Clearance folk came across to this isolated part from the Strathnaver region, followed by others who settled nearby and it is told me that on the Sabbath and Communion times, it was nothing for a thousand men, women and children to congregate in the hollows of the hills to hold their devotional services and to lift up their prayers to the heavens. It became a colony but as time went on they subsequently emigrated and today there are only two families living in that charming little bay. Recently a Captain John Ridgway has set up in this area, an adventure training school for age groups 14 to 25 intended (on lines with the School of Adventure near Applecross, Wester Ross) to feature rock climbing, hill walking, camping, map reading, geology, bird watching and marine biology. He plans to build a cedar-wood house for fifty students, and is being partnered by a fellow officer. Captain Ridgway is a famous Atlantic oarsman who attempted to make a round-the-world trip in his boat English Rose IV. Some few years ago he rowed across the Atlantic in an open dinghy.

So today there is a very different 'Adventure' than there was nearly two hundred years ago.

Then again, in far away Kintail, near Dornie on the way to Kyle, came another tale of emigration. During the very early 1800's, a great many were cleared from this area by Seaforth at the instigation of his factor Duncan Mor MacRae and his father, who themselves added to the land taken from the ancient tenants to their own sheep farms already very extensive. All over these snowball Clearances the factors seemed to be the prime movers of the cruelty—the moving forces behind the gentry. The people went to Canada and founded a little town there which they called Glengarry. I heard of one, a man of 93 years of age still alive, who was among the evicted. He had done well, and his three sons had three farms of their own. Hundreds of others from surrounding places had gone as well. Factor MacRae died in poverty in spite of his greed. They all seemed to get their deserts in the long run. The land he took from these tenants eventually fell into the hands of others who paid higher rents to the proprietor.

One of the most hated person who held land in this area was an Englishman, one David Kirk who had made a fortune in Jamaica and came to the parish in 1814. He took over the whole of the Ratagan area. He was responsible for building the house which is now a youth hostel at Kylerhea ferry near Glenelg. (Incidentally this is the one and only place-name in Scotland that spells the same backwards or forwards.) He was so hated by both people and proprietors alike that they threatened to shoot him. The story goes that one morning his horses were found dead at the foot of a steep cliff. They had apparently stampeded during the night—but there seemed to be no cause for a stampede. A man was arrested for this affair but as he had a cast-iron alibi of being many miles away when the incident took place, he was released—'not proven'. David Kirk was so terrified by this matter than he remained indoors in Ratagan House for many years and subsequently committed suicide.

Bringing matters more up to date, this time from the Rogart area (midway off the main road between Dornoch and Golspie, known as the Strath of Fleet) and near The Mound. This place is named after a causeway built for the Dornoch Light Railway —now torn up—to reclaim a strip of land from the shallow Loch

Fleet. A ceremony was performed in July 1968 by the Rt. Hon. John G. Diefenbaker (former Prime Minister of the Dominion of Canada who was holidaying in Scotland and who has strong links with the district) in the unveiling of a memorial cairn at Dalmore, to Sir John A. Macdonald, Canada's first Prime Minister, whose father was born in the valley of Fleet. And then a day or so later he went on to Kildonan, west of Helmsdale, to the tiny 17th century church there, to unveil a plaque in memory of his great-grandfather George Bannerman and of all the settlers from Kildonan who in 1812 and 1813 migrated to the Red River Settlement, which is now in the Province of Manitoba. Mr. Diefenbaker was the thirteenth Prime Minister of Canada. Very many of Gunns, Bannermans, Mackays and Sutherlands had emigrated to Canada during the Clearances. The landowner at the time was Lord Selkirk. When these settlers left they had nothing but their love of God and their desire for freedom. Their descendants are to be found all over Canada. The foundation marks of their old homesteads are discernible even today and all are close to the strath road. Lord Selkirk came to the Rogart district in June 1813. About five hundred people were sent away to the little unknown America's. They went, for they were a proud race. Lord Selkirk was at least good enough to help pay their passages overseas, which cost £10 a head. They were to have the land at 5s. an acre, or half bushel of grain per acre in perpetuity. Anything in fact to rid the country of them.

And so the lurid story can go on and on; it is simply a series of repetition all along the line of these 'burnt offerings'.

*   *   *

As a synopsis to this sorry chapter, I would mention the earls of Sutherland—possibly the oldest earldom in Scotland—were successively 'MORMAERS' (a Celtic title), 'JARLS' (Norse) and finally 'earls' or 'comes' as the Anglo-Norman influence began to prevail. This earldom was once in Gordon hands; then Gordon changed his name to Sutherland and thereafter, as I have previously said, it passed by the marriage of an heiress to the Leveson-Gower family. The 18th century saw the Sutherlands against the Jacobite risings and actively concerned in their suppression, and then in the Clearance days of which we have just read, the first Duke (Leveson-Gower) incurred hatred by his decision to clear the glens. Dunrobin Castle near Golspie, is the Sutherland home, and is a fitting memorial to one who was reputed to be the wealthiest man of his age. It also stands as a memorial of a castle built up on foundations of an infamous persecution and hate. It is now a boy's school, with 120 pupils, and a teaching staff of eleven. Both inside and out, Dunrobin Castle is redolent of history; on the wall above the main stair-way hang the colours of the 'Thin Red Line' regiment of Balaclava fame, the 93rd Sutherland Highlanders, and just beyond stands a bust of Garibaldi, a personal friend of the 3rd Duke of Sutherland. There was always a room reserved for the Prince Consort Albert. Be all this as it may, I feel the stigma of old will remain for all time.

An anecdote of the Clearance period tells of a crofter, threatened with eviction from his home that had been in the family's possession for long years past. He went to his minister for advice. The minister thought for a while and then told him the best thing he could do was to go home and pray earnestly. He did so, and two weeks later the crofter was back at the manse door. When the minister appeared he told him, with happiness radiating all over his face, 'Sir, the Lord's the boy!' 'What makes you say that Calum?' the reverend gentleman asked, somewhat taken aback at such language. 'Why do I say that, sir? Why indeed? the factor's deid!'

> We have no country left to fight for,
> You robbed us of our country and gave it to the sheep,
> Therefore, since you have preferred sheep to men,
> Let sheep defend you . . .

The above lines were said by the men of Sutherland, when in 1854 additional Highland blood was needed to fight for the British Empire in the Crimean War. Even the pompous Duke of Sutherland (a Sassenach)—George Granville Leveson-Gower, who bore no blood kinship to the once-proud Clan Sutherland—journeyed north from London to assist in the recruitment. He wanted to replenish the famous 93rd Sutherland Highlanders with new men. He was unsuccessful. The wrongs that had been done to their people were remembered by every true Highlander 'so long as grass grows and waters run'.

CHAPTER 10

THE KIRK

'*Don't leave it too late, I shall not pass this way again.*'

I think the above words are symptomatic of the Highlander's
Faith, for up in the north and north-west of Scotland the people
have deep religious principles and feelings and keep the Sabbath,
holy. Apart from their devotional duties, the day is observed as
one of complete rest. It is true to say, the Sabbath immobilises
all these scattered places like an anaesthetic. Practically every
household is wrapt up in Faith; Faith the substance of things
hoped for; the evidence of things not seen.

To honour a law that is older than all the statutes of men, that
is in fact an Ordinance of Creation, namely 'Remember the
Sabbath Day to keep it holy', is their sheet-anchor. The Divine
Creator has inscribed this law not only on Tablets of Stone, for
it is written deep and clear on all Nature. I remember Angus
the green-keeper of the Gairloch golf course, telling me, over
thirty or so years ago, that two Americans came to the course
and teed-up their balls one Sabbath morning. He said to them
(when, after attending service at the near-by Free Kirk, he was
told there were some people with golf clubs going along to the
course), 'What are you up to, my friends?' 'Oh,' they said 'we're
just going to have a game.' Angus replied, 'Well, if you don't
have the sense to know that you need a rest on the Sabbath, I

185

G

know that my greens need a rest.' Yes, all Nature needs a rest. Even the animal world needs a rest; 'on the seventh day thou shalt rest, that thine ox and thine ass may also rest'.

The word CHURCH in Scripture, has been understood in various senses. The root meaning of the term is *to call*, or to *call out*, and was applied to the assembly of Israel when it met to worship God. The word EKKLESIA was used by our Lord to describe the company who gathered around Him, and submitted themselves to His teaching (Matthew 16, v. 18). It is said the term church, however, is not derived from that word, but from the word KURIAKE, meaning 'belonging to the Lord'. The Kuriake designated the place where the church assembled, and this place belonged to the Lord, but did not manifest itself until the church gathered to worship.

Christianity is above all things, *a life to be lived*. It is not a church to be adopted, not an ordinance to be observed, nor a creed to be recited. All these things accompany salvation. But this life is mysterious—all life is. This life is spontaneous—all life is. This life is precious—all life is. This life is powerful—all life is.

At an early period a special sort of prosperity existed throughout the entire county of Ross-shire. Spiritual prosperity followed a great revival of religion in the middle of the 18th century; the same revival which paved the way for the deliverance of the Scottish Church from the blight of Moderatism, and then at the Disruption of 1843, emancipated it from State intrusion. Wester Ross was blessed with many notable servants of Christ. Godliness and a scripture-based morality bred integrity and kindliness. The Divine promise to parents was fulfilled, 'Train up a child in the way he should go; and when he is old he will not depart from it.' All too often nowadays, the absence of firm parental example accounts for the teenage minds of today.

The early Christians in the 1st century acted and preached in accordance with their belief that the end of the world and the Second Coming of Christ were imminent. Then after a century, they had to recognise that the world was not coming to an end and that the Second Coming was not imminent. So they had to adapt their theology and start to build a Church which would last in a world that was not going to come to an end—then.

The story is told of a little boy who was playing with one of his chums, and heard him boasting of his aristocratic relations, some of whom were Peers of the Realm. This boy turned to the lad and said pompously, 'Have you any Lords in your family?' He replied, 'I'm not sure, but I have heard my mother say that the Lord Jesus is our Elder Brother.'

Said the Syrians who had been routed by the Israelites (I Kings, 20) 'The Lord is God of the hills.' Up to that point they were right. Our God indeed is a God of the hills.

—On the hill of Ararat, Noah received the blessing of God after the flood.

—on the hill of Moriah, Abraham had his unforgettable vision of God.

—on Sinai, Moses, in answer to prayer beheld God's glory.

—on the hill of Carmel, Elijah called down fire from Heaven upon the sacrifice.

—on Horeb, he was raised above his dejection and given a new commission from God.

—on the Mount of the Beatitudes, Jesus proclaimed the laws of His Kingdom.

—on the Mount of Transfiguration, He was seen in Glory by the disciples who were privileged to accompany Him.

—on the hill of Calvary, He accomplished the work of which He alone was capable; the redemption of His people.

—and from the Mount of Olives, He ascended to the right hand of God.

The first translator of the New Testament in Scottish Gaelic, was the Rev. James Stewart, minister at KILLIN; and the first translator of the Old Testament into Scottish Gaelic was his son Rev. Dr. Patrick Stewart who succeeded him at Killin, and was afterwards minister at LUSS, Loch Lomond.

It is with words, as with the rays of the sun, the more they are condensed, the deeper they burn. When one remembers the Sermon on the Mount is told in three short chapters of St. Matthew's Gospel, and can be spoken at deliberate speed in some fifteen minutes, it seems possible surely to cut out a lot of high-falluting talk and writings, and massive wordage of reports and so forth, on such matters as 'Christian Unity'—*Ecumenical*, a 'oneness' that is being coined and constantly repeated these days?

In the bible there is a music in it which attracts the mind by its

richness and beauty.   A Pearl above all Pearls.   Just as a particular
disease in the world is treated by various medical methods, so
there are many religions designed and propounded to bring
happiness to human beings.   Different doctrines have been introduced by different exponents at different periods and in different
ways.   But I believe they all fundamentally aim at the same
noble goal in teaching moral precepts to mould the functions
of mind, body and speech.   They all teach us not to tell lies,
or bear false witness, or steal;   or take others lives and so forth.
Love is the corner stone.

*   *   *

Scotland as a whole is a Church-minded nation to a far greater
extent than England, so that in such a context the Church of
England is relatively the junior partner.   Church membership in
Scotland is 2½ times what it is in England.   It will appear galling
to some devout Scots ministers when the Church of England is
projected as 'the National Church in Britain'.   In fact, only
about 10 per cent of the English adult population can lay claim to
full Church membership;   whereas the Church in Scotland can
claim 66 per cent of the adult population to Church membership. Rather staggering figures.   It is predominantly Protestant,
and the smaller the religious denominations the more loyal the
members.

The Free Church of Scotland and the Free Presbyterian
Church of Scotland strictly adhere to all the Bible says.   Under
the name of Holy Scripture—or the Word of God, written—
are contained the Books of the Old and New Testaments;   all
of which are given by inspiration of God, to be the rule of faith
and life.   The Books, they maintain, commonly called Apocrypha
—not being of divine inspiration—are no part of the canon of
the scripture;   and therefore are of no authority in the Church
of God.

The Free and the Free Presbyterian Churches have, as their
acknowledged text-book, *The Confession of Faith*, dealing ex-
haustively with every aspect of scriptural life from the Creation
to the Last Judgement;   agreed upon by the Assembly of Divines
at Westminster as a part of the Covenanted Uniformity in Religion betwixt the Churches of Christ in the Kingdoms of Scotland,
England and Ireland, and approved by the General Assembly in

1647, and ratified by Acts of Parliament 1649 and 1690, as the public and avowed Confession of the Church of Scotland. . . .

> And these words, which I command thee this day, shall be in thine heart; and thou shalt teach them diligently unto thy children, and shalt talk of them when thou sittest in thine house, and when thou walkest by the way, and when thou liest down, and when thou risest up.—Deut. vi, 6, 7.

The Old Testament in Hebrew (which was the native language of the people of God of old) and the New Testament in Greek (which at the time of the writing of it was most generally known to the nations) being immediately inspired by God, they hold to be authentical, being by singular care and providence kept pure throughout all the ages.

The Greek name for papyrus was 'BIBLOS', and by the 4th century this was giving place to vellum and the roll form of manuscript to the codex. By the year A.D. 150 the twenty-seven books of the New Testament were ready for their transcription to the more durable quality of calf skin.

*   *   *

As I have said, Prayer and Faith are two of the characteristics of the peoples in the north-west. And that is why (in a later chapter) I felt constrained to bitterly attack the suggested new face lift to make the area into a multi-sports centre, proposed by a survey of the Glasgow Art Students. You will read in para. six of that letter of 19th July 1968, such a face lift—if we can call it one—would strike a mortal blow at all held dear up here. What a mockery in-comers would make of the Sabbath. It would result in a regular vendetta.

Prayer and Faith . . . *don't leave it too late.* If so, then, 'too late, too late, will be the cry; Jesus of Nazareth has passed by'. For hurrying along life's thoroughfare, we passed Him by and remained unaware, that within the very sight of our eye, unnoticed, the Son of God passed by . . .

Every Sabbath you will see families walking along the road to kirk, as well as cars conveying folk from far distances on the same errand. In the week-days, the ordinary crofter and those working on the roads, will be dressed in workaday clothes—but on the Lord's Day, everyone is dressed smartly, the women in their

Sunday best, and the men in dark suits, black shoes highly polished the night before. The children too in their Sabbath togs, and respecting graceful behaviour, walk quietly under their grown-up's eyes, their pockets full of pan-drops bought from the sweetie-shop on Saturday.

Prayer and Faith; and this reminds me of a moving story concerning the late King George VI. Once during the last war when the king was aboard a large warship, his steward called at his cabin. When there was no response to his knocks, he opened the cabin door and went into the king's suite, thinking no one was there. But kneeling by a chair was King George, deep in the act of prayer. Embarrassed, the steward withdrew silently, closing the door quietly behind him. He went back later, and apologised to His Majesty for his intruding on the king's private devotions. The king told him if a similar situation ever arose again, not to go away, but to join him. Such an answer would be typical of the man who won our hearts during his troubled reign, and whose Faith upheld by his prayers, enabled him to bear the suffering of his later years with such fortitude. Prayer, to the really devout, is not just a closing of the eyes and the mumbling of a few words. If that be so, I think there is a reference in THE BOOK to same, namely it is 'vain repetition'. Prayer is a bringing of our whole personality in humility into the presence of our Creator. And when we pray whether by ourselves or with others, there is always *Someone* unseen who joins us. For it is written in the Bible 'Where two or three are gathered together in My name, there will I be in the midst'.

. . . Here then was a young man, born in an obscure village, the child of a peasant woman. He grew up in another village. He worked in a carpenter's shop until he was thirty; and then for three years he was an itinerant preacher. He never wrote a book. He never held an office; he never owned a home; he never had a family; he never went to school; he never put his foot inside a big city; he never travelled two hundred miles from the place where he was born; he never did one of the things that usually accompany greatness. He had no credentials but himself. Whilst still young, the tide of general opinion turned against him. His friends ran away; he was turned over to his enemies. He went through the mockery of a trial; he was nailed to a cross between two thieves. While he was dying his executioners gambled for the only piece of property he had on earth—his coat. When he was dead he was laid in a borrowed grave through the pity of a friend. Nineteen long and wide centuries have come and gone, and today He is the central figure of the human race. I think it safe to say that all the armies that ever marched, or all the warships ever built, or all the parliaments that ever sat, or all the king's that ever reigned put together, have not affected the life of man upon this earth as has that *One Solitary Life*. . .

> And the lark said in her song:
> Often, often, often
> Goes the Christ in a stranger's guise.

In Tennyson's 'Morte d'Arthur', there are certain passages near the end that are today of real significance; the lines where Sir Bedivere regrets the departure of the good old days . . . 'For now I see the true old times are dead'—and Arthur's reply, 'the old order changeth, giving place to new, yet God fulfils himself in many ways'.

As one grows older, I am certain one grows more and more to love the way of life practised by these great folk up in the north. Old age is like everything else; to make a success of it you have to start young.

In reading through the New Testament I have often wondered what happened to the Wise Men and the Shepherds after that first Christmas? According to the Bible, these men had only a 'walking-in' part in the first act of the great drama, and were never heard of again in the story of Jesus. They never appeared in the group round Jesus during His ministry. Nor were they in the cast at the time of the Cross, or the Resurrection. The only thing we can be certain of therefore is they died, and their enthusiasm died with them? Is it not strange that the men who first saw the Star, and who in their great wisdom realised its portent, who journeyed so far to pay homage to the Infant King of Kings, should so quietly slip away from the scene? Again, is it not strange that the Shepherds who had such a remarkable experience in the fields at midnight, who heard the angelic choir, who hurried to the manger to worship the Babe of Bethlehem, should so quickly merge back into the darkness of obscurity? Is it not strange that such an emotional experience should have so little lasting effect? Yet after each Christmas, the decorations are pulled down, the fairy lights packed away till the next Christmas, the tinsel and all the bits and pieces associated with that joyful time, are thrown on the rubbish dump, and the spirit of Christmas, like the Wise Men dies. The many who had flocked to Christmas Eve services to pay due homage, have returned to their religious obscurity. For many—but not up in the Highlands—the annual pilgrimage to church has been made like the payment of a yearly premium for a comprehensive spiritual insurance policy. It is surely not enough to go to the House of God just on 'special' days; that makes it more of a theatrical atmosphere. The influence of the Gospel is not restricted to any traditional date or dates, for it is written He is able to help one on any and every day. What happened to the Wise Men and the Shepherds? That is of far less importance than what has happened to men and women throughout the ages who not only paid homage to the Infant Jesus, but gave their lives to the risen Christ.

To the Romans, the Christians were rebels, because they would not swear by the life of Caesar or adore his image; and so their cry was always *Christianos ad Leones*, 'to the lions, Christians'. The charge of rebellion against the State is one that has constantly been brought against Christians down through the ages for almost every persecution carried out against them.

I once read in an American magazine *The Carolina Israelite* the following: 'How could the Scots,' it said, 'have suffered the rigours of Knox and Calvin, if they were not directly descended from the Lost Tribes?' The strict unrelenting laws of Calvinism were based entirely on the equally strict laws of Judaism. Preachers up in the Highlands are without compare in their skill in opening windows which let us see into the Eternal World. They preach the sermon with a command of language and a justness of tone, action and reasoning, the like of which I have seldom, or ever, heard surpassed. And it is nothing for them to preach for an hour or an hour and a half without reference to a single note. And in the Gaelic services, the singing of the Psalms can be likened to a melody from the vestibule of Heaven. Words and phraseology in the Gaelic have a rhythm and grace which is quite absent in any translation.

The ministers in their endeavour to bring more into the

Faith, tell their congregation that the myrtle tree and the fir tree grew where the briar and the thorn had cumbered the ground.

The Scottish Reformation of 1560, was concerned chiefly with the errors and corruptions of the Church of Rome. Where the 16th century reformers in Scotland, following Luther, took as their watchword 'none but Christ saves', those of the 1600's, i.e. the 17th century, were forced by political developments to add further words 'none but Christ reigns'. The Covenanters emerged as the direct result of the Stuart theory of the Divine Right of Kings, which held that the 'legislative and architectorick' power of making laws resided solely in the king. The conception of Divine Right was a Byzantine product. In the early 14th century the Pope declared against Robert Bruce; the Scots replied that Providence, the laws, the customs of the Country and the choice of the people, had made him their king, and that if he betrayed his country, they would elect another. They cared not for glory or riches, but for that liberty which no man renounces till death. This Declaration made at Arbroath in 1320 is a landmark in Scottish history. After Bannockburn when Edward II escaped from its muddy reaches he got a small boat to Berwick; an ignominious end to his boast to wipe out 'Robert de Brus, who calls himself King of Scotland'. The victory of Bannockburn made all Scots feel they really were one Nation under God's guidance, and the aforementioned Declaration of Arbroath, and the subsequent Treaty of Northampton gave formal recognition to the bravery of the men who fought for the cause, and the freedom they won. It was James VI (James I of Scotland) who was responsible for the passing of the Black Acts, which declared, contrary to the teaching of Knox, that the king was head of the Church, as of the State; that there should be crown-appointed bishops in the Church of Scotland, and that ministers should not discuss public affairs under penalty of treason. Before the year 1688 was out the Stuarts were in exile. The persecution had gone. The Covenanters had either to obey God or obey the king; it was as simple as that. They chose God. They had no dividing line between toleration and submission. The Covenanters supreme conviction that their cause was right was illogically carried over to mean also that the course which they advocated was likewise right and justifiable. In this they made a tragic mistake. In certain verses of *Esther*, justification for retaliating against those who would destroy the faithful can be found. As I have said they had no dividing line; no differentiation. Those who were not for them, were against them. No compromise. Even if the curates appointed by the Crown had been saints, they too would have been regretted—such was the mood of carping criticism which the men of the Covenant for the most part displayed towards everything in any way linked with the Government. In this it seems clear, it was not the curate or bishop they objected to, but the main office. In dealing with opponents, the Covenanters never put themselves in the latter's place. All who disagreed with them, were promoters of 'Popery, Prelacy, Erastianism, Schism, Error, Tyranny, or Defection'. How unfortunate, to be sure. 'The Covenant' though right in spirit, and originally a protection of liberty, became hostile to liberty when subsequently they sought to enforce it to the letter. However, take away the Covenanting protest and regal despotism of an even more extreme type would have been speedily established in Scotland. So what? In another sense the Covenanters stand was neither unreasoning nor unreasonable. The National Covenant was a legitimate legal document by which the Covenanters had tried to obtain their legal rights. It had been declared unlawful to support it. But how could they depart from it, just because persecution was increased and when religious liberty—far from being given—was restricted to an intolerable degree? These were proud men, who when their enemies asked if they thought the king's power was limited, rightly pointed out that they knew of no power but the Almighty's to be unlimited. Charles II was the chief author of the persecution.

It was in 1563 the first ray of Reformation light broke through the darkness of Ross-shire. This Reformation found the Highlander an utter heathen in ignorance, a very fanatic in superstition and in his habits a lawless savage, rioting in the wild excitements of the chase, in the perilous adventures of plundering raids and in the fierce fights of rival clans and chieftains.

The Bishop of Ross, one of the Tulchan bishops (those appointed by James VI of Scotland on the express condition that they surrendered part of their income to the King) was deposed by the Assembly in 1638. He was one who was likely to use all his influence in suppressing the truth, and in oppressing the people who loved it.

On the re-establishment of Presbytery—after the days of the Tulchans—the people were found to be still grossly ignorant and superstitious and the state of their morals extremely low. During a tour of visitation by the Presbytery in 1656, even in Gairloch itself, the killing of beasts was in practice, and it is minuted in the Kinlochewe records (6th September 1656) of the 'abomination with the parish of Gairloch in sacrificing of beasts upon the 25th August as also in pouring of milk upon hills as oblations. . . .' Some years after the Restoration in 1660 (the re-establishment of monarchy by the return of Charles II)—in 1690 to be precise— the Presbytery began to resume possession, but only slowly could it do so. There were few ministers to whom places, occupied by them before the Restoration, were open. The reoccupying of the county of Ross-shire was found to be more difficult than to take possession of it at first. A strong political feeling was aroused and directed by the Jacobite chieftains, against the reigning sovereign and against the Church, which he had been the means of restoring. The number of people who rejoiced in the restoration of the Gospel to their land was small. In several parishes the first presentees had much opposition to encounter.

In 1716 the minister of Gairloch was compelled to leave his parish, owing to the ill-treatment he received at the hands of both the laird and the people. His crops were destroyed, his home robbed and he and his family were reduced to starvation.

It was only after about 1725 that the best days of Ross-shire began. At the climax of Ross-shire's spiritual prosperity the cruel work of eviction began to lay waste the hillsides and valleys of the north. The peaceful, virtuous peasantry began to be driven off by ungodly oppressors, to clear their native soil for strangers, red deer and sheep. The owners of the soil acted as if they were the owners of the people and they treated them without respect to the requirements of righteousness or to the dictates of mercy. Families by the score were driven across the sea. Wholesale eviction wastes were formed for the red deer, so that the gentry might indulge in the sports of the savages of three centuries before.

Other than the ministers of Ross-shire, there were 'The Men' of Ross-shire. 'The Men' were so named, not because they were not women, but because they were not ministers. It was necessary

to distinguish between the ministers and the other speakers at a
fellowship meeting when notes of their addresses were given.
And the easiest way of doing so was by saying 'one of the
ministers', or 'one of the men' said so; hence the origin of the
designation. In these days the designation has—in general—been
changed to that of 'missionary'.

One of the most significant events in Scots ecclesiastical history
was the *Disruption of 1843*, when what came to be called the Free
Church split from the Church of Scotland on the ancient and
sorry issue of patronage. That was an event of a most dramatic
order, the ministers so opposed sacrificing their livings with
selflessness that must be respected; and congregations suffering
forms of martyrdom—if only mild—for the sake of a conception
of religious liberty. The people rebelled when worthless men
were appointed to big parishes by lay patrons, quite regardless of
their being suitable or unsuitable.

In connection with the Reformation, the name of John Knox
(1505–72) stands out as being the great Scottish Calvinist and
Reformer. He wrote the History of the Reformation and much
polemical, controversial matter. Many south of the Border
looked on him as a dour ridiculous figure; but to his followers
he was 'the light of Scotland', a prophet sent by God to castigate
evil-doers, and reveal the truth to His people; to his enemies he
was a dangerous revolutionary—an agent of Satan. John Knox
was the man who made Scotland Calvinist, who did so much to
unite it with England, and whose doctrine of resistance to
authority had such a powerful influence on political thinkings. In
short he was 'a bold and heroical spirit'.

As to the Bible, a nameless and dateless document found
in Westminster Abbey said, a nation would be truly blessed if it
were governed by no other laws than the Book; for it affords a
copy for a king and a rule for a subject. It gives instruction and
direction to a senate, authority and council to a magistrate. It
cautions a witness, requires an impartial verdict from the jury,
and furnishes the judge with his sentence. It entails honour to
parents and enjoins obedience to children. In short it is a Book
of laws to show right or wrong; a Book of wisdom, of truth and
of life.

The Free Church of Scotland, at her separation in 1843, claimed
that she adhered to the Creed and Constitution of the Established

Church of Scotland in their entirety, and that she *had to separate* on account of the intrusion of the Civil Courts into the spiritual jurisdiction of the Church Courts, in order to maintain the lawful rights of the Established Church of Scotland. In one word, that she was the Church of Scotland, *free*; following the Church's original Calvanistic preaching to the letter.

When the Disruption took place in 1843, the party who contended for the spiritual independence of the Church of Scotland—for the non-interference by the civil courts (magistrates) in matters belonging to the spiritual jurisdiction of the courts of the Church—took every precaution to make their position crystal clear. The Claim, Declaration and Protest of 1842, regarding the encroachment of the Court of Session, leaves no doubt that the Disruption Fathers contended for the rights of the Church of Scotland as established by law. The two main claims put forward were (1) that 'there is no other head of the Church but the Lord Jesus Christ', and (2) that 'the Lord Jesus, as King and Head of His Church had appointed a government in the hands of church officers distinct from the civil magistrate, which government is ministerial, not lordly, and to be exercised in consonance with the laws of Christ, and with the liberties of His people'. In the law of Scotland the spiritual courts of the Church and the secular courts were co-ordinate, not subordinate the one to the other, in their own spheres of action.

The *Free Church* held this view unimpaired when she had in 1843, for truth and conscience's sake, to give up all the churches, manses, glebes and salaries, and all the remuneration which accrued to her from State connection, in order to maintain Christ's right to rule in His own Church by His Word in the hands of her own office-bearers. Those who fought for these rights recorded explicitly that they were compelled to relinquish State connection on account of the intrusion of the Civil Courts into the spiritual province of the Church by forcing ministers on congregations contrary to the wishes of the people and in defiance of the Church's courts, and *not* because they ceased to hold the doctrine of the Establishment of Religion by the State to be a Scriptural doctrine and highly valued by them.

This then was the position of the Free Church at the Disruption.

All office-bearers in the Free Church, when ordained to their respective offices as ministers and Elders, bound themselves to ordination vows and solemn declarations as being equivalent to an oath.

There were certain obstacles existing between the Free Church and the United Presbyterian Church (another body that had welded together certain other 18th century seceders, anti-burghers and such-like—burghers being the name of a sect of seceders from the Church of Scotland) and at the General Assembly of the Free Church in 1863 a large committee was appointed to see whether these obstacles could be removed so that a Union of the two bodies might come about.

Much bitter feeling arose in discussions, so much so that at the Assembly of 1867 five members of the Free Church committee resigned. There then arose two parties opposing each other known as the *Unionists* and the *anti-Unionists*, and as time went on these divergent positions and views began to unfold themselves. The Free Church party was led by Dr. Begg of Edinburgh and Dr. Nixon of Montrose; whilst the other party who were more for adopting a compromising solution was led by Dr. Rainy and Dr. Candlish.

Strife entered into the very heart of the Free Church. Instead of the Union that was contemplated in 1863, and so much desired, internal discussions and strife originated which at last broke up the Church into fragments.

A minority deplored the baneful effects of the union controversy on the peace and spiritual prosperity of the Free Church; of the Free Church being rent into two opposing camps.

It was in *May 1893* at the General Assembly that the Rev. Donald Macfarlane of Raasay, making strong protests over past events, separated from the Free Church and many applauded and followed in his bold step, and upon his preaching to a congregation worshipping at Millhouse, Kames, formed itself into the first congregation of what was to be known afterwards as the *Free Presbyterian Church*.

On his return to Raasay, Mr. Macfarlane received much encouragement and many meetings were subsequently held in different parts of the West of Scotland, when it was decided that immediate steps be taken to form a Presbytery. In July 1893 the Revs. Macfarlane, D. Macdonald (Shieldaig) and Mr. Alex. Macfarlane (Schoolmaster, Raasay) met and formed 'The Free Presbyterian Church Presbytery of Scotland'.

At a meeting on *14th August 1893* at Portree, the Presbytery adopted the Deed of Separation. At a further meeting that month (30th August) a call was moderated to Rev. John R. MacKay; and MacKay's ordination and induction took place at Gairloch in the golf-course hollow—the *Leabaidh na bà Baine*—on 11th October 1893.

He was the first minister ordained in the Free Presbyterian Church.

This, then, was the small beginning of the Free Presbyterian Church taken out of the Free Church. The F.P. Church then had but two ministers and a few students only.

On *30th October 1900*, the Union Act was passed; *i.e.* the Free Church duly united with the United Presbyterian Church, becoming known as the United Free Church of Scotland—or the present Free Church; a famous union and it produced the notorious litigation which gave the 'Wee Frees' their historical fame and which vested in this Union the bulk of the funds of the old Free Church proper.

The House of Lords declared in August 1904 that those who adhered to the Free Church were the 'True Free Church of Scotland' and therefore the rightful owners of all the property and funds.

This Union was heralded as one of the greatest blessings which had come to Scotland for years.

There still remained another union to be formed, the greatest of all, viz.: that of the authentic Church of Scotland and the United Free Church in 1929.

Concluding, it will be seen the Free Presbyterian Church and the Free Church accept the Bible as the infallible supreme standard; and the *whole* doctrine of the Confession of Faith as the subordinate standard because it is believed to be founded upon God's Word; and it is the desire of both these denominations to hand down their priceless heritage to their children and their children's children unimpaired.

*   *   *

The Communions in these villages up north are held twice a year. In Gairloch it is the fourth Sabbath in June, and the second Sabbath in October. The services commence on the Thursday right through to the Monday of the Communion Week, and during most of that time the stores are closed.

The general pattern followed is thus:

Thursday: 12 noon Gaelic 1¾ hour service
                          6 p.m. English 1½ hour service
Friday ('men's day'):   12 noon Gaelic 2½ hour service
                          6 p.m. English 1½ hour service
Saturday: 11 a.m. English 1 hour service
                          12 noon Gaelic 1¾ hour service
                          5–6.30 p.m. Prayer meeting (Gaelic)
Sabbath Day: Communion Day:
                          11.30 a.m. Gaelic at the Church 3¼ hour
                            service
                          11.30 a.m. to 1 p.m. English, at meeting
                            house
                          6–7 p.m. English at the Church
                          7–8 p.m. Gaelic at the Church
Monday: 11 a.m. English 1 hour service
                          12 noon Gaelic 1½ hour service

The Wednesday of mid-November is observed as Harvest Thanksgiving Day and church services are held. The stores and shops are all shut for it is looked upon as a Public Holiday (even for the post office). The public bar however, carries on as usual!

In the old days I remember witnessing these communions which were held in the open in the famous hollow at the Gairloch Golf Course, the *Leabaidh na bà Baine* (Bed of the White Cow, mentioned earlier), and thousands from near and far (50 or 60 miles even) came to join in the service. Days before the fast days every spare hole and corner was got ready to accommodate the throng of folk; every hut or shed with a roof over it was got ready by strewing it with straw to act as bedding during the five or six nights of their stay. Undressing or washing was never thought of. This hollow, a deep oval, was ideal for such a gathering and at one end was the preacher's 'box' affording him shelter from wind, sun and rain, so that his voice could be heard distinctly. It was never rain-sogged, for the soil was of pure, porous drifted sand; and the sheep saw to it that the grass was short. This hollow accommodated as many as 3000 people; and any stranger passing by, hearing these voices floating up out of the hollow, chanting beautiful and ancient Gaelic psalms, could not fail to be charmed with such utter solemnity; purely reminiscent of

our Lord's time? The assembly looked like a band of ancient
Covenanters.

What is it, the English ask, that moved in those olden days
such a multitude to walk miles and assemble, despite any weather,
over moor, mountain and stream—long before the motor car?
There can be but one answer; God's spirit had been moving
amongst them. They must have felt that the alternative to the
participation of that blessing was everlasting sorrow. They
gathered there, as it says in chapter 37 of Isaiah, to 'incline their
ears to hear and to open their eyes to see, and to learn that all
the kingdoms of the earth, may know that Thou art the Lord,
even Thou only'. The ministers then—as today up north—had
both oratorical power and spiritual fervour. *Don't leave it too
late.* 'Time,' said the Greek philosopher Theophrastus, 'is the
most valuable thing a man can spend.' Yet how often, instead,
do we let Time spend us? Leonardo da Vinci once said, 'Time
stays long enough for those who use it.' An eye surgeon once
attended a church, although he was generally too busy to do so.
The minister went along a few days later to see him, and to say
how pleased he was to see him at the kirk, knowing full well he
was so tied down by his work. He was surprised to see painting
after painting, all very lovely, on the walls of his sitting room.
'Who did these?' the minister asked gazing so intently at them.
'I did' said the surgeon. Knowing so well of his long hours at
duty and of his heavy responsibilities, he said, 'But how on earth
do you find time?' 'Find it!' the surgeon answered, 'I don't
find it, I *take* it.' Surely one can take time off, to devote the
Sabbath to rest and devotion? There is the making of music in
rest and devotion; but so many people these days are always
missing that part of life's melody.

Another story of a surgeon, who was on a lecture tour of
university medical faculties and the pace was beginning to tell.
'I'd give anything for a night off,' he told his driver. 'Why
don't we change places then,' his driver suggested. 'I've heard
you deliver the lecture so often that I could do it easily myself.'
Gratefully the surgeon accepted. He was relaxing at the back
of the hall at their next stop, and his driver was making a
magnificent job of the lecture. But at question time, to the
surgeon's horror, a keen young doctor raised an extremely
difficult point, but his stand-in didn't falter. 'I'm surprised that

such a simple point should give you trouble,' he told the student. 'It's so simple, in fact, that I'll get my driver, sitting in the back of the hall there to answer it!'

There is never any visiting on the Lord's Day, and no letters are written and none posted in the box even though they had been written on the Saturday previous—although the mail is not cleared till Monday a.m. Neither does one telephone, unless it be extremely urgent in case of sickness. Some of those belonging to the old order of things, draw their blinds on Saturday night, and even stop their clocks from chiming. No washing is ever left out on the line on the Sabbath.

At the close of the day, in many a house and cottage, amidst solemnity and the red light of the dying sitting-room fire, the household will kneel while the head of the family 'took the Book', and conducted family worship by reading a chapter of the Bible; and in some instances a Psalm would be sung, concluding with a Prayer poured out in a truly God-directed manner. And when we had the change to summertime, all clocks and watches were not altered to 'official' time till the Monday morning. All vegetables are prepared on the Saturday night, and no dishes washed up on the Sabbath. Where else in this country would we find such devotion, but up in the Highlands? And echo answers, 'Where?' In some of the old churches in the far-off spots you will still see the old paraffin lamps hanging from the rafters, or on the walls, although the electric light has taken over. With no lamps to fill with oil, no globes to polish or wicks to trim, am sure all this has proved a boon to the beadle. The people in the glens and far parishes must have experienced cuts in the electricity supply, and so the former lamps were there in readiness; and at any moment the kirk folk were ready to go back to the 'old ways'. In this connection it is wise, but in other connections it may be condemned. We have the case of the man who was counted as a disciple, but in the end Judas 'turned back' in his faith and loyalty and sold his Master for thirty pieces of silver. St. Paul had a companion in faith and service, yet later on he had to write of him 'Demas hath forsaken me, having loved this present world'. If after our confession of faith, we go back to the old ways, we make ourselves ripe for the judgement of God.

The 'cat-hold' and the 'Monkey-hold'; I am sure readers

will be asking what connection can this reference have to religion. I will explain.

In the Abbey at Iona, there is a replica of a carving on the VISHNAIVAITE Temple near VELLORE in South India. It is of a cat and a monkey. About the 12th century the followers of RAMANUJA split into two sects; the Northern School and the Southern School, the chief difference lying in the doctrine of the influence of divine grace on the soul. The first school's teaching was that it was 'Co-operative', whilst the other school maintained it was 'Irresistible'—a voluntary resignation. This was called the 'Cat-hold' school, because the kitten is carried by the cat (mother); whereas the other school was called the 'Monkey-hold' for the young monkey clings to its mother; so bringing in the old old problem, 'Does God carry us?' or 'Do we cling on to God?'

Strange that this carving has a place in the Abbey? Possibly it was brought back to Scotland by some warrior or other fighting a theological battle in Southern India as a souvenir at the time, viz. the 18th century.

*   *   *

Everyone knows the Old Testament story of the crossing of the Red Sea, but in Scotland, over a hundred years ago—in March 1865—there was a similar 'crossing of the waters' in the Aviemore/Boat of Garten area to Bigla's Castle, where a funeral procession was wending its way through a gloomy defile—the haunt of robbers. The procession came out unmolested making towards the Spey. At the head in a dilapidated cart drawn by a weary horse was a coffin bearing the remains of a woman. Tradition says, she was a Mackintosh or a Macdonald, and her Christian name was Mary, a woman renowned for her godliness. She was married to a farmer, and on her death bed she expressed the wish to be buried with her forefathers in the old churchyard of Dalarossie—more than twenty miles away on the far side of the Spey. Those near her told her that at this time of season the Spey would be in spate and neither man nor beast could ford it. But she was heard to whisper, 'Go to the river-side opposite Bigla, and a passage will be there for you to cross.' So they carried the coffin, taking it out of the cart, to the place where she had told them, and no sooner did they reach the bank, but the swirling black waters parted in front of them and the procession passed over on dry land. After offering up thanks for this miraculous crossing, the party made its way over the hills to Dalarossie Kirk, famous in legend as the sanctuary sought by the witch of LAGGAN, when she was pursued by the Devil. Later a stone slab was set up as a memorial to remind future generations of the miraculous crossing. The erection of this stone caused a deal of protest however. The Free Church minister condemned the folk, for a larger crowd went to visit the stone on the Sabbath rather than going to the church to listen to their minister. A climax was reached when one dark night, 'somebody' went and broke the slab into pieces and flung them in the Spey. And there it is supposed to be to this day.

A funeral nowadays is very different to olden times, when it was looked upon as a feast washed down with whisky. As a rule from the church the coffin is put on a tressle provided with a handle at each corner, the men walking and carrying the coffin on the tressle to the cemetery which might be a mile or so away. The followers take it in turn to carry the coffin, and without pausing, each moves alongside the coffin to take over from the other bearers who drop back to the rear, so that every man takes the body part of the way.

*   *   *

There is a very particular story I would like to tell of a missionary who had his 'parish' in the jungle area of Ceylon, who told me of a special incident that had occurred in his mission house. He had two servants, a cook (who was old and bad tempered) and a young boy who was the 'houseboy', responsible only for his master's room and the garden (compound, it is called out there). He was responsible to the missionary, not to the cook whom the boy disliked. The missionary managed to get some ducks and chickens which were put to roam the compound. The boy had a slingshot and he much delighted in using it and shooting stones. The missionary saw him one day at this game and told him he was not to carry on this practice for it was dangerous; he might even hit or kill anyone passing by, and also he might hit the livestock. The boy understood his master's orders and so he put the slingshot away. Some little time after the missionary was called away to a distant village to

hold worship. The boy then spent all his time in the garden,
keeping out of the cook's way. One morning as he was hoeing,
he came across a pebble or two and threw them out of the way.
Then he remembered his slingshot, went and got it out of his
room, and once again started up at his old game, for no one would
see him in the tangle of the trees and shrubs. Soon he found
himself giving more attention to the slingshot, than the garden.
However, as he shot a pebble a few minutes later, a duck came
walking in the line of fire. It got the pebble right on the head,
and dropped dead on the ground. What was he to do? No
one had seen him, so he dug a hole in one corner of the compound and buried the poor thing. He was at heart ashamed at
disobeying the words of the missionary, so put the slingshot back
in his pocket, went along to the kitchen to have a drink of water,
for he was thirsty, only to find the cook in his usual ugly mood.
'Boy, fill that box with wood', he said. But the boy said, 'I
don't work for you, cook, only for the master'. 'Oh!' said the
cook. What about the duck?' The cook had seen him after
all; and so he thereupon felt he must do all he could to please the
wretch, to prevent him telling the master when he got back from
the next village. Chopping and fetching wood, sweeping the
floors, and running messages for him. It was vain to protest,
for all the time the cook's words 'what about the duck' kept
repeating in his brain. The houseboy became the bondslave of the
cook. The little boy had no joy in the prospect of his master's
return. The missionary on coming back noticed the fellow
seemed to spend a lot of his time now in the kitchen. After some
days, the boy could stand it no longer, and ashamedly he sought
his master in his study and told him the whole story. Poor lad.
He told his master he had disobeyed him, and although he had
asked God to forgive him, his heart was sore, for he couldn't
forget his sin, and so he said, 'I want to tell you, my master,
all about it'. The missionary felt sad too, but he forgave the boy,
and kneeling together, they committed the whole matter to the
Lord. The little boy then left the study with a light heart, and
on his way back to the garden, passed through the kitchen.
The cook, sour as ever, barked at him, 'Boy, chop some more
wood, and fill this pail with water.' 'I don't work for you,'
came the quick reply. 'Oh!' said the cook, 'and what about the
duck? I must hurry and tell the master.' 'I've told him myself,'

said the boy full of confidence and happy, and left the kitchen. Confession to the master had freed him from all that bondage. Thus it is with all of us.

*   *   *

Faith! Faith is the one thing we cannot do without. Without Faith no matter what your religion—life is meaningless. Faith in your Doctor, your fellow man, your own self, is as necessary as the air you breathe. Faith in your God is your reason for living. We accept the world though we cannot prove what it is, or where it came from. We accept the air we breathe without knowing where it comes from. We accept the sun and the moon, the stars and all the rest of the Universe without asking for any proof at all. But—to many—not religion; somehow religion is different, or is it? Jesus cured a blind man, yet the Pharisees debated and queried it, even with the man himself, trying to lead him into the thought that he could not have been blind and that he wasn't really cured. With all the questions and thrusts at him, he simply declared once and for all on one thing he was clear, namely that 'once I was blind, now I can see . . .'

In the Oxford English Dictionary, Faith is defined with optimistic tautology as 'the spiritual apprehension of Divine Truth, apart from Truth'.

In the East, there is at the hour of prayer, a man stationed on the minarets of the Mosque, calling the Faithful to prayer and proclaiming 'There is no God but God, and Mohammed is the Messenger of Allah'.

. . . Before closing this religious (and I hope moving) chapter, I must tell you of a Mrs. Helen Steiner Rice, one of the greatest of all Inspirational writers I know of, and with whom I often correspond in America. She lives in Amberley, Cincinnati, Ohio.

This lady, who with her simple truths, has influenced and changed the lives of *millions* of people, not only in America, but in the world, has made this not only a vocation and an avocation, but a dedication, and she asks only one thing . . .

Show me the way,
not to fortune and fame,

Not how to win laurels
or praise for my name;
But show me the way
to spread 'The Great Story'
That 'Thine is the Kingdom
and Power and the Glory'.

To her, the acceptance of her books and work, and the response of people from all classes, creeds and countries is just a 'Modern Miracle'; for she says . . . 'tell me not that miracles don't happen anymore . . . for they happen in Believing Hearts, just as they did two thousand years ago . . . and nothing but a miracle wrought by God's mighty hand could place these simple words I write in hearts that understand . . .'

Helen Steiner Rice was born in the bustling little town of Lorain, Ohio on the shore of Lake Erie. Her father John A. Steiner was a railroad engineer. He died when she was sixteen years of age. At an early age she entered the business world as an associate of the Ohio Public Service Company. Her talents and winning personality (I have a very striking photograph of her) were quickly recognised. At twenty-five, she became Director of Public Relations, Chairman of the Women's Committee East Central Division of the National Electric Light Association, and Speaker for the Ohio Committee on Public Utilities Information. At the time, she was one of the highest paid women executives in the electric power industry. She was a personal friend of President Calvin Coolidge; and mark you she wasn't thirty years old then. She was primarily interested in making the part women play in the business world more significant and better understood. Working from her headquarters in Cleveland and New York City, she toured the nation, lecturing. Soon she was so respected for her alertness and acumen, she opened her own lecture service, addressing civic and social groups on women's contribution to industry and commerce.

One evening she spoke to the Annual Clearinghouse Association of Bankers at Dayton, Ohio, on the topic 'Do you know your job, or do you *love* your job?' The member delegated to meet her was a tall handsome young man named Franklin D. Rice, He was the most eligible bachelor in Dayton. After the meeting he took her out to dinner. Franklin had been a Lieutenant in the Air Force in World War I; he was then a director of the

Dayton Savings and Trust Company, and commuted a great deal to New York. He came of a family of outstanding ability and wealth.

Within a year they were married.

Everyone said she was the luckiest girl in the world; and she agreed. For the honeymoon, Franklin had arranged a cruise through the Caribbean, in a beautiful suite on an enormous luxury liner. About a week after the cruise began, her newly-found husband began getting daily cablegrams from his banking associates. The stock market was beginning to fall and the Great Depression was commencing. But Franklin never allowed himself to be anything but the perfect husband and host; gay and friendly. Instead of panicking over Wall Street's crash, he kept buying more and more stock, whilst others were selling. And for the next two years they lived more extravagantly than ever. Helen wanted to return to her work, but Franklin would not hear of it. Finally everything Franklin D. Rice had owned was gone.

Then, one terrible grey morning, Helen woke up to find that Franklin had gone too. He left her nothing but a note. Helen was then obliged to return to the business world. *So* many times since then she has wondered why she had to lose her husband so tragically, after just the two short years of marriage.

The President of Gibson, of Cincinnati, Ohio, who had heard her lectures many times and knew of her inspirational writings, asked her to join their company. She created her own niche, and worked unceasingly for more meaningful expressions of sentiment in greeting cards. After years of prayer and tireless effort to reach people through her verses, and her God-given gift of writing, Helen's prayers were answered in a most un-usual way. Just before Thanksgiving Day in 1960, famed orchestra leader, Lawrence Welk, chose one of her works to be read to millions on his nationwide television programme. The response was electrifying. Men and women, who had been seeking just such words of solace, wrote asking how they could purchase more of these selfless verses. As I have already indicated, millions of her poems have been printed and gone out to all corners of the earth. The term 'phenomenal' is really an under-statement.

The spark of her words had ignited a new concept of God,

His relation to man and of man's interdependence with Him. If the feeling that 'God is dead' is evident in the world today, Helen's verses help to dispel it. Since that day her audience has spread from continent to continent. Travellers have returned to their native lands filled with paeans of praise for her poems. Missionaries received assignments to far-off lands, and carried with them Helen Steiner Rice's verses of tranquility. Even servicemen in far-away outposts have found the miracle of God in her words. And so the story could go on and on.

As I have said, this truly remarkable lady has produced endless books, and thousand upon thousand special Inspirational Cards, all with Faith as the background. I would mention two special books of hers. One, is *Just for You* at 10s. 6d. and can be obtained in this country from Messrs. Kaye-Gibson Ltd., Shaftesbury Road, London, N.18. The other, published in November 1968, is called *Heart Gifts* at three dollars, fifty cents—about thirty-three shillings our money—it cannot (so far) be obtained in this country; only from Messrs. Fleming H. Revell and Coy, Old Tappan, New Jersey, U.S.A. It is really a beautiful book.

I am honoured at having met this lady and of being able to share her history with those who chance to read this book and to include her in my Highland pearls. She is a modest, humble person. In looks and build, she is very like our Queen Mother. As the lark that soars the highest, builds her nest the lowest; as the nightingale that sings so sweetly, sings in the shade when all things rest; as the branches that are most laden with fruit bend lowest; as the ship most loaded sinks deepest in the water—so those most holy are the humblest.

In one of her poems 'God's Jewels', and after her tragic experience, she ends it with the words 'We'll find the richest jewels of all, are crystallised from tears'.

This is *her* story; this is *her* song.

*   *   *

Living is like breathing; you need to breathe deeply to live. *Things* alone cannot bring happiness, and those who are always looking for something bigger and better, fail to achieve the realities of Life. This is well expounded in the following story: a young girl stood at the edge of a field of waving corn, where every stalk was tall and green and luxuriant; and the

farther the girl could see into the field the larger the ears became.
A genie told the girl, 'if you walk through this field, I will
reward you with a gift in proportion to the size of the ear you
select. But there is one restriction, you must start right where you
are standing, and you may go through the field only once. You
may not retrace your steps. The ear of corn you bring out will
determine the reward you will receive on the other side of the
field.' The girl was supremely happy as she started into the field.
Carelessly she trod on many of the stalks, thinking to herself:
I won't take any of these, for in the centre of the field are the
most perfect ears of all. I want the biggest reward possible.
She ran on and on, intent on finding the largest ear in the field.
Suddenly she realised that the corn stalks were getting smaller
and thinner; she was nearing the far edge of the field. In
desperation she looked for a good ear, but she could not bring
herself to pick any of those in sight. She kept thinking *there's
got to be another big ear before the end*'; but there was not. She
came out of the field empty-handed.

CHAPTER 11

THE TORRIDONS

THE Torridon mountains, which I look upon day after day from my bungalow in Gairloch, are supposed to be the oldest in the world; they were old before the Himalayas even started—older in fact than when the Children of Israel even saw Egypt. Everyday they seem to look different by reason of the angle of the morning light and cloud falling on them. There they are, everyday of every week of every month of every year; and yet no two days the same.

You approach Torridon village itself off Kinlochewe, the left turn-off at the village coming in from Glen Docharty. It is fourteen miles away, on a good road. Torridon lies at the western end of Glen Torridon, perhaps the finest and wildest of the Wester Ross glens. The road to Torridon is overshadowed by the might and majesty of Liathach ('the Grey one') 3456 feet above sea-level, a terraced mass of Torridonian sandstone topped with white quartzite (frequently mistaken for snow). Beinn Eighe ('The File Mountain', 3300 feet) and Beinn Alligin (3021 feet) also tower upwards, keeping the monarch of these hills, Liathach, company. Liathach is composed of more than three miles of steep terraces of red sandstone, most difficult to climb.

These mountains are of immense interest to geologists, who come from all quarters of the world to study them, for this Torridonian sandstone is some of the oldest rock in the world, so old in fact that no fossils have been found in it, an indication that the rock was laid down before life first appeared on this earth. This chocolate-coloured sandstone is about 4000 feet in thickness. Above this, the Torridon Red, lies a thick-bedded whitish rock referred to above, composed of quartz-grains plus a highly metamorphosed fine sandstone.

The Torridon mountains are known as 'sedimentary' rocks, as opposed to 'metamorphic' rocks, the product of alteration by various geological processes of rocks of diverse origin.

The phenomena of the glacial period are truly shown in this Loch Maree–Torridon area. The strata in general run parallel to the loch's axis, proving the existence of an immense glacier that moved to the sea down the deep hollow now filled with water. Further evidence of glaciation is the number of terraced thrust-planes which must have been borne by the ice sheet dropped from the parent rock in the line of the ice movement.

Torridon and Annat villages practically adjoin one another at the head of Upper Loch Torridon, which is part of Loch Torridon itself—a big arm of the sea—which also has Loch Shieldaig in its fold. The loch is broad, deep and lone-looking, crowned with these mountains of sandstone that glow like liquid gold in summer sunsets; and in winter present an eerie wildness. The loch also embraces the great Ben Damph forest.

The journey to Torridon takes you through wild scenery of loneliness. No sea-loch in Wester Ross is encircled by such terrifying massiveness.

When you are about halfway to Torridon you will not fail to see on the left side of the glen an extraordinary array of hillocks close together, rounded off; and this little fascinating area is called the 'Corrie of 100 Hillocks', or sometimes as the 'Valley of 100 Fairies'. These singular mounds are due to the natural action of ice and water in prehistoric times; the streamlets depositing a series of hummocks of debris, which gradually covered the ground as the ice retreated, leaving these corries behind.

Coming to the head of the loch, the road forks; left to Annat, a quaint-like village where a new 18-foot carriage-way road has been made connecting Torridon and Annat villages with Shieldaig, Loch Carron, and onwards to Strome Ferry. This new road some seven-and-a-half miles long enables tourists to cut out at least thirty miles in having to journey from Strome to Achnasheen and then on to Kinlochewe.

The new road, known as the Balgy (Balgee) Gap, cost £400,000, and was opened on 9th September 1963 by Mr.

Michael Noble, then Secretary of State for Scotland. Most times when I have been in these two hamlets, it has seemed to be siesta-time; either that or fast week, for no one appears to be out of doors! The big mansion house at Torridon is now an hotel. The Ben Damph Estate was owned by the fourth Earl of Lovelace until his death on 4th December 1964. Earl Lovelace was the ultimate heir of philosopher John Locke (1632-1704) whose writings influenced the drafting of the American Constitution.

Passing through Annat and leaving the Torridon Hotel on the right and along the Balgy Gap road you soon come to look down on the beautiful picture post card village of SHIELDAIG—a pearl if ever there was one. There is a sweet little restaurant/tea room, 'Ann's Parlour', in the village owned by two gentle-women, the Misses Hamilton and Hammond, who have the shop and post office adjoining. They also act as Registrars for the district. Then further on and making for Strome Ferry, there is the turn-off TORNAPRESS, for APPLECROSS, which is on the coast. Here again, you meet with another wild stretch to the remote peninsula of Applecross; ten miles of adventure, the road curling up and around a formidable mountainside, over the BEALACH NAM BO ('pass of the cows'). This sporty thoroughfare climbs 2000 feet in five miles, with hair-pin bends that are difficult to negotiate in one turn. Then you drop down to the sea—and Applecross. It is nothing unusual for this roadway to be blanketed out in the summer by swirling mist; and in the winter it may be blocked by snow for many weeks; and then the only com-munication left open is by sea. The Gaelic name for Applecross is A'CHOMRAICH—the sanctuary—and so it was in the 7th century, when the Irish saint (or monk) Maelrubha founded a church there (A.D. 673 I think is the actual date). St. Maelrubha was buried in the little church north of the village.

Applecross is arrayed along the shingle, its little stone houses looking out across the Inner Sound to RAASAY and RONA—and beyond, the north end of Skye. 'A free and easy life' is what the few crofters say of living there. They can shoot a deer if it ventures near the croft; they can fish in the sea if they want; and if they need any extra money, there's always the county roads department, they can look to for some spare work. They have no bustle or hurry to make a living.

The big glen of Applecross makes up the home farm of that

English gentleman, Major John Wills (of the tobacco family) who also owns 84,000 acres of surrounding land; and here of recent years Major Wills has established a West Highland School of Adventure—run on outward bound lines financed by the Dockland Settlements, of which the Major is Chairman.

The object is to foster the spirit of adventure whereby boys (between the ages of 16 and 20, who will come from industry, clubs, colleges and schools) may achieve strength of character through the pursuit of tough experiences. The course will last for three weeks, and the boys will get a chance to take part in outdoor pursuits, such as small-boat sailing, canoeing in the Inner Sound of Raasay, canoe construction, rock climbing, trekking, life-saving and seamanship. Also cultural classes, educational films, library, pottery and sketching. There is a warden in charge, and a team of skilled instructors.

Returning to Torridon village, which has the usual sub-post office, and a very excellent general stores with pretty, pleasant (Mrs.) Morag Macdonald serving you, we can take the eight-mile run over the mountain road to Alligin and Diabaig—where the road ends. I have mentioned elsewhere, what a great spectacular link with Gairloch it would result in, if even a single-track macadamed road were made (with adequate passing places) about seven miles only. This, with the Balgy Gap new road would make a marvellous journey, and would be a means of opening up Gairloch more. The inhabitants of these small villages or hamlets are really very few, Diabaig 50; Alligin 20; Torridon 70; Annat 25.

Should anybody reading this book, and come to this chapter, I would beg of them not to miss the journey to DIABAIG. It is one of the greatest scenic runs I know of anywhere in Scotland, and should you have a fine day, you will stand spellbound on the wee jetty at Diabaig. Time and Eternity, the Here and the Hereafter will seem to mingle. It is really overpowering to look up to the mountains and down at the lochs. Diabaig is a Norse name and thought to be connected with *dia* (God) and *aig* (a small bay) . . . so it may reasonably be interpreted as 'the small bay of God'. I was once there on a perfect October day. There was no one about save an old woman taking a few peats into her cottage that were stacked at the side of her dwelling; only her and two collie dogs. I shall never forget it. An unusual quiet;

a breathless silence; a silence that would have been the case 2000 years ago, when they parted His garments, and the Veil of the Temple was rent. You might feel a touch on your shoulder, and you would turn; but there would be no one there whom *you* could see. In Arabic I would call Diabaig, ROHALBI ('soul of my heart').

★ ★ ★

To a large number of people, even in Britain, the Highlands—and Sutherland in particular—is '*terra incognita*'. What a lot they miss. If in the past the Highlands were not more extensively cultivated, it was only because there were not enough human beings to do so.

CHAPTER 12

PRINCE CHARLIE AND THE '45

THIS chapter deals a little fuller with Bonnie Prince Charlie, and Flora Macdonald's subsequent life in America.

Glenfinnan, 19th August 1745.
Culloden, 16th April 1746.

The beginning and the end. And the end 'Gentlemen, I have flung away the scabbard'.

On 23rd July 1745, Prince Charles Edward arrived on the coast of Scotland with nine companions, few arms and little money. The news aroused both dismay and enthusiasm amongst his supporters, but they twice defeated the numerically superior and better disciplined government armies, before the Duke of Cumberland exacted a terrible revenge at Culloden. Prestonpans, 21st September 1745; Falkirk, 17th January 1746—and then Culloden.

The inspiration of that romantic adventure, from the raising of Prince Charlie's standard at Glenfinnan at the head of Loch Shiel, until after Culloden, is found in poems, songs and ballads for the past two hundred years and more.

The monument which has the statue of a Highlander at its

216

summit, has an inscription referring to the raising of the standard on that spot 'to commemorate the generous zeal, the undaunted bravery, and the inviolable fidelity' of the men who lived and died for Charlie. The inscription is in Gaelic, English, Latin and French, and commences with the words 'Traveller, if you wish to celebrate the deeds of former days, pay homage here now'; and then the fuller wordings:

> Let them tear our bleeding bosoms,
> Let them drain our latest veins,
> In our hearts is Charlie, Charlie,
> While a spark of life remains.

The setting of this monument is most outstanding. It was erected by Macdonald of Glenaladale early in the 19th century—about 1815 I believe—as a tribute to the clansmen who fought and died in the '45 Rebellion. The monument has been the property of the National Trust for Scotland since 1938.

The National Trust for England was formed as far back as January 1895, by a solicitor, Robert Hunter; a housing reformer, Octavia Hill; and a Cumberland vicar, Hardwicke Rawnsley; and its first property—a gift—consisted of $4\frac{1}{2}$ acres of cliffland near Barmouth, in Wales. The National Trust for Scotland, was founded much later, in 1931. Its growth has been most encouraging.

Glenfinnan (on the main road to Mallaig) is visited by many who would recapture the spirit of those far-off days; and on the occasion of the bicentenary, organised by the National Trust (who have a very nicely built office, showcases and toilet facilities, set back on the road and facing the monument) on 19th August 1945, there came a gathering of nearly 3000 people, including many from overseas. The Macdonalds, the Stewarts, and the Camerons, who attended, would have a feeling of pride in the blind devotion of their clansmen.

> And, see a small devoted band
> By dark Loch Shiel have ta'en their stand,
> And proudly vow with heart and hand
> To fight for Royal Charlie. . . .

The fiery cross had summoned the clansmen to Glenfinnan, but there were many difficulties facing the Pretender when he first anchored off Borrodale on 25th July 1745. The Young Pretender,

H

as he was called, to the title of James VIII and III, arrived with
little, as I have said. Only 1000 muskets, 1800 broadswords, a
few pieces of field artillery, 4000 Gold Louis and very few friends,
who became known as the Seven Men of Moidart. Very soon
he was to be worth £30,000 as that price was placed on his head;
but none of the Highlanders would sell their souls for thirty
pieces of silver, let alone gold. There were no Quislings in those
days. The fact that there was no one in the whole of Scotland
willing to betray the Pretender, was more a tribute to Scottish
character than to the universal belief in the Jacobite Cause.

Of course there are to be found some person, body or association, being more knowledgeable than average, who find out
errors in one thing or another; and in regard to this monument
the 'Forty-five Association, 1963' is one which disputes the
actual site where the standard was raised. Some of the older
people of the district will tell you their forebearers maintained
the standard was not raised where the monument stands, but on a
knoll. Indeed there seems to be no evidence, traditional or
documentary which claims the standard was raised at that
particular spot. I believe there are records that the tower was
that of a shooting box for use of shooting parties and fishers,
but there was no statue on the top when first built. About
twenty years later, the statue was erected. Although the inscription says 'on this spot . . .' this wording may be figurative,
meaning that the standard was raised in this vicinity, just as a
battlefield memorial indicates roughly that of the battle. I would
be prepared to let it go at that, but the '45 Association appear to
be wishful of delving more deeply into the matter.

It is known the Prince arrived at Glenfinnan at one o'clock in
the afternoon; about three o'clock Lochiel arrived with six
hundred men, and about two hours later the Prince ordered his
standard to be carried to the other side of the River Finnan where
it was displayed, which was done by the Duke of Atholl carrying
it, and one hundred of Clanranald's men with himself at their
head escorting it. As the bothy where the Prince rested before
the raising of the standard was at SLATACH, west of the River
Finnan, it would seem the Duke of Atholl led the Macdonald's
across the river to its east bank and halted there to raise the standard
among them with the Camerons mustered on the west bank and
facing the Macdonald's across the river. The Camerons had

marched down the west side of Glen Finnan, and would have halted there to rest at the mouth of the Glen until it was known where and when the standard was to be raised. The Duke could not have led the Macdonald's as far as the site of the monument because, if so, the Camerons on the west bank of the river would be too far off to witness the ceremony. It is also said that when the Duke of Atholl (or the Marquis of Tullibardine as he is also known) raised the standard he was so feeble that he had to be physically supported by two clansmen. If that be so, it seems surprising that he was capable of walking along the track leading the Macdonald clansmen from the Prince's bothy to the spot where the standard was raised, which would be a distance of at least half a mile. He was only fifty-seven years old but was troubled with gout. There is no evidence he was on horse-back. Many people think or assume that all or most of the clans who joined the Prince were present at the Glenfinnan ceremony; but actually there were only two clans present—the Macdonalds and the Camerons. Keppoch and his clansmen arrived later, and so only three clans set out with Prince Charlie from Glen-finnan. They came to *Laggan Auchentroon* on Loch Oich, and this is where the Glengarry men, commanded by Lochgarry, joined the Prince.

In a great number of references and records, it is noticeable that few, if any, tell us that the standard *was* raised close to Loch Shiel. The only spot which seems to agree with all the varying accounts referring to the topography of the ceremony, is quite a small knoll in the mouth of Glen Finnan on the east bank of the river Finnan between the main road and the railway viaduct. It is only really a small knoll, and since this knoll is never mentioned, it could be that to healthy Highlanders of the 18th century, they would not regard its ascent as 'climbing'. At the base of this knoll, there is flat ground sufficient to have accommodated easily, all the Macdonald clansmen, and on the opposite west bank there is ample flat ground where the Camerons could have been mustered. After the ceremony the standard was then delivered for safe-keeping into the hands of Keppoch's brother, Donald.

No blame is attached to Macdonald of Glenaladale for siting the monument where it is as we see it today, for as it originally formed part of a shooting-box, it had to be sited in a suitable position. The small knoll, is too small to have borne the shooting-box, and its site is not a conspicuous one, as it is somewhat hidden. And so Glenaladale quite rightly, chose for the monument the most inspiring site in the vicinity of where the standard *was* raised.

The statue on the top of the monument faces towards Glen Finnan, and the suggestion has been made that it is watching for the Camerons coming down this glen. But why not facing east? in the direction which the Prince and his men set out with such high hopes, and towards the scenes of the campaign?

And so, the question still arises in this 20th century, is the monument correctly placed? For myself, I think it is ideally situated.

*   *   *

After Culloden, the Prince was a fugitive for six months; and perhaps it may be handy to give a concise record of his flight.

1746	
16th April	Culloden
17th April	Loch Arkaig
21st April	Borradale
26th April	Sailed from Borradale
29th April	Benbecula
14th May	South Uist
28th June	Sailed for Skye with Flora Macdonald
7th July	On mainland again near Mallaig
10th July	Borradale
18th July	On Fraoch-Bheinn (above Glenfinnan)
21st July	Broke through cordon in Glen Cosaidh
24th July	Joined 'Men of Glen Moriston'
2nd August	Strathglass
16th August	Near Achnacarry, Loch Arkaig
29th August	In Badenoch
5th September	Cluny's Cage, Benalder
20th September	Sailed for France from Borradale on the *L'Heureux*

I have mentioned the price of £30,000 on the Prince's head, but he was never betrayed all the time he wandered through the Highlands and Islands.

> Tho' 30,000 pounds they'd gie,
> There was nane wad you betray. . . .

but it is not commonly known that two Highlanders (and ministers at that) made an attempt to capture him, but failed. These two who would have turned Judas were father and son, the Rev. Aulay MacAulay and the Rev. John MacAulay respectively. During a storm on the night of 29th April when the Prince and his followers reached *Barra Na Luinge* in the island of Benbecula, they took shelter in a deserted hut. The storm continued for about four hours. The party tried to remain warm, little realising that their arrival had been witnessed from the shore by a shepherd. The shepherd walked seven miles to NUNTON, on the west side of the island, home of the chiefs of the Jacobite Macdonalds of Clan Ranald. At that time old Clanranald happened to be entertaining the Rev. John MacAulay, Protestant minister of Barra and South Uist, who overheard the shepherd's description of what he had seen. He immediately grew suspicious and sent his own messenger to the shore to learn more details. In this way the minister learned that the Prince and his supporters were planning to make for Stornoway, Isle of Lewis, in order to obtain a boat for France. Immediately the minister sent word to his father, the Rev. Aulay, in Harris, telling him to get a warning to a third minister—the Rev. Colin Mackenzie in Lochs, Lewis—so that the Prince's capture might be arranged. Their plan was thwarted. Having learned that no suitable ship could be had in Stornoway, the Prince was taken for safety to the house of Donald Campbell, tacksman of the small island of Scalpay, at the mouth of East Loch Tarbert, Harris. Not to be outdone, the MacAulay's kept up their spying, and later they were able to learn the Prince's hiding place. By boat they arrived off Scalpay, bent on arresting the fugitive, but they were never allowed to set foot on shore. Brave Donald Campbell stood on the rocky jetty, armed with broadsword and pistol, and let flow a torrent of Harris Gaelic. 'Yes, the Prince is in my house,' he shouted, 'but before a hair of his head is hurt, it will be over my dead body. I am as much against the Stuarts as you are Mister MacAulay; and I would fight them in the field. But the Prince is foodless, homeless and friendless, and alone in my home; and the first man among you who comes ashore to seize him, I will cleave to the ground.' The two MacAulay's and their oarsmen wasted no time in turning their boat around and headed for calmer waters! The MacAulay's and their kin had been living in the Outer Hebrides (the Long Island as it used to be called) since before the 11th century; they also occupied much of Sutherland and Wester Ross centred around Ullapool.

*   *   *

It cannot but be accepted that the Prince's various victories on his march south and into England created much jubilation. To the Government their defeat at Prestonpans, near Edinburgh, on 21st September 1745 came as a severe shock. In Scotland, the outward result of the Prince's victory was that excepting for the castles of Edinburgh, Stirling and Dumbarton, the whole of the country was in Jacobite hands, more or less. In Charles's mind, Prestonpans implanted the fatal belief that his Highlanders were invincible. But Culloden was not so far off and by then the Prince's war-chest was empty, his men without pay, supplies of food and clothing were scarce and disorganisation appeared; and worst of all, the opinions of the Jacobite leaders were divided. But Charles remained a blind optimist to the end. The breach between himself and his long-suffering commander, Lord George Murray, commenced to widen. And Cumberland was on the march.

At Culloden the Prince saw with astonishment his troops— his invincible troops—flying before the enemy in utmost disorder and confusion, and in vain did he strive to re-animate and persuade them to return to the charge. But they were 'done' in more ways than one, and the mouths of Cumberland's murdering cannon spoke a louder and more persuasive language than all the Prince's promises and entreaties could do. 'Pray stand with me, your Prince,' he said, 'but for a moment—otherwise you ruin me, your country and yourselves and God forgive you.' Thus he addressed every corps he saw retreating. But all to no purpose.

Although Culloden was fought over two hundred and twenty years ago, legends have grown up around the battle; and believed by many. There is the persistent belief that the battle was waged between English and Scots; but this is hardly correct; for of Cumberland's fifteen regular battalions, no fewer than three regiments were Scottish (1st, 21st and 25th Foot). And to these must be added several other companies. Many of the atrocities perpetrated after the battle were *not* all carried out at the instigation of English officers. Some of the worst offenders were Lowland Scots. Contrary to popular tradition the numbers of men involved in the actual fighting were small, for although about 14,000 are estimated to have been present at the time, less than 3000 were actively engaged. Charles had spent the early part of the night of the battle at Gorthleck, about twenty miles from Culloden up above the south side of Loch Ness (on the Caledonian Canal).

Culloden, 16th April 1746. The Duke of Cumberland's fighting career ended in 1757 when he died aged only forty-four; but his name continues to be looked on in Scotland as a symbol of brutality. Culloden was 'The Butcher's' only real victory. At the time of the '45 people were heard to say . . . 'God save the King; God save the Faith's Defender! What harm in saving the Pretender? But who Pretender is, or who is King, God save us all, that's quite another thing!' . . .

Many a book has been written on the '45 Rebellion mostly connected with the land operations. But much happened at sea; and it was the vigilance of the British Navy, that put an end to the Prince's attempt to secure the throne of his ancestors. Coincidental, it was the seamanship, courage and persistence of French seafarers which saved him from capture after Culloden. The French ships made no less than *six* separate attempts to rescue him from the Hanoverian net, which was closing round him all the time. The last battle at sea after Culloden was on Loch nan Uamph, near Morar where a British naval force so damaged two French privateers that they had to make for home instead of trying to find the Prince then in the Outer Hebrides. These French attempts were organised by Irishmen in France (known as the wild-geese of Europe) in conjunction with the French King, who financed everything. There was a strong British Fleet on the look-out in the Channel, and King Louis was much afraid of this. Then up north in Sutherland at the Kyle of Tongue (mentioned in our northern travels) there was a two-ship action in March 1746. *Le Prince Charles* was carrying volunteers and £12,000 for the Prince's army, but it was intercepted and wrecked by the frigate *Sheerness*. The gold was taken off to be carried to Inverness, but under the shadow of Ben Loyal the men were caught by some Government troops, but before surrendering the foreigners threw the gold into a loch. It's a wonder the Tongue villagers haven't found it by now?

As I have said, the Highland army was then desperate for money; and with the Duke of Cumberland marching towards Inverness, they decided to put everything to the decision of battle. They did so on the wrong field on the wrong day. The man behind the French sea attempts at rescuing the Prince in his flight, was *Antoine Walsh*, a Franco-Irishman and the cruellest slaver of the century. He stood to benefit from the diversion of British Naval power; he was indeed the power behind the rescue operations.

As to the previous Rebellion, the '15 thirty years before the '45 there has been very little said; no pipe tunes or songs as with the later Rebellion. This is partly because events of the '45 are better documented and partly because of the glamour and romance attached to 'AM PRIONNSA' (the Prince). Prince Charles's father, the Old Chevalier of the 1715 seemed to have enjoyed less acclaim than his dashing young son. Through that Rebellion there were many who believed the Rising was doomed to failure. Also the Highlanders up in the north-west were superstitious, and an accident occurred at the very moment the standard was being raised by Castleton of Braemar; and *that* they said was a bad omen. It appears there was a strong gale blowing at the time, and when the standard was reaching the top of the flag-pole, a gilt ball got loosened and fell to the ground.

*   *   *

The 'King o'er the water', James III anxious to secure the Stuart line by marriage, sought a bride, and he finally, after a long search, married Marie Clementina Sobieski, a grand-daughter of King John III of Poland. Marie was the daughter of Prince James Sobieski who was the son of the aforementioned King John III. Her mother was a Bavarian of noble birth, so that the wife of James III (Marie) was the daughter of a Polish father and a Bavarian mother. James III, the son of James II was born in London (St. James's Palace). There were two children of the marriage, Charles Edward and Henry Edward, both born in Rome.

I will now turn to subsequent history.

It is an historical fact that Prince Charles entered the Protestant Faith in 1750 or 1751. Although he re-entered the Roman Catholic Church at a later stage, he was never at any time in his life anything other than a luke-warm Catholic, and was constantly at variance with the Papal authority; for example at the death of James III, the Prince desired that the Pope accept him as King Charles; but the Pope (Clement XIII) would not agree; and this displeased the Prince. One must always remember the hatred of the English then against the Papacy and the inescapable truth that the vast majority of the people were Stuart sympathisers. One cannot leave this matter without mentioning that Prince Henry, Duke of York and youngest son of James III entered the Roman Catholic Church as Cardinal, and this news was not, and could not be to the liking of the English people; and one can reason that this matter could not but harm the Stuart cause. It is certain Prince Charlie did not lose sight of this possibility and its connection with his attempt to regain the throne for the Stuarts.

When the subsequent marriage of Prince Charles to Princess Louise of Stolberg had broken-up, he went to live with Clementina Walkinshaw (of the battle of Falkirk fame) in Ghent. They registered as Count and Countess De Johnson in 1703; a daughter was born and she was registered as Charlotte Johnson, who eventually became Charlotte Stuart, Duchess of Albany; and the Prince nominated this daughter as the legitimate heir to the throne of England (imagine!). She was created a Knight of the Thistle on St. Andrew's Day 1764. In this nomination one can see the attempt to regain the Stuart hopes; for the next in line was naturally Cardinal Henry, Duke of York, and it would be obvious the English would not want a Cardinal as King. Then Prince Charles approached the Pope (Pius VI) to give recognition to Charlotte Stuart, but the Pope refused, only recognising her as Duchess of Albany. This action was done to placate the House of Hanover. And the point must not be overlooked of course that she was illegitimate; and another point was that the Pope had not forgotten the Prince had entered into the Protestant Faith; plus the fact that the limitations of members of the Catholic Faith that existed in Britain then, were something the Papacy wanted to see ended—hence the flirtation of the Papacy with the House of Hanover. There were many of influence in the Vatican who were opposed to the Stuarts merely on account of the religious advancement of Henry Duke of York who became a Cardinal without ever having been a Priest.

Charlotte Stuart—christened Johnson—afterwards left her mother, Clementina Walkinshaw and came to Rome to nurse her father, whose health was very poor. She made her peace with the Cardinal—a none too easy task. Eventually Bonnie Prince Charlie passed away and was buried in Rome. Charlotte lived but a little longer, about four years, dying of cancer of the liver. The Countess of Albany, the legal wife of the Prince went to London, and received a pension from the Court of St. James. She, prior to this, and whilst parted from the Prince, always insisted on being treated as the Queen of England, but the death of the Prince, and the offer of a pension effectively silenced her. (Money counted even in those days.)

There is the story that the Prince, whose official date of death was given as 31st January 1788, actually died on the 30th, and the reason that such a story gained currency was that the 30th January was an unlucky date for the Stuarts. He was conceded some importance by the Vatican in regard to his lying in State, but his brother Cardinal, Duke of York, requested the Pope (Pius VI) to accord him rites similar to those accorded his father James III. But the Holy See who had never recognised him as Charles III, and who incidentally had his eye on the main chance (agreement with the House of Hanover and the subsequent removal of the limitations against the Roman Catholics) refused.

The Prince was laid in State at a church within the Cardinal's jurisdiction. There was one motto in evidence displayed at the church wherein he lay, viz.:

AD INSULAS LONGE DIVULGATUM EST NOMEN
TUUM ET DILECTUS ES IN PACE TUA . . .

which being translated from the Latin, means 'Thy name went abroad to the islands afar off, and thou wast beloved in thy peace'. Such a motto, or inscription, is both impressive and appropriate.

The wording is taken from the Book of Ecclesiasticus.

This book was written after the time of Esdras, and is not in the Jewish Canon. Nevertheless it is considered as canonical by the Catholic Church, while the Anglican Church numbers it as one of the Apocrypha.

Chapter 44 begins: 'let us now praise famous men, and our

fathers that begat us' (Revised A.V.). The writer praises Enoch, Noah, Isaac, Jacob etc. In Chapter 47, Solomon is praised (verse 15).

> O how wise wast thou in thy youth
> And thou wast filled as a river with wisdom and
>   thy soul covered the earth (v. 16)
> And thou didst multiply riddles in parables; *thy*
> *name went abroad to the islands afar off, and*
> *thou wast beloved in thy peace.* (v. 17)

He was interred within the Church confines at a place called Frascati, near Rome, and laid there until final removal to St. Peter's, Rome, where all three James II, Prince Charlie, and Henry, Cardinal Duke of York, lie together. It is interesting to record that Henry, Duke of York always considered himself as Henry IV, the legitimate King of England, Ireland and Scotland; and I doubt very much if it is known he nominated as the heir to his crown, Charles Emmanuel IV, King of Sardinia, the great-great-grandson of Henrietta Stuart, the daughter of King Charles I. What is even more interesting is that this person—King of Sardinia—renounced his throne and entered the Church as a Priest; so we have two Clerics as heirs to the throne.

Again, when we consider the Prince, we must pay due thought to his nobility, and the nobility of his family. We need go no further than Charles I executed at Whitehall on that cold bitter morning of January 1619, for does not the poet of the time record 'that he nothing mean or spiteful did, upon that fateful morn'. James III never became King (*de facto*) for he would not renounce his Faith; similarly with Henry IX; on the other hand Charles III would and did renounce the Catholic Faith in his effort to regain the throne for the House of Stuart.

In a way, history has done scant justice to Prince Charlie. It is easy to condemn. He must have been a brave, dazzling and courageous man no matter what side you may be on. True he became an exile, a drunkard, a husband deserted by his wife—a weary half-forgotten exile in fact. All this is none too encouraging a description; but the legend of Bonnie Prince Charlie (I was almost writing Bonnie Prince *Charming*!) lives on, planted in the hearts and minds of the true Scot. He never intended to return to France, save as a *victor*; he was happy amongst the

Highlands and Islands—although a fugitive. Very significant are the words spoken by the Right Honourable Arthur, Lord Balmerino, as he stood on the scaffold 18th August 1746 about to suffer legal dissection and butchery as a punishment for his support of the Stuart cause. Just before his last words he said, 'I am at a loss when I come to speak of the Royal Prince. I am not a fit hand to draw his character; I shall leave that to others, but I beg leave to tell you the incomparable sweetness of his nature, his affability, his compassion, his justice, his temperance, his patience, and his courage, were all virtues seldom to be found in one person. In short, he wants no qualifications requisite to make a great man . . .' This from a man about to die on Tower Hill. This was a man who raised no demur when the Headman's axe was placed beside him in his carriage as he rode to his execution; but the people in their confounded ignorance (the curse of the mass) preferred Butcher Cumberland—even to the extent of naming a flower after him, 'The Sweet William'.

I thus come to the end of the Young Pretender. A portrait of Prince Charles Edward by Louis Gabriel Blancher is remaining in Great Britain, and is to hang in the Palace of Holyrood House. Although he has been known as the 'Pretender', he was the son of the legitimate king of this country—*King de jure*, if you like; but he could have been *de facto* had he been willing to renounce his Faith.

*   *   *

Flora Macdonald

I now turn to Flora Macdonald, the most illustrious woman the Highlands and Islands have produced. The story of her courage in aiding the Prince escape to Skye has been told a hundred times or more; but what is not so well-known, is her life after her release from a mild imprisonment in London; of her marrige to Allan Macdonald and their migration to America; to Carolina. It is an intriguing story.

Flora was born in Milton, South Uist in 1722. She died after a lingering illness, 68 years of age at Peindum (1½ miles north of Kingsburgh House) in March 1790.

She married Allan Macdonald at Armadale, Sleat Skye, on 6th November 1750. He died two years after Flora on 20th September 1792.

At the supposed birthplace at Milton, now in ruins, there is a cairn inside and the inscription on it reads that she was born 'near this place'; and it is said she was born at a shieling on the moor at the back of that ruined house, but for a time, she *did* live in Milton. The inscription on the cairn reads:

> ... Clan Donald raised this Cairn of Remembrance to their Kins-woman, Flora Macdonald, Daughter of Ronald, son of Angus of Milton, South Uist. She was born in 1722 near this place and spent her early life in the house that stood on this foundation. When pursuit was drawing near to the Prince in the Long Island she greatly aided him by her heroism and endurance to gain shelter in the Isle of Skye ...

What an attraction this cairn would be to tourists, if it were on the mainland? But only a rough track leads to the little knoll on which it stands. There is not even a sign-post on the main road to indicate the way. Alone it stands; just a heap of stones—with a touching reference. The Lost Glory.

Few people in this country know that after she married, she and her husband emigrated to America only to return after a short period there. Yet that time in the New World formed the second and in some ways, the strangest chapter in Flora's life. They emigrated to North Carolina, where Flora found herself a leader among thousands of emigrant post-Culloden Highlanders. Soon in a startling about-face, she helped raise many of them into an army—an army to fight, this time, on the side of their old enemy, the Hanoverian King. This was to be the American War of Independence. Children in North Carolina still learn how Flora, mounted on a white horse, reviewed her Highlanders as they set off to battle; how they were defeated, her husband and son captured, her possessions looted. It is really a story best told by the soft Southern voices of the descendants of those early emigrants, who today are farmers, cotton dealers, and housewives.

In North Carolina they are sure of one thing. If Flora's army had won those brief, almost forgotten battles, then the American Revolution would almost certainly have failed. That was Flora's 'Lost Glory'. Her husband Allan supported the English King (George) and suffered decisive defeat at the head of a company of loyal Highlanders. Imprisonment followed, and it was two years before he was united with his wife Flora. Home-sick, Flora returned to Skye, her husband rejoining her six years later. Both broken in health, Flora died in 1790, her husband in 1792 as I have said. History remembered them, but the Prince, she herself served so well, did not. That, in essence is the story . . .

Much has been said of Flora recruiting the emigrant High-landers to support the House of Hanover. It is true of course her husband Allan held the King's Commission as an officer in the North Carolina Highlanders, and fought against the rebels (the forces of the North Carolina Congress). He was taken prisoner at the battle of Moore's Creek Bridge in N. Carolina on 28th February 1766. He was, along with other Highlanders com-pelled to march all the way to Philadelphia jail, where he was imprisoned. It was on the 9th July he was released on parole and some time later he was finally freed and found himself in New York which was then a centre of British military activity. But after his release from captivity and whilst in New York he raised a company of Highlanders again. Flora's two sons Ranald (navy) and James (army) were serving with the King's forces at the time. Flora left America for Skye on a warship, *Lord Dunmore* in October 1779. At this time, Allan (on half pay) was fighting in Carolina again, under Lord Cornwallis. In Portree there is, in the Episcopal Church a tablet bearing the inscription perpetuating an incident that was supposed to have happened on her voyage home to England. A French ship attacked the *Lord Dunmore*, and the inscription records that she 'encouraged the sailors to make a spiritual and successful resist-ance, thus risking her life for both the House of Stuart and Hanover'. Flora herself wrote 'In our passage, spying a sail we made ready for action, and am hurrying the ladies to a place of safety, my foot skipping a step in the trap (presumably the hatch) I fell and dislocated my arm. It was set with bandages and strips of wood'. (How brave she must have been.) The arm was never properly set, and it remained through her life in a crooked fashion. Long after this, she wrote to Sir John McPherson, Governor General of India, a letter, seeking his interest in the welfare of her husband and herself, thus: . . . 'The casts in both my arms are living monuments of my suffering and discomfort, and the long jail confinement which my husband went through, has brought on such disorders that he has lost the use of his legs; so that I may fairly say we have both suffered in our person, family and interest; as much, if not more than any two going under the name of refugees or loyalists, without the smallest recompense' . . . This reference to her husband's legs has to be related to the hardships endured on the march as a prisoner from N. Carolina to Virginia, thence to Philadelphia—almost 700 miles. Flora lost the two sons eventually in the service of the House of Hanover.

On the termination of the war in America, Allan was given land in Nova Scotia as some compensation, but he failed to develop it on account of shortage of capital. He only got £440 compensation for losses in N. Carolina.

It is worth mentioning that the Highlanders recruited into the N. Carolina Highlanders numbered about 1500; amongst them were MacLeans, MacRaes, MacLaughtons, and others. There were Campbells, Camerons in smaller numbers; there were Stewarts, MacLeods, MacNeils and MacArthurs. The entry into the N. Carolina Highlanders was purely voluntary. One should remember that the Highlanders had left Scotland to go to a country that was a British colony and many of the leaders of the people were themselves officers of the Hanoverian army in receipt of half-pay, and it must also be borne in mind they had much influence over the emigrants. When the colonists rebelled against British control, a proclamation was issued by the Government calling on all to put down the rebels, and the last words of the Proclamation bore the ominous words, 'pronouncing all such as do not join the Royal call, as rebels and traitors . . . their lives and properties to be forfeited . . . God save the King'. These were meaningful words, that bore grim recollections to the Highlanders in N. Carolina, many of whom had supported and suffered for their support of the Stuart's and were in consequence, rebels, having in mind the repressive measures after Culloden. The trade between N. Carolina and Britain had reached good proportions, and the merchants of N. Carolina were anxious to maintain this. Republicanism, was foreign to the Highlander's way of thinking; and it can easily be understood that such circumstances could be effective in influencing the poorer Highlanders.

After the imprisonment of Flora's husband, Allan, in

Philadelphia, she had a very hard and difficult time, and whilst Allan sought compensation to the value of £1400, the Tribunal only granted him, as I have said, £440. Flora suffered greatly for her support of both Stuart and Hanover regimes. She had spent various periods in prison ships for her Stuart sympathies, and for her support of the Hanoverians had lost her all, her sons, and had experienced untold misery.

Flora returned to Scotland in July 1780; and there is a 'Carolina Hill' on Skye. There is also in the State of Carolina, a spring of water still known as the 'Flora Macdonald Spring'. The legend has it, that she used to sit for hours beside it, dreaming, dreaming and dreaming—and smoking her pipe! As a further matter of interest I believe in connection with the Vatican support of the Stuarts, every Sunday morning in every Roman Catholic Church, just prior to the end of the Mass (usually said in Latin), the choir sings 'God save the King'—the opening words being 'DOMINE SALVUM FAC REGUM NOSTRUM GEORGIUM'.

This American interlude of Flora and her husband's life is surely a very sad one. In as short a space as possible, I have given readers most of the story. Should I have made any errors, I may perhaps be excused, for I am no deep-versed historian. It is all enthralling, at the same time, heart-rending.

But . . . This is her story,
This is her song.

*   *   *

Reverting to the Prince Charlie period in Scotland, and the occasion of Samuel Johnson in later years sleeping in the same bed as used by Prince Charles Edward in Kingsburgh House in Skye, he left the following note on a table by the bedside . . . 'QUANTUM CEDAT, VIRTUTIBUS AURUM' ('with virtue weighed, what worthless trash is gold').

Neil MacEachen Macdonald (one of Flora's partners on the boat 'over the sea to Skye') subsequently followed the Prince to France, and married a French woman. Their son joined the French Army and attained great eminence in the army of Napoleon, and in 1809 he became Marshal Macdonald, Duc de Tarantum. His name was Jacques Joseph Alexander Macdonald. He was a distant relative of Flora Macdonald.

*   *   *

In the Lowlands there were thousands of Jacobites who found a thrill in meeting by candlelight and toasting 'The King o'er the Water'. But there were precious few of them ready to take sword in hand in support of their professed loyalty. The medal shown here was struck in London, and has the 'Butcher', Duke of Cumberland on the obverse; whilst the reverse (shown)

displays a battle-scene, with the date of Culloden, and the legend 'Rebellion Justly Rewarded'.

As an aside, the 4-poster six foot mahogany bed that the Prince slept in at Culloden House before the battle, was sold on 6th December 1968 at Sotherby's in London for £1100. The Prince took over the house with his officers forcing the house's owner, Duncan Forbes to flee for his life. After that it was Bonnie Prince Charlie fleeing for his life!

CHAPTER 13

HYDRO-ELECTRIC SUPPLY

T HE North of Scotland Hydro-Electric Board (or as we know it up here as *NORSHEL*, being more or less the initials of the undertaking, and not the name of an Old Testament prophet as some of you might think!) celebrated its 25th anniversary on 5th August 1968. They have a short, proud Gaelic motto 'Neart nan Gleann', which means quite simply 'Strength of the Glens'.

'Gun tigeadh solus agus neart an dealin dhionnsuidh gach croft'—let light and power come to all the crofts. With these words the widow of a crofter at Morar in December 1948 set the turbine spinning in the first power station of the North of Scotland Hydro-Electric Board; a mere 750 kilowatt production. It put an end to the famous waterfall by the roadside.

Over the last 25 years the Board has taken the Highlands out of darkness into the light, and brought about a complete social revolution at the touch of a switch. In this computer age, it is hard to remember that just after the second world war, the paraffin lamp still reigned supreme in the lonely places of Scotland; that 'electricity' was no more than a word in cottages and crofts on the hillside and in the glen.

The Board was brought into being by the foresight of Tom Johnston M.P. (who was Secretary of State for Scotland during the war years) in 1943 and it is hard to grasp the fantastic fact that since then, 96 per cent of the north has been electrified. Wherever and whenever their is pioneering, there is opposition. And in the early days of the undertaking, their efforts to build dams and make electricity, were occasionally met with antagonism. During one public inquiry, somebody claimed that a dam at Pitlochry would create fogs and bring rheumatism to the area, as well as malaria-carrying mosquitoes! Now, in that beauty spot, there would be a general outcry if anyone suggested taking the whole installation away. The Board, the oldest publicly-owned authority in Britain, has invested over £300 million in electricity supply and the development of water power resources, and its programme is today recognised among the major constructional achievements of post-war Europe. It is safe to say that had it not been for the Board, the future smelter development at Invergordon could not have become a reality. The undertaking is surely one of the most important lifelines in the Highland economic structure. The Board has made a tremendous contribution to the prosperity of the North of Scotland by building up a network of cables so that power can be taken to consumers wherever they require it; the greatest benefit the Board has provided socially. The complete electrification of the more remote areas has still to be achieved, but no one will doubt that in time the whole picture will be completed.

In 1946 a preliminary survey was made of the catchment area of Loch Shin, near Lairg in Sutherland. By the next year the nationalisation of the electricity supply industry resulted in the Board's becoming responsible for supplying the whole of that county. In 1947 the Board acquired the small non-statutory undertaking in ULLAPOOL and changed the direct current system to alternating current. That year construction commenced of a hydro-electric power station at Nostie Bridge (the village lies about a mile off the Dornie to Kyle road) with an associated rural distribution scheme to provide supply to LOCHALSH and the surrounding country. A submarine cable was also laid to connect with SKYE. The station was completed and power switched on in December 1948. Concurrently, a rural distribution scheme and the Kerry Falls Hydro-Electric Power Station were being constructed to supply consumers in the GAIRLOCH, POOLEWE and AULTBEA areas (Wester Ross) and supply was switched on in 1949 in the first instance from a temporary Diesel Power Station at Aultbea; the full supply from Kerry Falls came on in 1951.

In 1948 the Board acquired the undertaking operated by the Grampian Electricity Supply Company which had its offices in Dingwall, and thus there commenced a link which has since been maintained with DINGWALL. The Grampian supply was derived from a H-E Power Station at Conon Falls, Lochluichart. An extensive programme was then instituted to develop the hydro-electric resources of the area, designed to give supply to the whole county. The initial development was a station at Grudie Bridge, near GARVE, this station being commissioned in 1950.

The BRORA station was started up in 1950 at a time of national electricity shortage. Another contribution to electricity supply from Brora was the supply of coal from the pit there, and which for many years was used by the Board's steam stations to assist local industry.

In 1951 the Loch Shin scheme was published, and approved by Parliament in 1953. This great scheme began to produce power in 1958. Meanwhile, supply lines were being constantly extended. A supply was provided to the LOCHINVER area in 1953 REAY, STRATHHALLADALE and MELVICH (Sutherland) were switched on in 1954; and the extension to CAPE WRATH, KINLOCHBERVIE and BADCALL in 1957.

One of the most pleasing features of all these electrical schemes, has been that they have been carried out in an unbroken sequence. When the GLEN AFFRIC project was finished, there was the ORRIN one just across the Ross-shire hills; the Loch Shin scheme in Sutherland; and so it went on. When one scheme was completed, the Highland workers merely 'shifted camp'. It is true to say, all these projects—and of course more yet to come—'dammed' Highland depopulation quite considerably, stopping the drift south of many skilled and unskilled workmen. The comparatively new Pulp Mill at Fort William and the immense amount of electricity supply involved, brought new life-blood there, so that Hector and Calum could return to the love and labour in their native surroundings and under their own majestic hills.

All this vast work carried out by the Hydro-Electric Board, could never have been done without the generous support received from landowners and others in providing the necessary wayleaves for overhead lines and by the co-operation in planning and developing their works from the Town and County Councils.

In Wester Ross particularly—and where I live—there will always be feelings of gratitude for those intrepid pioneers of the development of electrical power here . . . the late Colonel Edward Blunt-Mackenzie of Castle Leod, and the late Mr. Tom Dalling and their staff, who so courageously set going the old Strathpeffer Company and paved the way for all later development.

The maintenance of supply in the more exposed parts of all these regions, is a major task, believe me, which could not be carried out but for the whole-hearted co-operation of the distribution staff, who in many cases in extreme weather conditions—to my personal knowledge—have performed wonders in their varied duties. I certainly 'take my hat off' to these 'hydro boys'. They are real sparks of genius.

From the moment the Board completed their first project at Loch Sloy, Dunbartonshire—after gruelling months in driving rain, snow and gale-force winds—they went from strength to strength. Their experts created more dams, more power stations and more power lines. Magic names like GLEN SHIRA and CRUACHAN, were scribbled on the drawing boards (and *what* a mass of complicated drawings there must have been made) and translated them into magnificent units, sending power coursing through the veins of Scotland. One needs to pause and think of all that was involved, when one switches on a light or a fire or a cooker, at one's home. The Scottish way of generating electricity began to excite other nations. Even Russia, that inveterate country of dam-builders, sent experts over here to learn.

Once a turbanned sheik came along seeking help. He had heard of the Board's research in the problems of de-icing equipment after blizzards. He wanted advice on the problem of de-sanding gear in the desert after a sand-storm! And all the time, records were being made and smashed again and again. At Breadalbane, a huge tunnel advanced by 600 feet in one week.

Something like 16,000 jobs and 300 new industries have come about in the north of Scotland over the years the Board has been operating. The job of powering the giant aluminium smelter at Invergordon, could not have come about if not for *NORSHEL*. Tom Johnston the far-seeing man who sparked off this great adventure, is dead; but he lived long enough to see his dream of a lit-up Scotland come true.

A few concise details will prove of much interest, I am sure.

Probably nothing less than a war, plus Tom Johnston's energy could have brought this great idea into being. Parliament had six times thrown out plans for the Board's promotion. Many of the crofters and villagers gave up their Tilley lamps and Calor gas with certain misgivings. Oil was so much cheaper than current and the lamps helped to warm a room, and when the first quarterly bills came in, the shock drove many a housewife back to old ways. Some people used electric light at dusk only for the five or ten minutes needed to replenish and prime their oil lamps. One can hardly grasp the immensity of the task before the Board. Its territory was packed with mountains, heavily indented all down its western seaboard by sea-lochs, where communication-lines were long and complicated, and the land sparsely populated.

The most interesting of all the schemes was at Cruachan (Argyll) at its south face. The construction of the dam at 1200 feet in the great south corrie, and more especially of the underground galleries, tunnels, pipes and vast machine-hall hewn out of the mountain's granite heart two-thirds of a mile underground (120 feet below sea-level) is perhaps one of the greatest feats of modern engineering in Britain. The dam itself is 1000 feet long and 150 feet high; but although eye-catching, it is nothing to what the marvels of the scheme are. These are hidden below the mountain and moor at a cost of £24m. This Cruachan venture was opened in 1965, and is the second biggest of its kind in the world; the biggest is in Luxembourg. It has an average yearly output of 450 million units. Its turbines are reversible and can drive the water back up the mountain into the reservoir behind the dam. What brains mankind has! In all the buildings of the power stations and staff houses, stone has been used instead of brick, and they all look superb and stimulate the social life of the communities. It also encourages the traditional craft of the stone-mason. Looking at everything in this sphere of creating energy, we are left with a sense of wonder that so much could have been achieved in so short a time. Life in the Highlands has certainly been transformed. Of course there has been a heavy price to pay for these benefits in the despoilation of famous glens and lochs. I remember in my younger days looking upon Glens Affrich and Cannich as the finest in Scotland. They are not so today. Even nearer home, at Kerrysdale in Gairloch, the work wrecked the beauty of the river, waterfall, and woods with huge pipelines running horizontally through the woods beside the road; and I ask myself if this ugliness could not have been less ugly? And certainly all over the Highlands pylons have added disfigurement to beauty. What of the future? The Board's main job has virtually been completed, but I suppose other minor ones will come along. There is a small one under promotion at Foyers on Loch Ness, to be used in conjunction with power from Dounreay in Caithness.

*   *   *

A few concise details will doubtless prove of interest showing the ramifications involved in this truly gigantic turnover from the old to the new up North.

Power Stations:
ANGUS, Carolina Port, Dundee
ARGYLL, Clachan, Cruachan, Lochgair, Lussa, Striven
DUNBARTONSHIRE, Sloy
INVERNESS-SHIRE, Fasnakyle, Invergarry, Kilmorack, Morar, Mucomir
LEWIS, Stornoway
ORKNEY, Kirkwall
PERTHSHIRE, Clunie, Errochty, Lochay, Pitlochry, St. Fillans
ROSS AND CROMARTY, Grudie Bridge, Torr Achilty
SHETLAND, Lerwick
SOUTH UIST, Daliburgh
SUTHERLAND, Shin

The staff of the North of Scotland Hydro-Electric Board numbers over 4000. At one time, 12,000 men were working on their road-making ventures. Something like £125,000,000 has been paid out in wages, and gone into circulation in the areas. Seventeen thousand (17,000) more farms now use the power they make; as well as sixteen thousand (16,000) crofts. Thirty-four more islands now have electricity. Refrigeration is another big outlet for current, from huge industrial installations right down to the deep-freeze you see in the shops, and in your homes too.

*   *   *

I think from the foregoing, it may be said the North of Scotland Hydro-Electric Board has brought new life to the Highlands. It has cost a lot to switch on to make life better and brighter. Both the colossal undertaking and ourselves benefit though. Agriculture too, has benefitted in being able to obtain the latest electrical technique and machinery.

When the great German poet Goethe lay dying in 1832, it is said that he kept uttering the words 'more light; more light'. This cry is even with us today—*fiat lux* . . . ('let there be light'). And this exclamation can, in this day and age, be translated into more senses than one?

CHAPTER 14

TRANSPORT IN THE FAR NORTH

ALL of us will, I am sure, have heard of MacBrayne's and
their steamers plying on the west coast 'twixt the mainland
and the islands and of the new car ferries introduced a few
years ago. The name of MacBrayne runs like a slogan throughout the western seas; they not only have steamers but buses,
lorries and piers—as well as a MacBrayne tartan! They are
lords of the island ferry services; they own them, they operate
them, they fix fares and lay down timetables, and nobody argues,
for as every islander knows, MacBrayne means the Government.
State subsidy keeps the firm sailing on an even keel and control
rests with the British Transport Commission and Coast Lines.
The company started in 1851, and in previous writings I have
given a full account of how MacBraynes came into being and
power.

But now I come to write about a very different concern—a
private company in so far it is not state controlled, that is widely
known and widely acknowledged as serving a most valuable
need to the community in Sutherland, namely The Sutherland
Transport and Trading Co. Ltd., whose head office is at Lairg,
with branches at Lochinver, Kinlochbervie, Bonar Bridge and
Ardgay. MacBrayne's can't run their steamers up and down the
roads of the far north, or across moorland tracks, so in 1878 the
above-named Trading Company started off in a small way, and
today with its wide ramifications its turnover is over half a
million pounds.

The company and its allied concern Pulford (Scotland) Ltd.
who are the fish salesmen at Kinlochbervie is owned by the
Grosvenor family (the Grosvenor Estate) who also own the
Reay Forest and Kylestrome Estates. This particular estate has
always taken a very long view of land ownership and in addition
to running these trading concerns to give local employment,
they have planted 3000 acres of trees and carry on many other

241

activities from the headquarters of the estate at Achfary situate
at the western end of Loch More.

Transport? . . .

In 1938 the Scottish Economy Committee made this report
'There is perhaps no individual element which has contributed in
greater measure towards the depopulation of the Highland area
than the inadequacy, or lack of, communications in many
districts. This is reflected in two ways, first by the existence of a
feeling of isolation, and secondly by the enforced submission to a
virtual tax upon existence due to this isolation in the form of
freight charges unduly increasing the cost of the necessities of
life.' . . . Thirty years is a long time for the learning of any
lesson?

*   *   *

The Sutherland Transport Company first started trading as a
partnership about 1878 under the name of Gray & Murray, the
partners being Mr. Gray of Colaboll and Mr. Murray of Achin-
duich; the descendants of these people are still living in the district. The Company's activities included the running of Mails
and Passengers by horse and coach to Tongue and Scourie and
Lochinver; coaching stables for the change of horses were at
Overscaig, Achfary and Altnaharra.

In 1905 the name of the Company was changed to the
'Coaching Company', and the first motor vehicle was used
on the Mail routes.

In 1906 the Company was sold to Mr. Wallace of Oban, who
completely motorised the business and at a later date started the
first garage in Sutherland. The Company was then called the
'Sutherland Motor Company'. By 1910 there was a total fleet
of roughly twelve Wagonettes carrying five passengers (who
were exposed to the elements) with a platform for the carrying of
Mails, Lobsters and Calves. These vehicles used to run into
Lairg on one day and out on the next. The trip from Lairg to
Laxford used to take roughly four hours. First and Second Class
Tickets were issued, second class fares were obliged to push on the
braes.

These open wagonettes continued on those routes until 1928
when the first enclosed vehicles appeared in the North West of
Sutherland.

It is a known fact that many of the drivers of these open wagonettes refused to leave Lairg with the mails unless they had a full hip flask to assist them; so they set out on their arduous trips and often failed to appear on scheduled time!

In 1920 the Company changed hands yet again, and became Sutherland Transport and Trading Co. Ltd., and it was in this year that the trading side of the business first commenced, mainly in motor spares.

The first lorry appeared in 1927 and was a Lancia, with a carrying capacity of roughly 3 tons. In 1934 three new lorries were purchased being Albions and carrying roughly 2 tons each.

During the 1930's new buses and lorries were purchased and the trading developed and in 1951 when the second Duke of Westminster took over the Company there was then a fleet of seven lorries and eleven buses. The Head Office was then at Lairg with a branch at Lochinver.

In 1956 the estate built a garage and workshop at Kinlochbervie and moved the transport, then operating as Pulford Estates, to Kinlochbervie from Rhiconich. At that time it consisted of three tippers, five platform lorries and three buses. They were occupied on the transport of fish and building materials for the work going ahead on the estate, and the buses were for the carrying of foresters who were working at Reay Forest.

In 1959 it was decided to operate the transport at Kinlochbervie as part of the Sutherland Transport and Trading Co. Ltd. although locally it has always been known as 'Pulford's Branch'.

In 1961 modern and spacious stores, showroom and workshops were completed at Lairg and opened in June of that year by the late Lord Fraser of Allander. From this point activities were expanded and a number of new lines undertaken.

In 1962 the turnover of the Company had reached nearly a quarter of a million.

In January 1965, the Transport and Agricultural business of D. J. Davidson Ltd. at Bonar Bridge was acquired and a comprehensive development with Board of Trade assistance was undertaken on the very good site on the A.9 close to Bonar Bridge.

The development envisaged a Petrol Station, Showroom and

Workshop and a building for the Transport and Agriculture activities and the future development of the large house as a tourist shopping centre with flats above. Owing to the recession in service business activities this development was curtailed and at present consists of a modern petrol station and a large building which is used as a transport depot and centre for agriculture sales and is being developed as a garage for both maintenance of its own vehicles and repairs for the public.

There is a specially constructed yard for coal stores and ground was acquired for the storage of cattle floats.

At the present time the turnover of the Company is in the region of half a million and a wide service is offered to the public in the north, covering transport, car sales, five workshops including a specialised body repairs shop, radio and television sales and repairs and electrical contracting, coal sales, agricultural sales of feeding stuffs and fertilisers, hardware sales in the various showrooms, motor spares and accessories, wholesale wine and spirits merchants, etc. Almost a hundred people are directly employed by the Company.

In addition to these services the Company operates mail buses which run daily into Lairg and back from Tongue, Durness, Kinlochbervie, Scourie and Lochinver. These buses carry passengers in the front half and the remaining half being for goods and the mail, a great variety of goods traffic including milk, laundry, requisites from the chemist and parcels forwarded from the railway, etc.

There is also a bus service from the Garage to Lairg Station two miles away, meeting every train, and a daily bus runs from Bonar Bridge linking the Highland Omnibus routes on the A.9 with the returning buses to the north-west.

This department also operates a hire car, a hearse and two ambulances which are stationed at Lairg. A further two ambulances are operated by the Company, one at Lochinver and one at Kinlochbervie.

The Company's Transport Fleet at the present, consists of six heavy lorries, a tipper and a four wheel lorry at Bonar Bridge, engaged on general and local transport. Also four four-wheel platform lorries and two tippers at Kinlochbervie, engaged on fish transport and local tipping work.

The fleet at Bonar Bridge is heavily overshadowed by the

Transport Bill at Present before Parliament as are all Highland hauliers, unless considerable freedom is given for back loads.

*   *   *

I now come to the history of Pulford (Scotland) Limited who are as I have stated, the fish salesmen at Kinlochbervie.

In 1951 the Second Duke of Westminster purchased the White Fish and Herring salesmen's business established in 1948 at Loch Clash Pier, and also the transport business at Rhiconich which was primarily concerned in the haulage of the fish.

Prior to 1948 virtually no fish had been landed at Loch Clash for 40 to 50 years.

The white fish are caught from three to twelve miles offshore, mostly by seine net boats. These boats are generally owned by the fishermen themselves often with shares held by the fish salesman and the majority of them come from the east coast of Banffshire and Aberdeenshire. The fishermen arrive at the port from home to join their boat at midnight on Sunday and return home by car on Thursday evening.

The boats leave for the fishing grounds about 4 a.m. and return to land their catches about 6 p.m. Seine netting may be briefly described in the following manner: On reaching the fishing grounds the boat drops a 'Dan' or buoy attached to many coils of rope on one side of her deck. She then steams in a straight line until all the rope on the one side is paid out, about 1080 fathoms. This rope is attached to the seine net which consists of a wing of 18 yards, a central piece with a purse or pocket (about 9 yards) and another wing about 45 yards in all. The other end of the net is attached to a similar length of rope on the other side of the boat. Now still steaming in a straight line and then in a segment of a circle, the net and the remaining rope are paid out until the 'Dan' is picked up on the initial side of the boat. Then full steam ahead pulling in both ropes on a double winch. The ropes shimmering in the water frighten the fish within an ever decreasing circle till they get into the pocket or 'moneybag' of the net. Finally the net is hauled aboard.

White fish are gutted and selected at sea and placed in boxes. On arrival at port the fish are weighed, iced and sold and then taken to the markets at Aberdeen, Glasgow, Fraserburgh, Leith, Hull and Grimsby by either Sutherland Transport and Trading Company's lorries or those of the buyers, arriving for the early morning market.

In 1949 the Second Duke of Westminster established an Ice Plant at Loch Clash capable of making 6 tons of ice in 24 hours, together with a deep freeze store and an ice store. This ice plant played an important part in the early development of the business.

In 1952 shortly after acquisition of the business, herring catches failed and the demand for white fish was very poor with the possibility of the port failing altogether. It was decided to purchase a fish processing business in Aberdeen in order to ensure an outlet for Kinlochbervie fish and guaranteed minimum prices were undertaken by the estate to support the fishermen.

In 1963 this business in Aberdeen was discontinued as circumstances had changed, the fish caught at Kinlochbervie being of a very high quality was too expensive for a processing business.

The Aberdeen processing premises were leased, the remaining half of the premises consisting of a yard and small office had been utilised since this time successfully collecting and washing the Company's boxes. This service is also provided for the port at Lochinver.

Salmon are collected through the Company Estate and many others are marketed through the Aberdeen premises, as are lobsters.

In 1961 the Old Ice Plant was replaced by a modern Sabroe Scale Ice Plant with a 36-ton storage room. This is being replaced by a still larger plant in the near future owing to the ever increasing demand for ice, due to the heavy fishings and the higher standards required.

In 1963 the Company undertook the management of Salmon Bag Net Fishing off the coast of Oldshoremore for the Reay Forest Estate. Approximately 1000 fish are caught each year.

In 1965 the Company obtained consent to establish as Ship Chandlers which has really been a useful adjunct. The Company obtain their principal income by auctioning the fish landed, for which they are paid 9d. in the £ commission. The Company also holds the oil concession from Shell Mex & B.P. Limited and fuels all the boats operating at Kinlochbervie.

Ten years ago, fish landings at Kinlochbervie were very small; the value being about £100,000. Today (1969) the value is well over £500,000.

The number of boats using the port varies from one month to another, depending on fishing conditions, availability of stocks and the demand from the Scottish Markets.

The greatest number of boats to be in Kinlochbervie at one time was fifty-five for a short period in 1964. The number is normally around thirty, reducing to around twenty at times. There are about twelve boats that always fish at Kinlochbervie, the remainder follow the fish and change their method for the different season.

In 1965 the Company produced a development plan for Kinlochbervie envisaging a covered market at Loch Bervie and moving its own offices to that site. It also proposed to form a Slipway and Engineering Company to maintain and repair boats, extra ice capacity and a number of other improvements including housing to get fishermen settled at the port; making the whole business a viable community.

All this, however, was dependant on the deepening of the entrance to Loch Bervie and its new pier.

At present boats may have to wait as much as two hours at certain times to either get out to the grounds or come in to the harbour. Both the County Council and the Company have pressed the Government to do this work estimated at £40,000 and a tentative agreement has been secured subject to certain tide tests being carried out.

At the time of writing (December 1968) the Government has now announced its intention of deepening the entrance channel, so the large fleet of seine-net fishing boats will be able to use Loch Bervie at all states of the tide. This will give Kinlochbervie and district a great shot in the arm. I wish all concerned every success.

CHAPTER 15

GENERALITIES

THIS chapter consists of several odd items such as THE
MOD; ROADS; A NEW FACE; PEAT; ACCOMMODATION
AND FOOD; SUPERSTITION; THE TARTAN AND THE KILT,
and will be taken in that order.

The Mod

This is a yearly festival of Gaelic music, song, dance, oral
competition and the like; and is held for a week at different
centres each year throughout Scotland, to which all Gaelic-lovers
(gentle Gaels with true speech on their lips) wend their way,
young—even the very young—and old. For music is a universal
language; a language which all the world understands be it
Gaelic or otherwise.

At one time and before I became so intimately acquainted with
Scotland, I used to imagine Mod was something you ate, like
haggis, or the name of a Cornish wine!

Every year these great Mods are held, Gaeldom abandons
itself to a week of glorious music and the renewing of auld
acquaintances. There is the thrill of the tartans, the joy of
meeting old friends and 'feeling' the soft touch of the Gaelic
accent, their lingering on the 'r's'; the softened consonants.
The Mod is a unique gathering; colourful impressive and electrifying. As someone once said, 'A gran' language the Gaelic;
profanity in it just sounds like poetry in any other tongue!'

The word 'mod' comes from a word 'mot', so Gaelic scholars
say, which is common to Norse and to Anglo-Saxon, but whether
it came to us from the Vikings is uncertain.

The Mod is not an entirely musical festival such as some would
suppose; for at the last Mod held, over 40 per cent of the entries
in the junior section were for the oral competitions, which is in-
dicative of the desire of Highland youth to become proficient in
the Gaelic language.

Invariably on the Sunday before the week commences there is a traditional Gaelic service held in the town's main church, attended by the Provost, Magistrates and members of the Town Council.

The word Mod these days is *not* to be associated with 'mods and rockers', such as teenagers appear to be involved in—many such activities reaching hooliganism. This sect might reasonably be termed Dom—Mod read backwards. And there is another corruption of Mod, reading Odm, such as the Monkees, Rolling Stones and other pop groups. It may be said a Dom is a crazy mixed-up Mod; and an Odm? An even crazier mixed-up Dom!

At the Mod meetings, people come who want to meet others similarly imbued; people who want to sing and dance in the old traditional manner, for to such folk these songs draw strength from their wild hills and misty moors; warm and fragrant from the heather; and amongst the whole assembly of such kindly folk, kith and kin are woven and knitted together like the strands of wool in the Fair Isle jerseys still being made by old knitters in out-of-the-way places.

These songs of the isles delight all ears—even English ears—as do the gaily-coloured kilts (with hues like the tint of heather, the greens resembling moss) swinging and swirling; that and the women wearing the brooches of their respective clans.

Tartan uppermost and everywhere; the shops making beautiful displays in their windows; and the Council 'goes to town' also, in stretching a banner across the main thoroughfare emblazoned with the words CEUD MÌLE FÀILTE (100,000 welcomes); a cheering thought even on a cold day.

Most of the elderly women who steadfastly attend these Mods, and who come from all quarters of the Highlands and Islands, are of a shy, retiring disposition; but the memories of song and laughter still abound in their bosoms. And as these women and wives (some mayhap bereft of their menfolk) listen to the young performers ('the young in heart'), they smile happily to the speech and to the tradition which, to them, is a sure and living force; for there are things which can be expressed only in Gaelic; truths in life that can only be put to Gaelic verse. For life in the Highlands is hard, as hard as the barren rocks that surround them and their crofts.

Young farmers have left their crofts for the week, and whilst

I

they are away their cattle will be roaming the hillside at leisure, crushing back the old invader—the bracken. Some of the youngsters only have enough money saved to come for the one day they are performing; and then back they must go to their homes which may be in one of the far-away islands of the Outer Hebrides. A hard existence; a stocky people indeed.

Young and old; junior choirs, assiduously coached by their Gaelic teacher, come to re-live, to revitalise one part—and to them *the* part—of Scottish home life which, to these young boys and girls, spells contentment of their own wee Highland homes. Until they grow up—aye there's the rub.

Yes, everyone of any note or having any Highland connections try to attend these Mods. No one ever seems to go to bed on such occasions; and meals are not the only things that 'stagger' during Mod week! Those behind cocktail bars work and sweat at high pressure—breakneck speed, for we are not west of Garve now! There must be a 24-hour licence, for they seem to work into the small hours of the morning.

So, after a week of tireless energy, tireless talking and tireless Slàinte Mhaths, the annual Mod closes down and everyone goes back to the Islands and Highlands—to the croft, the sheep and the heather. To extend this Mod idea, and promote even greater interest (and finance too) I think, if these Festivals embraced Gaelic, Welsh, and Irish songs, music and dancing, they would produce an immense impact on society generally.

The Mod-ites return to their homeland; to the crofts and cottages where the burn babbles round the back door, and is heard from the bedroom, lulling one to sleep; and then in the morning fretting like an infant to waken you up. Many have no water laid in to their wee houses; so they just go outside to wash under the tap in cold peaty brown-coloured water. Then come in for breakfast, glowing, and ready for the new-laid eggs picked out of the henhouse they've just opened up; warm oatcakes and oatmeal porridge, thick as can be; home-made marmalade—and the burn continues to babble. No luxury; just Highland life; no wealth—just a wealth of happiness and freedom. The mountains and lochs by day; the stars by night. IONNDRAINN—the longing for things gone beyond recall; the most moving note in Gaelic poetry. The Clearances cannot be forgotten; those days when the cream sailed overseas leaving the skimmed milk behind. But since those years, the skimmed milk has turned full circle; it is cream again. During those fateful days, man's greatest pleasure was when he was subduing rebels, defeating enemies wiping out all their kith and kin seizing all their property; causing wives to weep with tears streaming down their cheeks; burning their houses, raping the women and using them as pillows to sleep on.

Now, all that is over; though forgotten, never. The Highlander has a long memory, and a long life.

As a rule, the men are virile to a ripe old age. They die when their bodies wear out, and their hearts stop beating. They get more relaxed as they grow older—whereas townspeople grow more tense.

'AN COMUNN GAIDHEALACH' is the Gaelic for 'The Gaelic Society', and the very first National Mod was held in Oban on Tuesday, 13th September 1892. This first Mod only lasted for one day. Nowadays over 2000 entries are dealt with over a period of the week. It is very possible future Mods will run to the next week, following the Sunday opening. And who knows, as time goes on pop and jazz may find its way into it? With, such conviviality reigning and spirits flowing (whisky in particular), an American who happened to be present called it 'the Whisky Olympics!' A glance at the early office-bearers and patrons of AN COMUNN reads like an extract from *Who's Who*. Names such as the Marquis of Breadalbane, the Duke and Duchess of Sutherland, and the Marquis of Lorne appear. In 1892 there were about a quarter of a million Gaelic speakers in Scotland; now maybe only 70,000.

In 1892 at the first Mod, the '45 Jacobite Rebellion and Culloden, had not even then been erased from public memory, and socially Gaelic was regarded as an inferior language to Scots as a whole. There had also been a mass movement abroad and into industrial towns and cities, so disrupting the cultural pattern. Nowadays the platform of the Mod is veering towards youth— young Gaeldom looking to the future; the children of the Highlands and Islands. They represent junior choirs, and the hope of AN COMUNN in its striving to preserve Gaelic culture.

Man cannot live by bread alone—nor can a nation. As well as the butcher, the baker, the candle-stick maker we must have art and music, and it is not enough to import this art or music,

for no community is complete without the same living in its
midst. By long tradition the Tuesday of Mod week is 'Children's
Day', and at the last Mod almost a thousand youngsters came
along to test their skill in story, recitation and song—fluent
speakers and eager learners; and it is on these youngsters shoulders
competing today that the future of the Gaelic language largely
depends—these children from the scattered crofts and remote
communities of the north-west coast (and islands where Gaelic is
so uppermost). It means a welcome break from their school
desks too! Several fringe innovations have recently been introduced such as a children's quiz, a folk-group competition and an
old-style ceilidh (cayley). A ceilidh used to mean simply an
informal fireside gathering where any old songs and stories were
exchanged, and general matters discussed, trivial or profound.
The host (*fear-an-tigh*) had to tell the first tale and then the guests
provided the rest of the entertainment. Today ceilidh has assumed
a different connotation—a more sophisticated programme of
music and song, either in a neighbour's house or a village hall.
A ceilidh is for remembering the best of yesterday and forgetting
the worst of today; and designed to make something better out
of tomorrow.

Roads

The north of Scotland, like the Highlands in general, has its
share of worthies who frequently come out with sayings which
in time achieve local immortality. One comes from a County
Council road worker. Asked by a visitor, what he did for a
living, he replied, 'Who, me? I do nothing. I'm with the
County!'

When I first visited the Highlands—and Gairloch—in 1914,
the roads one had to travel were nothing much more than tracks;
narrow, overgrown with grass, and passing places say one every
quarter mile, and it was quite the thing, upon spotting a car
coming towards you to get out and wave your handkerchief,
letting him know you had stopped at a stretch wide enough to
allow passing, and for him to come on. Of course there were
few cars in those days. Now, how different it all is. Mr.
Macadam and the roads' departments have seen to all that, and
motoring is a pleasure. Up in Sutherland I find the roads to be

even better than in Wester Ross in that there are more straight
stretches; no awkward bends or corners, in fact you can, in
some cases, see miles ahead.

In the very early days, the name of General Wade stood out
first and foremost; and I don't know how many times I have
quoted this couplet to visitors, viz:

If you saw these roads before they were made,
You'd go down on your knees and thank General Wade.

He was a pioneer if ever there was one. He was an Irishman in
the red coat of the Hanoverian army whose dedicated task was
to subdue the Highlands by building roads. You see many of his
hump-backed bridges (Wade's bridges) to this very day—like the
back of a cat as it stretches itself on wakening. He worked with
his squads of mercenaries under appalling conditions, yet how he
succeeded. They rolled boulders aside with crude levers; they
forged northward at the rate of a mile a week, cutting roads
through rock, moor and marsh. He was a genius; a stubborn
genius. After the 1715 Rebellion, in July 1724 to be exact,
Major-General Wade was instructed to proceed to the Highlands, and in December of that year he received his Commission
as Commander-in-Chief of the forces in North Britain. He
reported that money would be required for the mending of the
roads between Garrisons and Barracks for the better communication of His Majesty's Troops, all over the north. By the end of
1725 he had begun the construction of his great military highway
through the Great Glen from Fort William to Inverness. This
was followed by the making of the road southwards, Inverness
to Dunkeld. In 1731 he commenced another gigantic job, the
road from Fort Augustus over Corrieyairick Hill (3000 feet) across
country to Dalwhinnie and thence to Aberfeldy and Crieff.
During a period of only eight years he constructed a total of
250 miles of major roadway. What an effort! With the
construction of the Tay Bridge at Aberfeldy in 1733, Wade's
work as a road and bridge builder was virtually completed. He
was relieved of his command in 1740 and died eight years later
on 14th March 1748, aged 75; and was buried in Westminster
Abbey. A Major Caulfield was appointed successor to Wade
to carry on; and he continued in office for thirty-five years.
Later on, we find the name of Thomas Telford—another colossus
of road-makers—looming up in the early 1800's. He opened up

a road on the *north* side of the Caledonian Canal from Inverness
to Fort Augustus via Dores and Foyers. This, too, effected vast
changes in the conditions of travel throughout the Highlands.
And today, as I have said, all roads are kept in excellent condition;
so there is nothing to fear.

A New Face

Early in 1968 it appears the Scottish Tourist Board in conjunction with the Secretary of State for Scotland, sought assistance
from the Glasgow School of Art Department of Planning to make
economic surveys of nine regions in Scotland—an academic
exercise in fact; but strangely, neither the Inverness office of the
Tourist Board nor the Highland and Islands Development Board
were concerned, connected or consulted in this Wester Ross
survey. The report seemed to be entirely devoid of any sensitive-
ness relative to the inhabitants thereof. The Highland and Islands
Board's complete staff numbers eighty-six, and the Tourist Board
executive consists of twenty members all of whom (except three)
are men of letters akin to what one is accustomed to see in an
Annual Bank Report; O.B.E.'s, C.A.'s and such like, but
none with any mechanical or civil engineering experience—no
expertees.

Far reaching proposals by these five senior students for the
development of Gairloch and Wester Ross as a major holiday
area was envisaged—in fact it emerged as a $£4\frac{1}{2}$m 'Plan',
suggesting new hotels, indoor heated swimming pools, covered
games areas—if necessary in inflatable portable buildings (how
would *they* stand up to winter's gales here, I asked myself) more
halls, cinemas and schools utilised for crèches and children's
playgroups. Gairloch was to become a 'holiday village'—a
vast Butlin's camp as soon as you passed Achnasheen; bowls,
tennis, fencing, judo, boxing. And I suppose lots of one-arm-
bandits dotted along at strategic places. A territory of fun-fair
amusement. One new hotel was shown looking right on to the
tombstones over the cemetery wall. No locals, except perhaps
in a casual way were consulted; nor were the Lairds. In fact
they seemed to run riot, and maybe would have thought it good
fun suggesting the planting of palm trees around tables outside
in the Strath (Gairloch) square so one could sit on a sunny day
sipping an aperitif, watching the pretty Highland girls passing.

They made only four brief visits in thirteen months (November 1966–December 1967) to assess the picture. If fully implemented we would have big supermarkets—and no staff to cope with everything, unless it be imported Cypriots or Spaniards. And what fun then for these foreigners and the teenagers?

The loose-leaf book of 136 pages expounding all these wonderful ideas, complete with drawings, resembled a pattern-book one gets in a wallpaper shop; weighed 2 lb, and a tab gummed on the last page proclaimed the price at 21s. I chanced to steam off this tab, and found underneath, the figure of 15s. in the original print type. So at the outset the authors were 40 per cent out of their initial reckoning. That being so the £4½m could easily reach £6m. A £4½m plan? almost double the loot taken in the Great Train Robbery of 1963!

We were, in dear old Gairloch, to have a 'NEW FACE'; a 'NEW LOOK'; and all this expenditure to bring more tourists to the area when, during the season the place is packed out. To say nothing of the country's balance of payments deeply in the red to the tune of hundreds of million pounds. But I suppose the Government attaches great importance to all this spending, arguing that it is no pie-in-the-sky stuff, as all these proposals form a vital part of the blueprint designed for Scotland. These planners may have swallowed a deal of wisdom, but it would seem as if a lot of it has gone down the wrong way. Their brain power needs sharpening on the pumicestone of the moon.

This survey came out on 1st May 1968. I was on my way to spend a month at a house in Oldshoremore (near Kinlochbervie) on 2nd May, arriving at Scourie Hotel for lunch. Parking the car with ease, in the courtyard of this very excellent hotel for few if any visitors are about the far north then, an aristocratic gentleman in a green velvet jacket and plus fours came out to talk to me. I took it he was a landed-proprietor of the district. When I said I was only stopping for lunch as I was going further north, we went in to the hotel to have an aperitif, and he asked me where I was from. Upon saying Gairloch, he said, 'My! my! What a beautiful place that is, but had I heard the news?' No, I had not heard the news; and then he told me of the £4½m scheme, which had come over the radio that morning. I was dumbfounded; I am afraid it spoilt my lunch and that together

with coming over some 3½ miles from Laxford Bridge along
heavy road reconstruction work, put the lid on everything.
However, I decided to wait to see more details before getting
any hotter under the collar. Papers and details filtered through
and I thought something strong needed to be said via the Press,
but I put it all aside till the end of May. When I left Sutherland
I called upon the Editor of the *Northern Times*, Golspie, whose
paper covers the whole of the north, and handed him the following letter which appeared in the issue of 7th June; under the
caption 'THE OTHER VIEWPOINT'. (All the following Press letters
appeared under my own name and address; there was no need
of camouflage.)

I have just returned home to Gairloch after spending many
weeks in North-West Sutherland around Oldshoremore and Kinlochbervie, and I feel I would be failing if I did not pen this short
letter to your paper saying what a delightful, enchanting countryside it all is; even more scenic than Wester Ross. Mountains, lochs
and lochans are everywhere you turn, and the Highland folk with
their cheerfulness personified, outclass those anywhere else in the
North.

The atmosphere of peace and contentment prevails, and it is to
be hoped no grandiose development schemes—such as the Highlands
and Islands Development Board appear to be bent on regardless of
spending millions of taxpayers' money—will creep up on the area.

Visitors will never appreciate any so-called 'new-look' of the
Highalands; they want it all 'our way' in this land of 'fàilte' and
'slàinte mhath'. The superb settings to be found need no further
gilding; its gold leaf is there for the taking, and to tamper with
nature will spell ruin. Scenery and quiet thoughts involved are the
tourists' magnet, refreshing them from their towns' everyday mad
rush.

I have written much about Highland life, and the thousands of
letters that come to me from all over the world stress a common
point—viz., that nothing should ever be done to spoil what exists
up here today.

Upon nearing home, I had a long chat with the Editor of
The Ross-shire Journal in Dingwall. The *Journal* covers all
Ross-shire; indeed it seems to have subscribers all over the
world (from letters I subsequently received), and gave him the
following for publication. And this appeared also on 7th June
—caption being 'QUO VADIS'.

Quo Vadis

Chariot racing up and down Slioch, with a petrol pump on top; a scenic railway along the jagged Cuillin range; a bingo-hall on Beinn Eighe!

Why not? for our so-called planners seem to be bent on spending tax-payers' money on Highland development of grandiose scale.

The latest is the massive idea of spending £4½ million on 'developing' the Gairloch area of Wester Ross. This brilliant (?) scheme appears to have been born on the drawing boards of the Glasgow School of Art.

No one in the district has been approached—not even the Lairds of Gairloch, yet I seem to remember the chairman of the Highlands and Islands Development Board saying publicly in 1965, that nothing can be done in the Highlands unless the Highland people were with them, and knew what was being done. Today it would appear everything turns on the political screw, and out of the blue comes a comprehensive plan of huge dimensions, aimed at revolutionising the very way of our gracious life here.

Such senseless ideas, if put into effect, will ruin—not improve—an area of Scotland that over the years has safeguarded its peaceful, quiet atmosphere (quite unknown elsewhere) and which makes it increasingly inviting to those who cherish such a holiday.

The Highlander is a worthy, if not a wealthy person. There is no poverty, and everyone is happy making a living as at present. There are no hard and fast barriers of wealth and station; the society is characterised by a well mannered equality. Above all, they keep the Sabbath—a practice sadly lacking in our land today. To foist something upon a community quite foreign to its way of life is sheer lunacy and courting disaster long before even one pound is spent of the £4½ million.

I have just returned from over one month in the north-west of Sutherland, within easy reach of Cape Wrath. A wonderful scenic sea-board, with mountains, loch and lochans everywhere you turn. Here too, is to be found even more peace and restfulness than in Wester Ross; and here too, the Sabbath is respected.

Should the waves of progress creep on and up to Sutherland (the land of the Clearances years ago) and when its ripples are seen advancing, I am sure the folk there will extend their stone walls (dykes) across the main arteries, and only those who mean to fall in with their outlook on life will be allowed to enter.

To attempt to boost a place by artificial means, trying to make it urban, is just throwing money down the drain.

The heritage in the Highlands is the tradition of humanism,

which came down from the Greeks and the Judaic-Christian
philosophy of man's unique nature.

Socrates taught that it is not knowledge or skill in a craft or
science that makes a man fully human; it is wisdom and virtue, and
we need this wisdom more than ever before in all this breathless
propaganda of the Highlands. In short, man with a true sense of
proportion becomes a princely person. Quo Vadis, indeed! Rural
ruin, indeed!

I then followed this up with a longer letter to the *Ross-shire
Journal* which appeared on 19th July 1968:

THE GAIRLOCH PLAN—AN APPRAISAL

My former contribution to your columns merely skimmed the
surface of the £4½ million plan for Gairloch and district. Frankly
when I first saw the brief reference in the Press in May, I was
disturbed, but later appalled as I read the full survey set out by the
Glasgow School of Art Department of Planning, commissioned by
the Scottish Tourist Board (Edinburgh).

The loose-leaf book of 136 pages is unwieldy, weighs 2 lbs., and
priced 21s; it resembles the pattern books one gets in a wall-paper
shop.

The report describes Gairloch as without winter snow with a wet
climate and cold sea (forgetting these shores are washed by the Gulf
Stream!). Nevertheless it proposes indoor heated swimming pool,
shop, clubhouse, covered games areas, the building of at least 100
more houses, chalets, caravan and camping sites (one situated on a
marsh), schools utilised for crèches and children's play groups—a
new holiday village with new hotels (one adjacent and looking on to
the graveyard, the tomb-stones significantly shown!) new golf
course, bowls, fencing, boxing, tennis, coupled with water ski-ing,
sailing, a large hall for conferences, judo, air inflatable buildings—
the lot! Though not at the moment a trampoline arena, which is
the latest 'jumping jimminies' sport at Aviemore. The whole is
aimed at a much lengthened season—though I might add a family
holiday season cannot be extended here for it is tied up with school
holidays. Even beautiful, secluded Flowerdale House, the home of
the Mackenzie Lairds of Gairloch for generations, is thought of as a
possible hotel or training centre.

It would take far too much space criticising all the points; the
authors must think everyone here is not making a worthwhile
living. But the plain fact is, everybody is content, and by the time
the season ends in October, there are sighs of relief from the constant
rush and stress.

And so, I will confine myself to the following conclusions, *sans peur et sans raproche*.

1. The whole concept is academic, stream-lined with theories, fanciful ideas and hopelessly out of balance. No analyses of costs are given, just £4½ million—it's as simple as that. Of course, we cannot blame them, for none of these so-called planners have any skilled degrees such as Civil or Mechanical Engineering, so necessary in covering such a project. To my mind, if fully implemented it could run to £8m. And all this, when the Government is up to its neck in debt.

2. How can a report involving such gargantuan expenditure be given any serious thought, when only four brief visits in 13 months were paid the whole area, and that by five art students? One asks what does the School of Art know of the Highland way of life and its heritage, that has been handed down through centuries?

3. It would be a flagrant abuse of taxpayers' money to attempt to alter, desecrate or prostitute the uniqueness of this countryside. A balance between sentiment and pragmatism is essential, with the accent on sentiment in the regions.

4. The scheme is set at urbanising Wester Ross. This would be tantamount to erecting a merry-go-round with organ and old type naphtha flare lamps in the forecourt of Holyrood House. As such the whole work put in by the Art College (which I am sure has given much interest and fun to all) to say nothing of a lot of money spent in preparation, printing and so on, is to be deplored.

5. If any study were needed, it would have been far more to the point if it had been conducted by two members of our local District Council and two members of the County Council, under the chairmanship of an independent fully qualified dynamic person, who had solid business acumen, massive common-sense and sure instinct for the Highlanders' wishes; and one with a true sense of proportion. If our Council and the County Council don't know what is required, then who does? I say again we don't want students, academics, theorists, lecturers, professors or what not, engaged on these practical and aesthetic aspects.

6. Not one word is said as to the people's religious observance; obviously the planners are unaware that Sunday (the Sabbath) is sacredly kept as a day of rest, when one can lay aside one's cares and anxieties, and attend the many services (both then and on week-days) in 'giving thanks'. To make the area into a 'multi-sports' development centre would strike a mortal blow at all we hold dear. What a mockery incomers would make of it all. It would create a regular vendetta.

7. I now come to the incidence of crime, which nobody seems

to have thought of with the supposedly influx of a further 2000 or 3000 people attracted by all the many 'improvements'. Should this area be over-run by adventurers, there may well follow in their wake undesirables of such character and violence (the violence of an aimless, drifting generation) as we so frequently read of in the Press —vandalism, robberies, murder, rape and so forth. If so, Wester Ross's blessed peaceful nature would suffer irreparable damage. Glen Docherty could be another Glen of Weeping. Many may say, this would never happen; but—it could. Who knows?

8. The people who come to these parts, seek what they cannot find elsewhere—tranquility. This would be completely rocked, and Dr. MacGregor and his wee black bag would be working overtime dispensing tranquiliser pills!

9. But I think this is enough. Ours not to reason why, but to try and put reason wise. We have politicians, but no statesmen. Surely those who live here and whose roots have been firmly established for generations, are not going to sit back and sell their birthright for a mess of pottage?

The finger of guilt and shame would be pointed for all time at those who decided to go through with this pointless scheme, should it ever come to pass. Such a tidal wave would creep on like cancer reaching Sutherland and Cape Wrath, where it would overspill to the ocean. It will be of no use then going down on one's knees imploring Heaven's help, for it will be too late to stop this second flood, the second Clearances. In short, we simply cannot afford to allow the North West of Scotland to lose its individuality. Anyone who should welcome this incursion can only be motivated by greed.

I think it would serve a very useful purpose if those who are against this violation of the Northern Highlands, write me. I would keep all names and addresses strictly private, making use of the comments when the right time came along.

I got a crop of letters from all quarters, one even from New Zealand, all whole-heartedly agreeing with everything said. This letter occasioned a certain amount of press replies, some of which were in favour of development so that one's pay-packet would be increased. Greed seemed to be the gist of those correspondents.

Mind you, whilst I am strongly in favour of progress, there is all the difference in the world between Development and Improvement; even 'balanced development' can find a useful place. In and out of season over the years, I have said various improvements were needed in Gairloch. To cite a few: an attractively built Information Bureau, Public Conveniences (I believe there is only one such building between Strathpeffer and Ullapool), a decent Village Hall on lines of the one at Poolewe, a road, Diabaig to Red Point (I advocated this to the Secretary of State for Scotland in 1965), and a few others of a minor nature. But to spend something like £4½m plus, is beyond all reason. It is a pity we people who live here were not consulted, and meetings arranged on lines of Isaiah, chapter I, verse 18 'Come now, let us reason together'. The majesty and serenity of this area would be utterly and finally lost by applying the lip-stick of such a development scheme. Just fancy suggesting swimming pools, when there are nine superb beaches at hand. I considered it to have been a piece of sheer cheek and impertinence—a slight on our intelligence—to have issued such a survey. There is the movement to 'Save the Argylls'; there must be a movement to 'Save the Highlands from Spoilation'. If not, and Planners have their way, it will result in catastrophic disaster. These designers need to think and walk warily; otherwise as an M.P. once said in the House Commons in 1960, they will have 'gone over a precipice and must walk warily!' I think he must have been an Irishman?

Then in August 1968 the chairman of the Highland and Islands Development Board had some scathing remarks to make of Highland landowners and I took that opportunity to have the following letter published in the Press on 23rd August . . . Caption being THESE MEN MUST CHANGE.

In opening the exhibition at Moy Hall, the chairman of the Highland Development Board 'took a swipe' at some Highland landowners inferring they did not accept the need for change, the caption in a Scottish national newspaper being, 'These men must change'.

I am not connected with business or owning land, but I disagree entirely with the learned Professor's jibe.

These so-called Planners (urbanisers of the countryside) are creeping into the Highlands all too fast with unsavoury ideas, and unless sanity prevails the time-honoured way of life in the Highlands will vanish; and with it, respect.

In the years to come, quiet will be priceless. The time to stop, look and drink in the never-ending panorama of the golden areas of Wester Ross and North-West Sutherland, will be gone. Pearls of a great price scattered through highly-paid supercilious officials dictated by Whitehall orbiting in cloud-cuckoo land.

Just think; agricultural land to the tune of 700 acres being filched for the Invergordon smelter plan!

People come up north to 'unwind' from their every day city strains; to seek what they are unable to find elsewhere in Britain. It is a fact that never before has this country been hit by such a prevalence of mental illness.

The Highlanders seem to be looked upon as sheep. Let me say, whatever failing we may have, we have not got sheep's hearts. Those in authority appear to be more concerned with their own image than with the country's image.

The magic of the Highlands, which Queen Victoria so passionately loved, is on the verge of extinction, should these 'magicians' continue to wave their wands so freely.

After this I went overseas to the Islands, and under the caption THE WIND OF CHANGE the following letter appeared in *The Stornoway Gazette* on 31st August 1968. I particularly did this because there are thirteen Councillors from Stornoway and other islands who are members of the Ross and Cromarty County Council.

I am sure the people of Lewis, and indeed all the Outer Isles, will have read with dismay of a recent academic survey made by students of the Glasgow School of Art, which in effect suggests Wester Ross be converted into a comprehensive 'multi-sports' area; and to cost at least £4½m.

In the Ross and Cromarty County Council there are 13 representatives from Lewis; and I feel sure they at heart will be appalled to think anything so foreign to the Highlands should have ever been given thought. It is certainly no credit to art to attempt to alter, desecrate or prostitute the uniqueness of this wonderful countryside.

People come up North and to the Isles, to 'unwind' from their everyday city strains; to seek what they are unable to find elsewhere in Britain—and they come back, time and time again.

In the years to come, quiet will be priceless; pearls of great human value scattered through highly paid planners with unsavoury ideas orbiting in cloud-cuckoo land.

Unless a firm stand is made, in another decade the Highlands, their villages, and above all the Sabbath, will become a vanished way of life. It is really very sad to think in the future we may see an aimless drifting generation turning tranquillity upside down. There will be many Glens of Weeping should that come to pass.

It is not given to the wisest of us to know where our destiny lies; but it is given to all of us to know where our duty lies.

This then completed my Press network over the entire north. All these extracts were sent to the various Depts. of State, and drew the usual replies of course, that my views had been noted with interest.

I had one personal letter from a noble Lord (amongst other titled personages) that I feel I should quote here, without divulging his name, viz.:

> I agree entirely. Some time ago as a Fellow of the Ancient Monument's Society I received their annual booklet and was struck by the remark of a prominent architect to the effect that it was difficult to calculate who had wrought more destruction to the centres of the most beautiful cities of Britain, the developers or urban town planners. Sad to say some of these ill-mannered louts are creeping into the Highlands with their unsavoury plans supported by the very organisations supposed to guard the Highlands. Of course most of them come from the same background as the above-mentioned people.

On the 18th May 1968, a Canadian citizen (of French origin) living in Ontario had a very pertinent letter in the the *Northern Times* to the effect of his horror at learning on his recent visit to this country of the proposal to erect a large electrical power transmission line across the Kyle of Sutherland and of the havoc caused by other forms of development, all of which he brings under the term 'desecration'; and he finally asks the question as to whether tourists or other forms of developments which have the durability of the pyramids about them, are more destructive of natural amenities?

So we are not alone!

No doubt these students on their whistle-stop visit would have seen a restaurant and shop here, called 'The Wild Cat'. It is a wonder this did not give them a cue to other colourful channels in their quest for further fanciful projects, such as Polar Bear Ice Cream Bar; Ben Hope's Panther Swimming Pool with Ben (3040 feet) trying to keep his distance; lady's seal-skin handbags as one of the store's special lines, since the Gulf Stream washes our coastline and seals are constantly bobbing up; and noticing something blue flitting through the birch trees imagine it to be Tarzan (in a boiler suit!). And going along further into the village of Strath, to the butcher's shop, finding deer carcases hanging up, and this could suggest a great local industry in producing deer-skin rugs? Then again, the square at Strath could lend itself to a nice Club building entered by swing-doors; to the right 'The Sheep Drovers' Club where the men, wearing black wide-brimmed hats and home-made hook-and-eye suits, could foregather to discuss all matters of sheep raising (in the old days it would be the rustlers on the look-out for stealing cattle), keeping their spirits up with the necessary amount of medicine as the atmosphere hotted-up; and through the swing-doors on the left—the ladies' club-room, appropriately called 'The Listening Post'. But at £4½m, perhaps their imagination had petered out?

Peat

A very large part of Wester Ross and Sutherland is covered by peat bogs, and to the casual visitor these bog-lands with their characteristic vegetable life seem uninteresting except for just a passing glance, to say to their friends back home, they had seen peat growing! and to say what a lovely smell pervades a room with a peat fire burning.

Peat-cutting for the winter fires. Peat is the centuries-old fuel in many parts of the Highlands and Islands. The vast deposits that remain, hold a great potential industry—there for the taking. One acre in ten of the land surface of Scotland is covered with peat. On the land-reclamation side, some 10,000 acres of moorland have been converted to green grazing sward in Lewis.

Peat is evidently a post-glacial deposit, and in the long ages past with the weather cool and wet, the growth of sphagnum moss would be encouraged and this is the main formation of peat. So it grew and accumulated over the long, long years. Peat deserves to be classed among the most interesting natural phenomena of the Highlands; not only the peat itself but the many objects preserved in it. At some depth at the bottom of bogs, hazel, birch, alder and willow have been found in perfect state—after centuries of time.

In some bogs hazel-nuts have been unearthed deep below the ground, as perfect as the day they dropped off the trees; some peat fields are full of the rose-beetle wings, still glittering in metallic lustre, which must have lain there embedded in these black, airtight 'silos' long ago; and from the masses discovered in many districts these beetles must have swarmed like the locusts in the old Egyptian days. It is very evident that in those far-off ages a different vegetation covered the earth when peat began to form and that the land was full of plants and insect life now extinct.

The usual impression of peat is that it is a very modern growth and quickly formed. Nothing could be further from the truth. Forest upon forest; peat upon peat; and so it came to pass.

Peat is also found at the bottom of some lochs—submarine peat bogs; and these too must be thousands of years old.

The Scottish Peat Committee have been investigating this peat problem for the last twenty years, and in their early 1962 final report, state that a peat industry providing jobs for 4000 workers and reclaiming tracts of land for farming, could be developed in Scotland.

More than 1,600,000 acres in Scotland are covered with deep peat, and workable deposits are put at 600 million tons of peat solids, equivalent to some 500 million tons of coal. One of the attractions of large-scale peat utilisation is the prospect of agricultural reclamation of the basal soil after clearance of the peat.

The calorific value of dry peat is about 8000 B.T.U./lb, some two-thirds the value for coal. The market garden value of peat used in Britain for horticultural purposes and for gardens is about £1,000,000. Peat has one key virtue in that it can soak up many times its own weight of water, and hold on to it for long periods. Nutrients added to peat make for strong growth, resulting in better plants, earlier flowers or crops. Peat can be compressed into such forms as briquettes, enabling transport costs to be cut. In Dublin about 50,000 tons of briquettes each year are used as a clean, easy-to-handle fuel. All in all, real positive attempts should be made in the Highlands to exploit this valuable natural asset; instead of just Reports and Findings.

In going over Struie Hill to Bonar Bridge, you will see near Altnamain, quite a big attempt at peat cutting—mechanically planned. An endless belt conveyor is used to put the peat cuttings right into lorries for despatch. In Sutherland you can pass miles of peat stacked neatly, almost at the roadside. These stacks are perfectly made—quite an art really—and many have nets thrown over them (weighted by stones at the four corners) to prevent the stacks being blown down by the winter gales.

Yes, I am sure, this industry could be developed on a big, profitable scale.

Accommodation and Food

The villages up north are more or less honey-combed with bed and breakfast (B. and B.) signs, and these spotlessly clean houses or crofts give you a nice cosy bed and a real hearty breakfast—porridge or cereals, crisply cooked bacon (and you're often asked if you'd like more than one egg and how you'd like it done), toast and butter, scones, oatcake, home-made jam and marmalade, and anything else you fancy (including a nice herring fried in oatmeal), and you generally get up from the table 'too full for words'. Few give lunches nowadays, and not so many give a full evening meal but compromise with high tea. And there's lots of hot water for washing or shaving as a rule. What is high tea?—just tea with something to it! and that something can be a lot; it is not only—even with the locals themselves—a family meal, but a real party piece. (In England, tea is just bread and butter and jam with a few cakes.) The perpetual tea pot, a big brown one as a rule in these old houses, is never off the hob. 'Scones—in living memory' you'll say.

> Lean and thin
> We stumble in;
> Fat and stout
> We waddle out!

You should never put sugar on your porridge. The old folk always had a cup of fresh milk beside them, taking one spoonful of porridge and then a spoonful of milk. And they had it well salted. Porridge in the grim old days was the barrier between poverty and malnutrition. Many old folk take a plate of porridge last thing at night. Oatmeal to the Scots is very much what rice is to the Chinese.

Now, coming to hotels, by and large they are good, but to my mind a large number of them fall down on the sweets. Some can't get away from just ice cream with a peach stuck in it and a wafer—'Peach Melba'; and a bought Arctic Roll, or jellies and fruit salads. Whereas there are endless nice tasty sweet dishes if the chef will only go to the necessary trouble. At one Highland hotel, as I didn't care for the choice of sweet, I asked for biscuits and cheese. Although it was lunch, the mini-skirted young girl came back, saying cheese was only served at dinner at night! And then coffee is too often charged as an extra. A good waiter or waitress should always be able to advise you as to what meat dish is good (and fresh) or whether it's coming to you out of the deep freeze. There's also the point that the *Chef's Special Dish* may not be quite the same if it happens to be the chef's day off! or if he is on duty, he may have toothache or a bit out of sorts which makes his expert touch with a sauce not quite so piquant as it should be.

In one Highland hotel, I made mention in a former book as to sitting on a settee in the small lounge, and the springs came through the worn-out upholstery as I plonked down, to give me a hard foundation, letting out a twang like Big Ben striking the hour. Four years later I called in at the same hotel for lunch. The same settee was there and I sat on it gingerly. Big Ben still struck the hour! Some of these hotels have to take in bus parties to equalise their finances more. Some of these parties can be quite noisy and as soon as thirty five of them get out of the coach and into the hotel, it would seem the whole place belonged to them. One man had his dinner wearing a woollen cap with a toorie on it. Another was eating his trifle with a knife and fork. And then you get the waitress carrying three or four different orders around the party's table and you can hear the following casually asked with a smile 'are you the ham, madam?' 'Yes.' And another young lady said 'She was the trifle,' whilst a robustly-built tall chap said he 'was the chicken'! Quite amusing really. And then as to having your whisky, someone I remember once said 'there's no bad whisky. It's just that some is better than others.' Regarding this beverage, it's a common saying 'not to drown the miller', and one man when asked if he took water with it, said disdainfully 'Ah didna' think whisky could swim'.

Then the coach leaves, and they all go on their way rejoicing to visit the various scenic spots that have been marked out for them by their English tour promoters; and they'll be sending off picture post-cards by the dozen telling their friends perhaps, that viewing from the top of a hill or glen into a grey swirl of rain 'we viewed the mist, but missed the view'. Either that, or 'forty-eight hours of Scotch mist—some day it will be fine'.

In their travels up in Sutherland, they will pass shepherds with their stick and collie dogs, remarking how quaint it all is—a sight they never come across in the cities. But whether they could understand the few gibberish words their master says to these beautiful well-trained animals, such as 'Waira mi bosh', we will never know. Nor will their friends.

There is another thing that I find fault with in these various hotels; namely the prices charged for drink. When travelling I like to indulge in a small aperitif before lunch, and I keep to the same routine. Up to a year or so ago the general charge for my meagre requirement was 3s. 6d. Granted the cost of liquor has risen slightly the last two years, the prices charged vary considerably for the self-same aperitif. In Dingwall it was (last year, 1968) 3s. 8d; in the Lairg area 5s. 6d.; in Durness region 4s.; in Fort Augustus 3s. 9d.; in Fort William 7s. In drawing attention to such discrepancies, I am generally told it is due to transport, or head office laying down the prices. There should be a standardisation, and the point as to transport is ridiculous. I could understand that if you were ordering a case or so; but for a small drink in a small glass—well!

It should be remembered the average American tourists like to surround themselves with home comforts; expecially central heating. They look at the hotels for service lavishly dispensed by traditionally-costumed waitresses; and this aspect never seems to occur to the management up in the real Highlands. They will expect—and pay for—a toilet sealed with a piece of paper carrying the legend 'this seat has been sanitised for your personal protection'. Yes, this *is* the case in America. Apart from 'I'm Backing Britain', a slogan like 'I'm Eating Scottish', at our Highland hotels should be the password. No need for a 'I'm Drinking Scotch' slogan, for people are doing that already.

There is difficulty, to my mind, in getting *real* Scottish meals in both restaurants and hotels. True, you can get roast Scotch beef, steaks etc. but what's wrong with good wholesome mince and dough-balls, *and* haggis (and fish haggis too), cod puddings; home-made steak, kidney and mushroom pie? And what about the luscious herring? There is too much warmed-up tasteless meat and chicken. And what about calf's brain—in other words cervelles—a most delicate dish, served fried with asparagus and mushrooms. More often than not, if you ask the chef or waiter (or mini-skirted girl again!) as to such a delicacy, you may be told the butcher doesn't have enough brains to go round! As though there are not thousands of sheep in the Highlands. Perhaps in this day and age, and with so much agricultural science floating around, one asks the question if our sheep and cattle are being raised without heads at all. Something tasty, and away from home, makes an enormous difference. I have found these days that in serving roast beef, no Yorkshire pudding comes along.

In a report made December 1968 by the Tourist Board, after an exhaustive personal survey of over 400 establishments it was found that many of the Highland hotels were much out-of-date to current needs; in fact it was said some had been found so deficient that they would not be included in their accommodation guide.

This makes sorry reading. I have hinted my own personal experiences, and agree; though at the same time—as in England— in travelling around, you soon find the right places at which to stay. The others, you just give them the go-by. Heating—or rather the lack of it—is a failing; and I strongly object having to put a shilling in the slot-meter for a radiator in my bedroom if paying a high price for condescending to stay in mine-host's hotel. Electric blankets should be universal in all decent hotels; the day of the hot water bottle—rubber or stone—is long past, and what a saving it makes in the chambermaid's duties. Bath-rooms/toilets are far and away inadequate, especially if the toilet is part and parcel of the bathroom. There should be separate toilets and separate bathrooms. At one fancy-priced hotel in Sutherland, there was only one such combined convenience for a whole corridor; and sometimes one had to go downstairs to a convenience that outsiders could use. Many kitchens need modernising.

It is *not* a case of building a whole lot of new hotels in the Highlands and giving lavish grants right and left; it is a case of bringing those that advertise for custom in the usual flowery manner, bang-up-to-date. It's as simple as that; and these particular places should not look to the Highlands and Islands Development Board for major assistance. Private enterprise should take that upon its own shoulders and initiative. After all, these hotels *do* make a profit, and its no use spoon-feeding all and sundry.

And what a tremendous difference it makes, if you have a pretty cheerful waitress attending you—not one who can't care less. At one hotel, in ordering my pudding course, the girl came with it and smilingly said, 'Your sweet, sir'; to which I said, 'And you're pretty lovely yourself!' She altered my short week-end to a long week-end!

In some 25 guineas-a-week hotels you seldom get thin wafery toast (Melba toast); and I was in one place for a whole week, and there was never anything but unattractive boiled potatoes served, and some mornings, no bacon.

Superstition

Although I have previously touched upon 'Second Sight', this heading comes more under Superstitious Beliefs. At one time it was customary for a sixpence to be put in a baby's bath water, or sewn into its vest to keep away The Evil Eye. Another method of banishing evil, was to bore a hole in a knotted part of a walking stick, and occasionally peep through it. Fishermen going to their boats, should they speak to a minister would assuredly have bad luck, and no fish. To ensure good luck in the home, it was deemed necessary that beds be in line with the floorboards—never facing the door. Another superstition was that a child's hair cut at new moon, kept in good condition. A Brora lady was visiting a friend who lived in an old house on the outskirts of that village. She was sitting beside an old-fashioned fireplace, when the door opened of its own accord. Her friend said 'Don't worry, it is only the ghost; she often does that'. Sometime later the house changed hands, and when the fireplace was being replaced, the bones of an infant were found behind the stonework. The bones were buried, and the ghost no longer opens the sitting-room door. It is said that in one of the upstair windows of the same house, a light shines out from a room that has no lamp.

Superstitious beliefs used to be rife amongst village herdsmen up north, who on 1st May of every year, gathered on an open piece of land to celebrate the annual BEL-TEIN. It was quite unheard of for any man present to arrive empty-handed, and consequently there was a plentiful supply of eggs, butter, oatmeal, milk, beer and whisky for the occasion. The ceremony opened with a square trench being cut in the ground, but with care taken to ensure that the turf in the middle remained undisturbed. Here a fire was lit, and on it was prepared a caudle consisting of the eggs, butter, oatmeal and milk. When ready, a few drops were spilled on the ground by way of a sacrifice. Next the herdsmen took a piece of oatcake, shaped in a most unusual manner. When prepared for baking, nine raised pillars of oatmeal were added to the normally flat biscuit, and each one was dedicated either to the supposed protector or destroyer of the various farm animals. Facing the fire, each herdsman broke off one of the raised pieces, throwing it into the fire, at the same time reciting 'This I give to thee, preserve thou my cows; this to thee, preserve thou my sheep' . . . and so on. The performance is repeated a second time, but on this occasion, the dedications are directed to such animals as birds, fox and eagle in the hope that it might dissuade them from attacking the domestic birds and animals. The ritual completed the participants feasted and this was washed down with the beer and whisky. In some areas and on the first Monday in every quarter it was customary for Highlanders to sprinkle the cattle with urine.

There are certain old Highland customs to mark a death. As the end of an old Islesman approached, he gave urgent instructions in Gaelic to the nurse who was attending him; and she took all the measures that he required of her. Beside the bed, on a small table, she laid a saucer which contained bread and some salt. These were for his provision on his Long Journey. Beside the saucer she set a tumbler of water, and, also on the table-top, she put a lighted candle to light his road. Next she opened the top half of the window, to allow his soul free passage. Lastly she stopped the clock on the mantlepiece, and then turned all the glass fronted pictures and a mirror face to the wall. The dying man watched these preparations anxiously and when they were finished he sighed with relief; and waited patiently for the end. Soon after his death, the nurse snuffed the candle leaving it and the provisions beside the bed till next morning. Then, the window was shut, the clock restarted, and the pictures and mirror returned to their normal positions. The reason why all the glass had to be turned round was lest anyone should happen to look into the glass or mirror and should see Whoever-Might-Come to escort the soul onwards.

Funerals on an island used to be big social occasions for the

men, where people took a long time about dying. Fathers and
sons left ploughs, sheep and fish hooks, and came along eagerly to
renew old acquaintances; to exchange news and views, to spit
reflectively and enjoy the unaccustomed wearing of a gold watch
and chain. Uniformity of wear was observed; bowler hats and a
half bottle of whisky in the hip pocket! Islanders wore bowler
hats only for funerals and their own marriages, so that a nono-
genarian might go to his rest, without having had it on his head
more than a dozen times.

In the old days the people used to say 'Better a good funeral
than a poor wedding'. Then it was necessary to carry provisions
when men had to travel long distances on foot carrying the
coffin across rough and hilly country to the place of burial.
And the provisions carried were the proverbial oat-cakes, cheese
and whisky. The more important the person the bigger and
better was the banquet.

To ward off evil spirits, witchcraft and the like in olden days
up north, one practice was for two of the household to collect a
bucket of water running under a nearby bridge on New Year's
Eve, carrying it home, not speaking to anyone they met. Then,
on New Year's Day, the man of the house would give each
member a drink of the water, then sprinkle it around the whole
house. In that manner it was supposed evil would not enter
their dwelling.

Closely allied to superstition is witchcraft; and here is the
story of one Donald Mackay of Golspie who was the last person
to be hanged in Dornoch in the year 1738.

He was working diligently on the road, when up leaped a
hare from under his feet. He lifted his spade and struck catching
the hare a blow and knocked it over. But it recovered, getting
into the cover of some bushes. Later that day an old woman who
had the name of being a witch, was found dead, and her body had
an ugly wound similar to that which Donald's spade had inflicted
on the hare. It was clear to most people that the witch had been
masquerading in the shape of a hare, and she had only herself to
blame.

So there was some surprise when Donald was arrested on the
charge of murder; for it was generally expected that after a formal
trial he would be acquitted. But he was sentenced to death, and
was hung on Cnoc na Croiche, the Gallows Hill in Dornoch.

Then there is the 'Curse of Scotland'—the nine of diamonds, and superstitious beliefs are many over this.

Mary, Queen of Scots introduced a card game to her court, *Comette*, in which the nine of diamonds was the winning card, and this is said to have reduced many noble families to penury. In another game called *Pope Joan*, the nine of diamonds represented the Pope, and since the Pontiff was said to be anti-Christ by the Scottish Reformers, the context of 'curse' can be seen. The word 'curse' seen as a corruption of 'cross' gave rise to the nine of diamonds seen in early sets of cards as the saltire of St. Andrew's Cross. Another version says the nine of diamonds was known as 'The Justice Clerk'—a reference to Lord Justice Clerk Ormiston, who was reviled for his severity during the 1715 Rebellion.

Since Campbell of Glenlyon played cards with his Macdonald hosts the night before the Massacre of Glencoe, it was natural that a belief should arise that made the order for the next day's butchery to be written on a playing card. The Duke of Cumberland is alleged to have written a 'No Quarter' order at Culloden on the nine of diamonds playing card. There is also a connection between diamonds and monarchy, *i.e.* every *ninth* King of Scotland was a curse to his country. John Dalrymple, first Earl of Stair, and the real villain of Glencoe had an heraldic coat of arms, and on a saltire azure *nine* lozenges of the field (*i.e.* the nine of diamonds) appeared.

Mary Queen of Scots (Mary Stuart) 1542–87, fascinated men in her time, and has fascinated poets and historians ever since. She sheds very bright rays of light from the centre of a very dark legend. In her character she is a peculiar mixture of victim and villainess. She was no 'Pearl'. She was a victim because she was caught in the national, the dynastic and the religious crosscurrents of her time. From this viewpoint, there is much pathos in the story of the child betrothed at the age of five to 'the French Dauphin and kept under the care of the Guises' for ten years; then after the death of her husband, sent back as Queen of Scotland. She was a Catholic having to rule the country of John Knox, the only man to resist her charms. As Queen of Scotland she was a menace to her cousin Elizabeth on the English throne ('Defender of the Faith') by her potential role in the ancient feud between Scotland and England, and as an arch-plotter and emissary of Rome and France, threatening the civil peace in Protestant England. She was deeply involved in the murder of her husband Lord Darnley (whom she married in 1565 when only 23 years of age) by Bothwell. Then she married him within six months of the crime in 1567. She was later forced to abdicate, imprisoned at Fotheringay Castle awaiting trial for her supposed involvement in the plot of Babington to murder Queen Elizabeth; and was duly executed.

Now to End in Lighter Vein

Many of the Hebridean place-names can give rise to a certain amount of amusement in the way they are given a twist. 'Once upon a time there was a man called Ben Becula who was much Harris-sed lest he might Lewis his life. Soay took a cocktail of Eigg, and Rum, though it seemed Eriskay drink, especially as he wasn't Uist to it, and anything he thought might Appin. Shortly he said, "Iona feel a little Tiree"—and he knew he Shuna swallowed the Muck—"so Islay me down and en-Jura little pain". Later he was heard to Colonsay, "I hear my final Coll". So his soul went to Skye and they took his body away in a Barra and made it into a Little Minch. As for his poor wife Lis-more, she Canna bear being so a Knoydart. Indeed it's a wonder the shock of his being thus Stornoway has St. Kilda'.

I hope this has caused a little merriment; just like the stoat and the weasel? 'What's the difference?' I was once asked. Not knowing, I was told, 'well a weasel is (w)easily distinguished, but a stoat is (s)totally different!' I hope readers managed to ferret that out? Slàinte Mhath!

The Tartan and the Kilt

The Tartan of the Gael, long since adopted by other Scots as a national symbol, and reluctantly acknowledged by the War Office for use within the British Army has now invaded the world of fashion and 'haute couture'; imitated today from Paris to Peking. The Gaelic word for this material is 'BREACHAN', and the word tartan is derived from the French 'tartaine'— originally given to a certain kind of fabric, regardless of colour. Before the '45 Rebellion, when tartan of one sort or another was almost universally worn in the Highlands, the yarn for the 'breachan' was spun and dyed by the womenfolk. The weaving, too, was done by local craftsmen, and the design carefully made. The casual observer seldom realises just how few colours are actually employed in a tartan.

With the destruction of the clans after the '45, and the ruthless devastation of the Highlands, the Act prohibiting the wearing of the tartan was but the seal on Whitehall's determination to root out and destroy the Celtic Highland way of life. And so, the great majority of so-called clan tartans in use today, cannot be ante-dated much beyond 1800.

The Highlanders have worn a form of tartan from as early as the 16th century. The ban imposed on the tartan in 1747, was repealed in 1781.

The length of the kilt? It should be worn to *just* above the knee, or if kneeling down, then about one inch from the floor. If a kilt pin is to be worn on the apron of the kilt—although this is not essential, it should be of a simple design. Then there is the *Sgian Dubh* worn on the outside of the leg in the right stocking.

It is interesting to learn how the kilt came into use. Originally the Highlander wore a very simple, utilitarian garment, and the kilt as we know it today, all arose from a certain Thomas Rawlinson, an Englishman (a *Sasunnach*) who became a legendary figure in the 18th century, about 1726, eleven years after the first Jacobite rising of 1715.

Thomas Rawlinson, a Quaker, who had iron foundries ('bloomsmithies' as they were then called) in Furness, was born in 1689, and was a man of unusual vision and energy. In 1726 he launched a project for the smelting of iron in the Highlands; in Glengarry in the Great Glen. His selection of this spot was on account of the great wealth of timber there. Unfortunately this venture was a failure, due to high freightage costs and poor quality ore; and it only lasted ten years. He had an agreement with John Macdonell, 12th of Glengarry, to restore Invergarry Castle (which had been burnt down by Government troops, as the Macdonells had supported the Stuart cause) for his own occupation during his lease. The idea of a *Sasunnach* living in the Chief's castle was bitterly resented by Glengarry's followers, and many attempts were made on his life.

In 1729, Highland dress consisted of the belted-plaid (*breachan-feile*), a single garment gathered in and belted at the waist, covering the upper and lower parts of the body. It consisted of a single piece of cloth, 12 ells in length. Although Rawlinson thought this dress was attractive and maybe just the thing for their moorland life, it was extremely awkward whilst working in his foundry. That they should wear trousers, like an Englishman, would be unthinkable to these dour Scottish workers. One night, some soldiers sought shelter from a storm in Invergarry Castle; and there was one, a Private Parkinson, who was a Regimental tailor from England, who was very taken with seeing this Highland dress. A Highlander came in, wet through, took off his belted-plaid to dry it at the fire; and then Parkinson saw it was but *one* single garment. Rawlinson mentioned to this tailor how awkward the dress was for foundry work, and wondered if it could not be made into two garments; a garment pleated as before, attached to the belt, and an upper garment to be used as a cloak or blanket? Parkinson took the necessary measurements, and thereafter the *feile-beag* (the little kilt) came into being. This 'crime' of altering the national, Highland dress, proved at once popular and became the official dress of Highland regiments.

Rawlinson returned to England in 1736, and he died the following year, only forty-eight years of age; yet it was he, an Englishman, who designed the kilt.

Closely associated with the tartan are the GAMES. The Highland games held nearest to Gairloch is in Skye, at Portree, and take place generally the last week of August in a hollow—a natural amphitheatre—only five minutes' walk from the square. The brae to the hollow is generally lined on both sides with tents put up by gypsies professing to have the power to tell you your fortune, as well as selling many odds and ends. You sit around the hillside looking down on the hollow where platforms have been built for the Highland dancing contests. Near by, in the specially reserved seats, sit the gentry—the judges—all bedecked in their full Highland regalia, sashes and kilts, the whole setting a veritable colourama.

I have seen some athletes of wonderful 'frame' at these games; some who can lift and throw a 28-lb weight as far as 70 feet or so, as though it were but a small stone; nae bother at a'. I think some of the porridge-makers must have photographed these giants for their carton covers; Tarzans of the Tartans we could rightly call them.

Thousands attend these games and the contestants come from far and near. These games continue to be a magic draw to all and sundry.

Of course, Braemar on Royal Deeside, miles away from here, is the hub of the Highland games, and with Royalty present, it dominates the world in such sports. 'Cabers and capers', a wonderful day of events, personalities and splendour, the like of which you will never see in any other realm of sport. August and September are the most colourful months in Scotland when all the various clans foregather and wage war in the tossing of the caber, putting the weight, throwing the hammer, dancing Highland flings; the tug-of-war, playing the pipes, and in so far as Portree is concerned the 20-odd mile marathon race up the mountains and down the glens.

The tossing of the caber is really a terrific athletic effort; for it weights about two hundredweight of larch, fifteen to twenty feet in length, and is about ten inches diameter at the thick end, tapering to three or four inches at the top. 'Some piece of log?'

CHAPTER 16

THE NEW YEAR

NOLLAIG CHRIDHEIL; BLIADHNA MHATH ÙR. In whatever language, a Happy Christmas and a Good New Year, is the universal theme of the age-long greeting which heralded the dawn of Christendom, and all the joy involved. The glad tidings and the good wishes accompanying them all through these centuries engender goodwill amongst us all—a pattern that has been a salient factor in Christian society ever since; and it is even more necessary today as at any time in the past. It is the season when the old and the young, the sick, the needy and lonely are remembered. It is the season—or it should be—for Peace combined with happiness; it seems incredible that mankind has not yet been able to erradicate forever what has been so foul a blot on the escutcheon of each succeeding generation—War, with all its misery and horror. The Peace promised to mankind is still far from being supreme; and so the warmth of feeling at the beginning of a New Year is therefore all the more necessary if only to remind us of what our lives on this planet should really mean.

*   *   *

Taken as a whole, Scotland pays little attention to Christmas in relation to what it pays the New Year. Of all the days in the year, *Hogmanay* (New Year's Eve) stands out first and foremost; the eve of Scotland's greatest feast. 'Hogmanay!' the very name savours of intrigue. Many overseas visitors must think it is something to eat or drink! Another form of haggis maybe? And Scots are born with the conviction that New Year's Eve was the invention of their own native genius; so 'tis well to bear that in mind when you go to a real Scots party in the

Highlands, where you'll be surrounded by strapping tall Highlanders and pretty buxom lassies. Nollaig, Nollaig, Mhor.
Yule was unknown as a name for Christmas in the more Celtic
parts of Scotland, where the name is NOLLIG, a term derived
from the Latin ecclesiastical name *Dies Natalis*. Nollaig Mhor,
(big Christmas) was used to distinguish this festival from Nollaig
Bheag, little Christmas, or New Year's Day. Candle Night
(OIDHCHE CHOINNIE) is now a name given to Christmas night.
The period during which the New Year festivities occurred, and
sometimes before and after Nollaig, was popularly known as
'The Black Cuttings of Christmas', from its liability to tempestuous weather. Similar sayings are current in the Highlands,
as in the south. 'A green Yule makes a fat kirkyard' has its
counterpart in a Gaelic proverb, viz. 'Christmas without snow is
ill-favoured'.

*   *   *

In the old days, New Year's Day in the Highlands was
celebrated on the 12th January. Some Highlanders however
seem to keep it from the 1st to the 12th inclusive! The very
old custom of 'first-footing' in the Highlands (*i.e.* Hogmanay,
the eve of visiting and wishing one another a 'Guid New Year')
was that you gave the 'letter-in' a coin in exchange for something
he or she brought in; and after a drink and a bite, you then let
the first-footer(s) out by the back door. On the morning of
each New Year's Day, be it a Sunday or week-day, the Free
Church and the Free Presbyterian Church hold a service, which
is more in the nature of a discourse than of an ordinary Sabbath-
day worship; a means of prayer in fortifying oneself for the
ensuing twelve month's worldly affairs and pitfalls of life.

New Year's Day is a monument to error and human fallibility;
although a holiday, it is in no sense a Holy day. Its only God is
two-faced Janus, who belongs to the whole of January. It falls
seven-twelfths of the way between Christmas and Twelfth
Night. In terms of the most elementary logic, it should coincide
with the winter solstice when the solar year completes its cycle,
and starts anew; but instead of coinciding, it misses the solstice
by ten days. In different parts of the world, New Year's Day
or its equivalent has in years gone by been observed in almost
every month. It has been governed by planting time, harvest, the

phases of the inconstant moon, the return of migrant birds. Not until the 16th century was 1st January commonly accepted as the beginning of the New Year. Now, it is a fixture on our calendar, essential to the accountant and the tax collector—but otherwise of little significance. Perhaps that is why we tend to load the day with symbolism? It should have a new snow cover to hide the past year's errors and provide a fresh page in every strath and glen? With the sun shining with the promise of a better tomorrow; and the wind just that bit cold enough to temper man's arrogance.

And there should be a fire on the hearth, so we can draw on our pile of logs from the garage or coal shed and get a blaze going at this seasonal time; and relaxing, the sweet hissing made from the open fire lends and adds itself to the festivities of food and drams, turkey and rum-butter for the plum pudding. Different logs give different glows. Birch is my particular favourite for it does not spark or spit like larch. The former gives off a yellow flame, the latter more orangey. Beech is stubborn in its deeper orange. And outside, if true to form, white prevails—snow-white, but no dwarfs, only the fairies! If the logs be mixed then my mind turns to the rainbow; the 'End of the Rainbow' in fact. From the kitchen comes smells galore, soup, turkey, stuffing, freshly made mince pies and the plum pudding gently rolling on its cushion of steam in the inner-steam-pan. And after the logs, later peat takes over as a final curtain at the witching hour of midnight when the fairies *do* come out to play and you hear the strains of *auld lang syne*; and *we'll tak' a cup o' kindness yet*.

This is not a smokeless area, and so logs and coal don't come under the hammer, and the bowl of water beside the electric fire in the whim of humidity has lost its place up here. Heather can, and will, be burnt at large to help produce better and more tender food for the grouse, and we are free of diesel oil fumes from the No. 12 bus. In short we can live as we like; we might be as far off from authority as the astronauts rounding the moon. We are outside the general orbit of science; the moon can keep on rolling round, the tide can keep on ebbing and flowing, the salmon will continue to leap, and our good old logs will continue to glow till well past midnight. And Heaven? it is still beyond 256,000 miles away. And Life? it is very close at hand here in the stillness of the Highlands—in fact a year closer than it was this time last year. And we say to ourselves 'may He who was able to wrap Elijah with His mantle, guide us safely through the years that are yet to be—and may they be many and happy'. At this time and season, we look backward with gratitude; we look onward with hope; we look upward with confidence. Twelve months (a new year) is not a long time really, and yet how utterly unpredictable it is. How often are we taken by surprise in the year that has closed; sometimes to the increase of our joy, and at others to the deepening of our sorrow. All this goes to the weaving of life's pattern—which is not always fair-isle—but we are taught to accept our providential changes in humble submission to the sovereign Will of a higher order, whereupon all things shall work together for our good.

The New Year usually heralds the coldest days of winter, when the streamers of the Northern lights dance overhead, and the frosts seal the watercourses, and drive the wading birds to the saltings.

How this planet once looked can only be surmised; how our part of this planet looks now can only be appreciated and enjoyed by living to the full in its unique individuality with strings of pearls around us.

The Highlanders are like the Chinese; they put more accent, as I have said, on the New Year than on Christmas. On all their festival dates, fireworks, crackers etc. are let off by the thousand. We don't do that here though. The county road men always work on Christmas day; it is just an ordinary day to them. But New Year's Day is a holiday all round. Only the last two or three years, have the local stores closed on Christmas day; before then, they kept open. The shepherd pays no attention to these special festival days, nor to any other festivals or holidays. He's always on duty and at some periods working overtime. No unofficial 'down tools' for him. Not the least attractive sight to a visitor in the summer is that of a weather-beaten man, crook in hand, dogs at his heel, striding across the moors; his shrill whistles are understood by his collies and with ears and eyes they capture his every command, huddling the sheep together and bringing them back downhill. In fact the hills themselves seem to be in unison with the dogs. The overall picture has an air of romance about it. This may well be through

K

the summer, but then not so romantic when autumn comes along with mists, followed by the icy winds and drifts of winter, and then the anxious days of lambing. Hard work, long hours, a remote house; and certainly he doesn't work by the clock, for animals don't understand what B.S.T. means! There are many superstitions about seeing the first lamb of the new year. If it is standing still, it means a year of tranquillity; if feeding, a year of hunger; if lying down, a year of sickness. Should the lamb happen to be romping about, then a year of ups and downs. But the most favourable omen is to see your first lamb with its head towards you. This means prosperity.

These, then, are my general comments on The New Year; most likely the supplies purchased with painstaking foresight at pre-Jenkins' prices were consumed (although 'drunk' is really the operative word) prematurely—unless they had been pad-locked and put out of sight. Of course if the contents *had* dis-appeared beforehand, then the excuse for dashing out for new supplies would be that Hong Kong 'flu had crossed the McLellan Line, and one had to have something in the house to combat it; and alcohol (100° proof if possible) is the generally accepted medicine prescribed by the B.M.A. for such a plague!! Syrup of figs, or prune juice would be of no avail in such circumstances; at any rate not to the hard thinker, for there must be something handy when the grandfather clock strikes twelve, and the foghorn of the north-west—'Radio 5 Sandwood Bay'—blasts its sweet music in your ears, and your mind turns to ghosts and more ghosts and phantom sailors, and you find yourselves lifting glasses and talking Double-Dutch; to say nothing of Esperanto-Gaelic in a Brittany accent. You've eaten and over-eaten; in fact the whole household has eaten as much as would feed all the Biafrans for a week, or more. And should you have a TV set, it would result in Cilla Black, Lulu and company singing pop songs and Billy Smart's Circus performing to a sitting room of sleeping beauties! With snores as off stage sounds. Then you wake up and say Happy New Year, and wait for the echo coming through, loud, though not quite clear—a bit muddled you ken, due to atmospherics—'the same to you'; whereupon you say 'the same to ourselves', and the voice over Radio 4 Scotland says, 'shall I repeat that?' Then, for the sixteenth year in succession in the last programme before the Watchnight

Service, my friend Jack House will be looking back on his own personal year in 'The Year That's Awa'.

. . . Farewell to the old year; the last page is written, with each deed recorded. The record now stands. So hail to the New Year, let each precious moment, be counted a pearl beyond value or cost; and spend not one hour in useless endeavour; for time that is wasted is time that is lost. . . .

And so another year is ushered in; and as you wander back home, you'll hear lots of 'Guid nicht's', lots of 'Guid nicht Hector', 'come awa' Sandy' and the strains of 'Should auld acquaintance be forgot' gradually dying out as you put the distance between yourself and that merry gathering. The lights in the various windows, are flicked off . . . then silence.

> . . . and the night shall be filled with music
> and the cares that infest the day
> shall fold their tents like the Arabs
> and as silently steal away . . .

The crofter and his wife will just sink into the cosy chairs by the fireside embers, for 'twill not be long before the man of the house has to be up and doing—this time working, not 'New Yearing'; the hens to be let out, and water and a good hot mash given them; snow to be shovelled away from the door and paths, and maybe a few crumbs put on the window sill for the robin.

*   *   *

So far, I have made little mention of Christmas, only to the effect that Scotland as a whole, and the Highlands in particular don't look upon Christmas Day as anything special; and they certainly don't foster the Santa Claus belief in their children, albeit to my mind it is a beautiful, kindly belief; for the youngsters open to Santa, the floodgates of affection to his generosity and simpleness, since the kindly spirit of Christmas spreads its radiance far and wide. The priceless gift of Christmas is meant just for the heart, and we receive it only when we become a part. The season for joy and merry making; for giving and taking.

> To take His priceless pearls of Love, *reach out and you receive,*
> For the only payment that God asks, is just that *you believe.*

'Silent Night', perhaps the world's most famous carol was actually composed by accident, because the church organ in the tiny village of Oberndorf broke down on Christmas Eve. It broke down, of all the curious reasons, because a mouse had gnawed a hole through some worn leather bellows. When the organist Franz Gruber, a 31-year old village schoolmaster sat down for a rehearsal on the morning of 24th December 1818 (a hundred and fifty years ago) not a note came out—just a soft breathy sigh. Gruber conferred anxiously with the assistant priest, Joseph Mohr. How could they have a Christmas Eve Mass without music? There was no chance of repairing the organ quickly, for the organ mender only came with the melting of the snows in spring. Gruber and Mohr were quite ordinary men, but each was unconsciously blessed with a strand of genius. As they contemplated the mute and useless organ Father Mohr said, 'I have no idea, but I have written a little poem, but perhaps if you set it to music—two parts for your voice and mine, perhaps a chorus for the children with guitar accompaniment...? Gruber was a competent musician; he could improvise, and he could compose in a hurry. At first he tried to find a theme, but as his fingers wandered over the spinet in his study he suddenly realised that this was a simple lullaby, 'sleep my child and rest; I am watching over you'. Pretty soon a piece of paper was covered with a rough score. And then Gruber took his guitar from the wall and transcribed the accompaniment. It was then easy to put together a plain, home-spun cradle song. When 'Silent Night' was performed that night in the tiny church, its impact on the world was no greater than a grain of sand; in fact the score and music were almost thrown away. But when the organ-mender, Karl Mauracher came in the spring, he displayed a casual interest and took the music away. For years the carol remained unknown. Then a Dresden music publisher heard a performance by a wandering quartet and transcribed it. For the first time 'Silent Night' was published as 'Tyrolean Folksong', authors unknown. Like a stone in a placid pool the circles made by the modest hymn spread ever wider. German emigrants took it to the New World, where it was plucked on the banjos of the westward-bound pioneers; even missionaries took it into every foreign tongue from Hindu to Eskimo. Yet Mohr died unknown and destitute in 1848—there was not even enough money to bury him. By the time Gruber, who had become a choir director died in 1865, his part in the composition had been discovered. King Frederick of Prussia, intrigued by the carol, ordered the score to be traced to its source. But even then Gruber earned nothing from it.

How strange that this apparent trifle, dashed off in an emergency, should have achieved imperishable fame. Stranger still to think that a cold and hungry mouse perpetrated a deed and initiated a chain of events that was to resound to the ends of the earth.

> Christmas and New Year . . .
> And in God's Holy Sight
>   No man is yellow, black or white,
>   And Peace on Earth cannot be found
>   Until we meet on common ground.

We stand once more at the end of the year with mixed emotions of hope and fear, Hope for the peace we long have sought, Fear that our hopes will come to naught. . . .

The Holly. . . . Because holly grows in most parts of the world, for centuries it has been used as a decoration at festivals. In ancient times people believed that anyone who wore a wreath made of the berries would be gifted with second sight. Holly bears fruit and stays green in winter; thus it became a symbol of immortality. During the rise of the early church, many Christmas legends were linked to holly. One says that holly was the burning bush from which God spoke to Moses in the wilderness. In certain early yule celebrations holly represented the male, and ivy the female; and whichever was brought into the house first at Christmas told whether the husband or the wife would rule the home for the next year.

CHAPTER 17

HIGHLAND PEARLS

WHAT irritates the oyster makes the pearl; but not up in the north-west of Scotland, nor I hope in reading through these pages, has any sense of irritation been caused in uncovering the many pearls of beauty, both in respect of places and the life led by the Highlanders and their families—unchanged in an aching, changing world.

Millions of years ago northern Scotland slipped. It moved sixty-five miles south westward forming what is now known as the Great Glen; along the line of the fault, three lochs mirror its mountain walls, and boats pass along them for twenty-two miles of artificial waterway, linking them into the Caledonian canal. Striking still northward you come into the Highlands proper, through the wide sweep of Glencoe traversing the 'great fault' of the Great Glen you are then bound, for miles and miles and through vast moorland, ready to explore the timeless beauty of the innumerable lochs and lochans and mighty mountains of the far north-west. Here you come across the poetry of place-names that produce a golden ring in the vast area of Sutherland. Moorlands purple with heather, forests blazing with autumn's firey tints, beaches white and golden under the September sun; blue seas and sparkling streams wherever you turn. Small wonder late summer and autumn in these parts has its devotees. Once seen the extraordinary mountains and landscape are never forgotten. It is not their geological antiquity alone which impresses most visitors, but their massive shapes towering above the surrounding and seemingly endless moors; Suilven, Canisp and Stac Polly are three of the outstanding chain that run inland behind LOCHINVER. Suilven especially standing guard behind this small township of 280 souls. To say nothing of the other notable mountains further north, Ben Loyal, Ben Hope, Arkle, Ben Stack and the peaks (Sail Ghorm and Sail Garbh) of Quinag, this latter near Kylesku ferry. I may have missed naming many more, but what's the odds in such a land so full of Nature? Through all these panoramic views you cannot but realise you are in a land of quiet efficiency, into a peace untouched by the world's panic— a deep satisfaction and rest in hospitable surroundings; memorable mountains, lochs and lochans—the richest of memories, the priceless pearls, not only of Nature, but of those who inhabit it all.

The English lakes could be plonked into Rannoch Moor easily and not be seen. Snowdon, 3500 feet, would be dwarfed by Ben Nevis at 4400 feet odd; the Macgillycuddy Reeks in southern Ireland cannot be compared with Liathach, 3456 feet in the Torridons, or An Teallach, 3500 feet in Ross-shire; let alone the Cuillin range in Skye. Scotland is not 'multum in parvo', but 'multum in multo'—overwhelmingly vast and endlessly varied. Scotland's land area is two-thirds that of England, and yet London and district alone out-numbers Scotland's population. I often feel we do not fully appreciate our heritage; as that grand Scottish song has it

> . . . For these are my mountains, and this is my glen
> The braes of my childhood will know me again;
> No land's ever claimed me, tho' far I did roam
> For these are my mountains, and I have come home . . .

In respect of Scottish mountaineering one often comes across the word MUNRO. A 'Munro' is one of the 277 separate mountains in Scotland over 3000 feet; the other 268 points higher than this are called 'Tops', . . . a tally of 545 'bumps' above this magic altitude. 'Munro's' is purely a Scottish term, the name coming from Sir Hugh Munro, who first listed (and very nearly climbed) them in leisurely Victorian days.

Some people are prone to exaggeration with barefaced disregard for the truth that would make Baron Münchasen whistle with envy; but for myself I have not exaggerated one jot or one tittle. The Highlander has what the Germans would call gemütlichkeit—a friendliness which is irresistibly endearing, and lives 'midst overpowering natural beauty and romantic associations.

A lot of visitors look upon the far north-west as always raining or misty; and some think we have webbed feet! They term it as 'straight up and down rain'; either that or 'real Highland brew stuff'. Give a dog a bad name? But this is really not always the case, and so recent as last year (1968) when most of England had continuous cold, heavy rain and wholesale floods, we commenced having a summer that prolonged itself into an Indian summer—not a drop of rain from late May to end of September. It became truly monotonous. And yet I have never seen such a variety and wealth of blossom in the garden since 1955. The hospitable sun didn't go to bed whilst any guest was still awake; and one can very often read the paper out of doors past midnight on an ordinary fine summer day. Even the trout, during our phenomenal spell, seemed to be grilled as soon as they were fished out of the loch.

But naturally there's no disguising the fact that in the winter we *do* get arrogant gales brawling in from the Atlantic (I have even known the storm-shutters of the front windows being torn away, and the $\frac{3}{4}$-inch iron bar going across them, buckled nearly double), and rain bucketing down; leaves dancing about performing their own particular ballet, the choreography never being the same one act after another. And when such storms are around the crofter says to himself, it's best to go into the byre to smoke a pipe and put your feet on the cow's backside, to warm them. Then, it is, that the old folk tell you, nothing but the stoutest kirk or the stone-built cottage will come through the elements unscathed. But floods? No. For the terrain is not level and the water just overspills the roadway into the moor and gets away to the sea through dykes or culverts made big enough to cope with exceptionally heavy amounts after the snow melts on the hills. However, when finer spring weather is at hand, we who live here soon forget we ever had any winter trials; and with such improvements in the roads, extra passing places, and with the magnificent new car ferries plying to the islands of the north and west, the magic of the whole Highlands, wet or dry, opens up again.

On fine summer evenings there are long lingering sunsets such as you can only compare with those places near the equator. This is no tall talk, for I have lived for years in the East, as well as up in the Highlands, so I ought to know. Without the rain, which outsiders think is always with us, there would be no tumbling waterfalls (such as depicted on the book's cover-jacket), no salmon leaping, for the burns (streams) would be dry; and perhaps the distilleries would run dry also. And *that* would be a calamity!

In spite of all the beauty and way of life such as I have commented upon in these pages, I have a warning to give . . . If you come to Wester Ross and north-west Sutherland and travel around the many places I have told you of, you are at times in GREAT DANGER. And why? Because you may never want to go anywhere else EVER AGAIN for your holidays; and so you have to seriously ask yourself 'is the risk worth taking'? I hardly think you need ask me for the answer.

The crofter and Highlander in out of the way places may be poorly off in some cases, living in wee clean and tidy cottages through whose doors luxury, as we know it today, may have never entered. Yet all the same, the love of life lies deeply on their chiselled faces and they still live in *Tir Nan Òg* . . . the land of the ever young. Yes, indeed, they are a worthy if not a wealthy folk. You never come across a bombastic, loud or foul-mouthed Highlander. This in itself—if nothing more—can be considered surely as 'pearls of character'; for in England where you constantly come across gangs of workmen, every other word seems to be a swear word.

Considering the dire trials and tribulations the Highlander has gone through and suffered over the centuries, it is nothing short of sheer determination and grit that their land and their life is what it is today. I would instance but a few of these hardships (though that word is somewhat an inadequate one).

There was the disastrous Darien Project which was akin to the South Sea Bubble, and reared its form in the late 1600's. It was a great dream thought up by one William Paterson and is said to have touched most homes in Scotland; a rich trading company on the Panama that was to be the commercial centre of the world and was to send back to Scotland ships ladened with silks and spices plus Spanish gold. But it turned out to be a fever stricken swamp that swallowed up Scottish money to the extent of about £400,000 and Scottish manhood; and the English promoters and merchants, and even the English King, William III himself (although he was also King of Scotland) paid scant attention and very little regard for this disaster which fell heavy on Scottish youth and which brought along in its wake economic ruin to countless families. Much bitterness occasioned the Scots against the English who appeared to be obstructionists at every turn, up to the time of the project's collapse in 1699. It was a bitter pill.

Then came 'BLIADNA THEARLAICH', or as the Highlanders called it Prince Charlie's year, 1745, and the subsequent tragedy at Culloden on 16th April 1746—sorrows which echoed down the centuries. After this defeat (the last war fought on British soil) the wearing of Highland dress was forbidden by law; the clan system in the old familiar sense, namely a 'family', not a social hierarchy, was completely shattered by merciless measures. This was followed by the Clearances, already referred to; the glens being emptied by deportation or emigration. By the rigidly repressive Acts of 1746 and 1748 the old ties of clan kingship were cruelly broken. Henceforward until 1782, except by stealth, the tartan was unseen in the hills and glens, where before it had been the people's pride and joy. In 1782 the Duke of Montrose fought nobly for the repeal of the hated Disarming Act and was successful; but it was not until forty years later, towards the middle of the 1800's that a romantic interest in Highland dress was reborn. During this truly melancholy period the oppressed Highlanders dourly and silently endured their wrongs, brooding upon the loss of their ancient heritage; but powerless, very similar to Czechoslovakia today.

As if this were not enough, there came the terrible potato blight and famine around the 1850's. The shaws of the potatoes turned black and the potatoes rotted in the ground; and a vast number of people were left starving since their main food then was potatoes and herring. In Ireland too, the famine swept over that country like a plague, leaving behind it over a million new-made graves. The wolf stood at every door as it did in the Highlands; though not quite so shattering as in Ireland. Many efforts were made in the north to afford relief to stricken families, particularly in road making as a means of providing work, food and money for the starving Highlanders. In respect of Wester

Ross the disease came about in mid 1846.   Government steamers used to call in at Gairloch bringing food and enquiring as to the poverty and distress caused by this widespread calamity.   A Destitution Committee was set up in Edinburgh and funds made available to help all involved.   Eventually all these mentioned hardships were overcome but, for the Highlander, the old-time proverb still remained, namely 'ye've put yer han' t' th' plough, ye must niver, niver take it away.   All through life ye'll have them plough handles in yer han's an' ye'll be goin' down the furrow, though ye may crack a stone here and there.'   And so it came to pass, but despite all this, today we find the Highlander and the people full of vitality, hope and hospitality beyond compare.   What a transformation from the former days of trial? Pearls of priceless value, and the superb settings to be found 'midst their surroundings need no further gilding; its gold-leaf is there for the taking.   The scenery, the quiet thoughts aroused in drinking in everything, the feeling of 'timelessness' is a magnet to young and old.   It should be known the Highlander thinks that anyone who lives elsewhere is unfortunate.

People come up North and to the Isles to 'unwind' from their everyday city strains; to seek what they are unable to find anywhere else in Britain—and they come back, time and time again.

There are many references to 'pearls' in the Bible in both the Old and New Testaments.   Two verses in St. Matthew chapter 13, verses 45 and 46 are very significant of the Highlands and the life enjoyed there, viz. 'the Kingdom of Heaven is like unto a merchant man, seeking goodly pearls: who, when he had found one pearl of great price, went and sold all that he had, and bought it'.   After a strenuous and varied life in many parts of the East, I am happy to have followed in this Holy teaching, and bought a pearl of rare price in Gairloch, Wester Ross; and here I shall remain till I behold the last sunset dipping o'er the bay . . . at least I hope so.

The Scots have a great sense of humour tucked away in them; quiet, dry humour—but nevertheless good humour; seldom ever seamy.   And for quick-wittiness they are all there.   A man rushing into a shop said, 'Can I have a mouse trap, I'm in a hurry, I've got to catch a bus'.   'What size of bus?' Kenny ironmonger asked!   And we've all heard of the Aberdonian who cultivated a wart to grow on the back of his neck, to save him the expense of buying a collar stud.

And of course haggis is often the subject of much leg-pulling with tourists who don't know what it is. I saw a notice in a Highland butcher's shop 'Freshly killed chickens 7s. 6d. each; freshly shot haggis 2s. 6d. per pound'. In another shop a lady asked hesitatingly 'Er, have you any, er haggis?' 'Yes,' the light-hearted butcher said as he picked up a couple and showed them to her. 'How do you sell them?' she asked. 'Oh,' he said, 'dead, we sell them by the pound. On the hoof by the hundred-weight,' he beamed. 'Oh, well,' she said, 'I'll just have a small one.' 'Sure, madam. Do you want a male or a female one?' She turned to her husband, but he was no help; and I suppose after mumbling and buying a small one—male or female—they hastily got out of the shop. It was their first haggis hunt. Scottish humour generally arises out of the 'situation', than out of any planned idea. Surely the secret of keeping young is to have a joy in living coupled with a highly developed sense of humour.

The butcher could have elaborated still further on this 'Great chieftain o' the puddin' race', by telling the good lady, the haggis could only be shot by the light of the full moon in January because of the Scottish Game Law; or that the haggis when young has to be fed on porridge for the first six months of its life!

There are of course instances of a certain amount of simpleness in some of the unscholared folk, which in turn cannot but reflect a great amount of humour, if it were not so wrapped up in either innocence or ignorance. I call one incident to mind. There was a mother who, when she lifted the children's family allowance at the local post office, put a cross X on the pay slip, for she couldn't sign her name. One week instead of the X, she put a little circle, O. The change was at once spotted by the tight-lipped spectacled postmistress in Sutherland and queried. 'Well,' replied the mother, 'I forgot to tell you my husband and I had a row last week, and we separated, so I'm just going back tae ma maiden name!'

And naturally enough there is always one or more who like to put over a 'tall' story to their fellow-men. There was a man who was fond of his dram, and every year used to go along to help his neighbour lift potatoes and carry them to the potato pit.

This time he was carrying bags backward and forward to the pit, and after dumping each sack, he would take a nip from a half bottle he had tucked away in one corner of the pit. This went on for a while, when he got so imbibed with his work (putting it mildly) that in empting a sack he fell right into the pit. His pals ran and picked him out and he told them, 'You know, chaps, I get these dizzy turns now and then, and I had one turn like this last year. But believe me, it was a day earlier than this!'

Another man who had sheep, went out one morning with his collie dog—so he was telling his crofting companions one night in the local bar—but couldn't see a trace of any up or down the hill. So he put his telescope to the dog's eye, who immediately rushed off. The beast was away two days before coming back to the croft with all the sheep!

In a land where so many folk have the same surname (in Wester Ross, it is full of Mackenzie's; in Sutherland the Mackay's and Murray's) and christian names also, it is very difficult to speak of, or refer to anyone in particular without resort to nicknames; and up in the Highlands you come across dozens of such. In the South this is quite an unheard of thing, but with there being so many Kenny's, Calum's, Sandy's, Willie's, Hector's and so forth, you really cannot get away from nicknames for identification. Some are very apt and amusing, and one wonders how on earth they first came about. They are never used in any derogatory, or disparaging manner. Indeed, they can all be classed as pearls of Distinction?

One thing about Highland folk in general is they never complain. They may be suffering pain, rheumatics, fibrositis, neuritis, fallen arches and what not, but should you ask how they are, the invariable answer is 'I'm fine'. I fancy it may be they don't wish to bother you with any detailed diagnosis. It is a wonderful spirit of course to be suffering and yet not moaning, even though it be only one's own family that is around. Pearls of consideration to be sure. Everyone seems content and happy, untroubled really by life's worries that exist in the world at large. The words 'Highland' and 'problem' have been coupled for many a long year, and we are constantly being reminded of it today by our many politicians, development boards, and the like who seem to be more concerned about their own image than most other matters, but the Highlander doesn't appear to be unduly ruffled. There is no poverty, although the Scots have learned the lessons of poverty in the past—that nothing comes without effort and that one values most what costs most. Everyone is content in making a daily living. There are no hard and fast barriers of wealth and station; the society is characterised by a well-mannered equality (vide my Press extracts).

Of course there is always plenty of gossip knocking around to make life more interesting, and if anything unusual happens the villager seems to make the most of it weaving up his or her own story as to the whys and the wherefores. And then it snowballs! Should anything be told you and you're not supposed to know it, you are asked to 'treat it as news' should it eventually come to your ear. And should anything be given you in strict confidence, they will say 'they don't want to put their tongue in it'—but just passing it on for what it is worth. 'Och aye; 'chust that! Believe me, love and scandal are the best sweetners of tea. News is news; gossip is for those who have time on their hands (and I don't mean a wrist watch!) and whose conscience means little to themselves, let alone to others. The rumour mills are constantly lubricated by a few gossipy-living folk. There isn't much to see as a rule in a small village, but what you hear makes up for it!

> Man flies at supersonic speed
> To suit the modern humour
> And science hopes that some fine day
> Who knows?—perhaps he even may
> Exceed the speed of rumour!

And again

> If you know some dreadful scandal
> Such as gossips always court
> And could add a few words to it
> When they call for your support,
>   Don't say it!

Jealousy also provides a good runner-up to gossip.

In the Lochcarron/Applecross district of Wester Ross, there lived two men, Donald and Angus who both had humpbacks and were slightly deformed. Although close friends, the one was always jealous of the other. One Hogmanay they were going the rounds of the countryside into the early hours of the morning when they came across a hollow and found the fairies singing and dancing. But they all seemed out of tune and out of step. Donald noticed this and loudly shouted out 'Wednesday', whereupon the song and dance assumed a correct and regular rhythm. The fairies were so delighted they tore Donald away from his pal and took him with them to the hillside opening. They kept him for a year and a day; and when he came out to the world again he was as straight as a rod, and no hump. On his return to Lochcarron, and Angus seeing such a transformation in Donald, he was consumed with jealousy, and knowing of the secret he went along the next Hogmanay and coming across the fairies dancing at the hillside spot, went up to them and shouted out 'Thursday', forgetting that it should have been 'Wednesday', as the password. The fairies took on a furious look and dragged him in with them to their cave. But after only one day they pushed him out. Angus came back to Lochcarron with two humps; his own and that of Donald's; and his body bent almost double.

*   *   *

As to visitors being enchanted with the Highlands, I would comment on two particular incidents of which I was personally aware. There was a family who took a rented house for a month. The house, approached by a side road off the main road, had no parking facilities for their two cars inside the house fencing, and so they left the cars just outside at the top of the roadway. There are in fact few houses that do enable cars to be contained in their own grounds. During the summer and the nights so bright, sheep wander around, and if they come up against a car and see their reflection in the bodywork, they imagine it to be a sheep from another fold and are apt to bump its image, scratching and denting the car framework. It is a most embittered experience to have one's car damaged through no fault of one's own. For myself, I would see red. But these good people to which this happened, told the old lady of the house they didn't really mind and would still come back next year. They were not meaning to have the cars repaired, for it would remind them of their visit to the Highlands! Another party I knew, got their tyres *deflated* at a garage as soon as they crossed into Highland territory, asking the attendant to pump them up again; for when they returned to England they would be able to say to their friends 'We've got Highland air in our tyres; beat that if you can old dears'. Aye, and maybe 'och aye.

In touring Sutherland's vast area, a vibrant region of space and beauty (so vast really that you can travel 40 miles or so Lairg to Tongue, or Lairg to Laxford Bridge, without seeing one litter bin, let alone a house, ruins excepted), though there is plenty of moorland to offer 'relief', one is struck by the fact as to why there should not be far more sheep around. Those that are there, are mostly of the Cheviot breed, as opposed to the black-faced ones commonly grazing in Wester Ross. They appear to be very hardy, yield more and better wool and meat than their black-faced cousins. I am not a farmer, but considering there are unlimited acres of good moorland and grass in north-west Sutherland (better than in Wester Ross, or so it would seem) I am left wondering why it is that crofters there don't go in for sheep in a big way? Instead of only having fifty head or so, why don't they go in for thousands and make their county a real sheep-ranching area? After all, 10,000 sheep and more covering such an immense acreage would be a most valuable asset to both the crofter and the country as a whole. Unlike those in the South, the sheep here are not fed with fatty food. In the South I am told they even give them pills to fatten them up! Government officials appear to have been tearing their hair out in getting the Invergordon smelter; but this will have little impact on the north-west, for the young people living there do not relish going into industrial work in a town.

The general land survey in Sutherland can be classified into three tiers; the lower ground for cattle, the middle for sheep, and the high ground, forestry and deer. There is most money in cattle, but crofters seem to be more at home with sheep. I am told that difficulty of tenure is an obstacle to sheep grazing on a large scale; but surely those in authority, and the crofting commissioners could sort that out satisfactorily? As it is, it seems to me to be a sheer waste of good land.

I have made reference to deer—an animal that is indigenous to these northern parts. Its antiquity extends over many centuries. Certainly changes have come about since those early days of stalking; the telescopic sight was then an unknown quantity; the deer pony of old has been superseded by the

Landrover and so it goes on. It is estimated 194,000 red deer roam Scotland's seven million acres of deer country. Roe and fallow are also to be found in the glens and hills. There is even a small herd of reindeer in the Aviemore district.

I now turn to the subject of venison, which appeared to be one of the staple foods in Old Testament days. But travel the Highlands as you will and when you will, seldom do you have venison served up to you in hotels. It is true there are seasons when venison is good and when it is not considered good for eating; but in these days every hotel, and many guest houses, have deep-freezes, so there should be no excuse for it not coming up as a dish at any time.

When I first came to Scotland I used to think it tasted awful, like dried cork; but that was accounted for in the way it was cooked. When properly done it can be held in very high esteem. The deer is a choosey eater, living upon heather and luscious grass and shrubs met with on the moors and hills. Being such a clean eater, there is very little fat on it, and so it needs very slow cooking. Unlike beef, venison should not be served underdone. When properly cooked it is far superior to lamb or mutton chops; infinitely more tender. In fact it is a very tasty 'pearl'. In its own gravy, fried potato croquettes and green peas make it a regal dish. When the weather is cold if the venison is fresh it should be hung in the larder for a fortnight before cooking. If warmish weather, then a few days will be enough.

I have already devoted a chapter to The Sabbath, remarking what an utterly priceless pearl this can be, and how few—if any —other parts of Britain observe the Lord's Day as up in the north. It is part and parcel of the countless other pearls of beauty. Whilst the day is held in solemn account, the ministers on their visits are sometimes able to tell you in simple language, some amusing stories; and indeed many of the older generation of preachers were constantly drawing interesting analogies from everyday life and incidents. There are some stories which come to my mind, which are in no wise blasphemous, but all the same, significant.

There was a wee boy who had a pet cat but could not cope with all the kittens that came along; and when the last event came to pass, he took two of them to the Church of Scotland minister to see if he would adopt them and give them a good home. The minister was not keen to have them and so the boy went away. The self-same pastor chanced to meet his fellow cleric, a Free Church minister in the village a day or so later, and told him of Johnny's visit to him with the kittens. About a week later Johnny rolled up to the Free Church manse with the two kittens, asking that minister if *he* would take them in. The minister was rather abrupt and annoyed, saying he was a rascal to go to the Church of Scotland, and then come along to him on the same mission. Howbeit, Johnny was unabashed and said when he went to the C. of S. minister, the kittens had their eyes closed; but now these few days later, their eyes were opened, and they thought they would be better cared for in the home of the Free Church!

This is the story of two parrots. One was owned by an elderly lady and was a comfort to her in her old age, until it began saying over and over again 'I wish to goodness the auld body would die!' This hurt her very much, for she began to imagine that her family, with whom she lived, were talking aloud behind her back and within hearing of the parrot, and wishing her dead so they could come into her money. One day she shared her distress with a friend who said the wicked old parrot might improve its manners and speech if she brought her brother's parrot along for a time. His bird was a pious one, for her brother was a minister of religion. So the second parrot was brought, and the two cages placed side by side. Eventually the old lady's parrot shouted out 'I wish to goodness the auld body would die'; and immediately the second parrot intoned 'O Lord, hear our prayer. Amen'.

Yet another parrot story. An old religious spinster had a beautiful South American parrot given her years ago by a sailor, and its language from time to time was very nautical! But she didn't worry too much, but when the Sabbath came round she always threw an old blanket over the cage for that seemed to keep the bird quiet and not talkative; and the wise old fellow always knew what to expect on the seventh day. It was the one day the lady was never disturbed in her reading of the Bible by unholy exclamations. So all was well. However, one Tuesday afternoon she saw the vicar coming up the garden path to call on her. She was in a flurry thinking of the parrot's language, but suddenly thought the best thing to do was to put the blanket over the cage as per the Sunday routine. This she did, and the vicar and she were having cups of tea and cake and chatting away quite nicely, when the air was rent by the parrot's cry 'Well, this is a blooming short week anyhow!'

*   *   *

In respect of the north-west of Scotland, the position of the Gaelic Highlands is very like being a nation within a nation; and this has existed over the centuries. Many people have come from far and wide to see what the Highlander is like and what he represents. Many such folk have written about him and his way of life. But unless you live permanently among them and so have daily contact with them, these writers can at the most only give a superficial picture with their words. You need to be able to live *with* them to penetrate their wonderful make-up; if not, then the author is looked upon as a complete outsider—the 'Gall' of Gaelic heritage and history. I have been privileged to know this area for some fifty odd years, and feel a just claim to know a little—if not more than a little—of what I say and put on record, with feelings of pride and certainly devoid of all fanciful expressions. The Editor of a Hebridean newspaper once wrote 'one cannot understand a people and why they act as they do unless one knows the content of their memories. One cannot understand also, the paradox of the naturally gay in heart, seeking religious consolation in a grim Calvinism; neither can one understand why Lewis which clothes the world in such colourful tweeds, clothes most of its womenfolk in black'!

That the Highland way of life is not hard is too often accepted without the realisation of just how much hard work and determination is needed to make a reasonable living in these parts. For many decades amid much tribulation, as I have previously recorded, their once fertile lands were left to revert into a wild state, with the bracken as the chief invader; and government aid in the past has been very reluctantly given to help bring back fertility and productivity. The crofting system even today is characterised by marginal production. There has even been the alarming decline in crofter-fishing of seventy-five per cent in the last few years. In the last five or ten years there are signs of revival such as land reclamation in Lewis, new possible uses for peat, uses for seaweed, bulb and plant (shrub) growing, new and extensive areas of afforestation, and very recently a firm employing nearly a hundred people making spectacles . . . and of course the gallop made in tourism.

Every day in the crofter's life is a busy one, both summer and winter; and he is often left with the thought 'the day ends with so very little done'. Albeit they refuse to make any concessions to old age, and they continue to live in gratefulness for the present, and tell you the cure for everything is salt water—sweat, tears or the sea. In this frame of mind, the philosophy given in a Chinese proverb may be enlightening . . .

. . . Until tomorrow becomes yesterday, men and women will be blind to the good fortune of the present . . .

In looking back over the years, they will tell you that once the water has flowed under the bridge, it is gone. No good wasting any tears to add to the stream; only the future matters from now on.

Certainly in this area where Time is of little account, we cannot hope to alleviate the Highlander's isolation by adopting a 1st or 2nd class postage system. But possibly by the time this book is published this infamous racket may have been replaced by some other form of irritation thought out by some smart Alec in Westminster. Who can tell, for nowadays it would seem mankind is fast coming to grips with the mysteries of the universe, and landing a man on the moon within the next year—but it cannot cope with the ordinary problems of day-to-day living; not even of those in the Highlands. In living for the future, scientists are forfeiting Today. Perhaps there is too much money with too little time to spend it; too little time to seek out the Pearls in the overpowering natural beauties that I have endeavoured to unearth through these many chapters. In these regions that are nourished by the warmth of the Gulf Stream, there is scope for all, and its roads are for enjoyment, not speed; as we are far away from the concrete-slab school of architecture, thank goodness.

What is this life if, full of care,
We have no time to stand and stare?

The fate of human civilization will depend on whether the rockets of the future carry the astronomer's telescope or the atom bomb. Man can comprehend neither infinity nor eternity, though he uses the concepts intelligently enough in all his intricate mathematical calculations. We're so far ahead of ourselves, we'll catch ourselves up before we've left! Controlling the universe may be all very well until we look nearer home and find elementary problems of living too big to handle. I put the question, is man running before he has learned to walk? And the rich pearls—the *strings of pearls* in fact—I have chanced to depict, may well be smashed one day into powder, and then we come to the point of further atoms being available for splitting. So it goes on, and will continue to go on—until FINIS; the point of no return. Then this land which we treasure so much in the north will *not* be for us 'richly to enjoy'. (1 Timothy 6 : 17, vide Dedication). We know the Highlands as silent, simple, majestic and resistless. Such was the Reformation; such were the revivals in Scotland under the Fathers of the Covenant.

People come to the Highlands for various reasons. Thousands of Americans and Canadians link their visit searching for the croft or village whence their forebears emigrated. Teenagers come to marry at Gretna Green! Most visitors come in the summer when the days are long and lazy; when the air is laden with the rich smells of the good earth. It is then the sun is the busy-bodied gardener working overtime supplying the alchemy that turns a dormant country into a living miracle. As every crofter knows one must make hay while the sun shines. A crofter looking over his cattle and sheep expresses this miracle in a homely, understandable way when he says 'it's been a good summer; with the rain we've had, there has been good grass, and we'll be sending big fat cattle to the market'. Summer to him is a very personal matter, and whilst he expresses his sentiments in a mundane laconic way his simple words are a glowing tribute to the growing season—good grass!

The deeply carved coast line of the north-west is the result of tremendous earth shaking and vibrations, seismic upheavals, volcanic capers (and Highland reels!), the erosive action of water, wind and glacial ice and the ever patient work of Time. So the cutting, the gouging and slashing continues giving the whole landscape of the west coast and particularly the north-west region, a characteristic personality of its own. Nature at times can be

very vain—an old show-off, when she holds up a looking glass
to reflect her own loveliness. Mirrors for these reflections are the
hundreds of lochs and lochans seen at every bend; and created
in these mirrors by a delicate balance of earth, sun and sky. At
times you can never really photograph the mountains, for they
are for ever changing in colour and perspective—never the same
for very long.

One must be very much of a dullard to come to the Highlands
and go away unimpressed; after all, to say there is an embarrassment in so many rich pearls, is a masterly understatement. In
this (God's own country) there is ample space to ramble—more
than in any other area of Britain—so much so one might term
it a vast 'Rambling Reserve'.

If I had my way . . .
> For all leaving Britain, pleasure to seek
> A tax of one hundred pounds a week;
> Then those booked abroad, would come to Gairloch
> 'Our economy's saved', cried Calum and Jock.

If I had my way . . .
> I would round up the strikers, and give them a trip
> Down in the hold of a dirty old ship,
> 'The Clearance; the Clearance' is echoed again
> We can do without lazy, truculent men.

If I had my way . . .
> I'd bring back the birch, so once and for all
> The rowdies would know just where it would fall,
> And gallows put up as in days long ago
> The murderer left to be picked by a crow.

If I had my way . . .
> I would scrap all the Planners, and substitute men
> Who knew what a strath was, and what was a glen,
> For as it is now, ART seems to be hot
> On making our Gairloch, just what it's not.

If I had my way . . .
> Then Minister Harold would rush up one day
> His pipe and his papers and say, 'look Bee Jay
> You keep to your Pearls, I'll look after the mob',
> So I got some more star-dust, and finished the job.
> . . . Highland Pearls . . .

*   *   *

As only God can make a tree
So lochs and lochans maketh He,
We can but see them as a whole
Through the windows of our soul.

I hope these pearls with pride of place, will get affection, love and grace; if not, my Heaven will all be wrong; t'will *not* be my story; it will *not* be my song.

In my humble way, I have portrayed the timeless magic beauty you constantly run up against in the north-west. But until I really saw and became immersed in it all, I confess I was not prepared for Nature's soft and quiet beauty—a country 'living in so many mansions' so to speak; so stirring. I think the majority of us take all these things for granted; we are prone to do so. But for myself, I see something different each day from my house that Love built—something that didn't seem to be the same yesterday. To visitors, whose first time it is to come so far north, I am sure it must be above their expectations. I know it must, for hundreds have told me so. It could not be otherwise if you pause and think and meditate, getting the firm handshake and warm welcoming smiles. The Highlands are an escapist's dream paradise. The peace of meditation indeed; for when everything is quiet, and we're lost in meditation, our soul is then preparing for a deeper dedication. . . .

There is an old Chinese saying 'In the noise of the market place there is money; but under the cherry tree there is peace'. There may be no cherry trees in the north-west—only mountains; and under their shadow you can find peace and quiet in plenty.

All the wee Highland villages/hamlets are *oases* to men and women in this frantic, tearing life we live in. For life is simple, and seems to stand still in the midst of the spacious moorland, and the mountains guarding them. Truly, on a clear day you can see Forever. . . .

'*Chaque pays a son savoir vivre*'. . . each land has its own way of life, as the French say. Sometimes when one views these different Highland surroundings, finding oneself alone in the Alone, it all seems to come straight from the Rubaiyat of Omar Khayyam. Once in the Egyptian desert going and coming back with a friend from somewhere (I forget where, for it is over 30 years ago) we passed the same two men plodding beside their camels. 'Why don't they ride?' I asked our French-speaking

Arab guide. '*Ils ne sont pas pressés,*' he said . . . 'they are not in a hurry'. So it is in the Highlands.

Whenever I leave the north-west of Sutherland, I hear myself saying in Arabic, *wahshani* 'I miss you'. And if the wind is blowing from the north, as I journey home, I feel the answer wafting back, *wahishni* 'I miss you too'.

In the far-off days along the many rocky shores and bays of N-W Sutherland, the villagers used to pray thus: 'We pray Thee Lord, not that wrecks should happen, but that if any wrecks should happen Thou wilt guide them into these lochs and rocky shores for the benefit of we poor folk.' In the Clearance days, I can hear the old people, in turning to the Book of Proverbs, invoking the Gospel's words where in Chapter 22, verse 28, it is recorded 'Remove not the ancient landmark[s] which thy [our] fathers have set'—apparently to no avail at the time.

As I write these lines, the earth continues to spin, and will continue turning. The sea will also continue to ebb and flow and produce white-horses (and not phantom white horses) as and when it pleases—and nothing we can do will stop it.

The Scottish Highlands have not a bit of everything, but masses of everything. Like St. Paul, Wester Ross and Western Sutherland has the gift of being all things to all men; for all around there is a world of warmth in many senses, and seas embroidered into islands with golden beaches and virgin white sand far too numerous to have listed or recorded through these pages. Scenic shrines galore, for we should remember Nature is not only the master creator of big things but of little things as well. Like a great poet, nature produces the greatest results with the simplest means. There is just sun, flowers, water—and love.

* * *

Most of my life (till 1939) was spent in Ceylon (the 'Isle of Delight' and supposed to have been the Garden of Eden), and the Far East, but no beckoning fingers of the Tropics, the fragrance of oriental flowers or even the scent of spices in the native bazaars have any power to call me back from where I am in the Highlands today. As the Irish say 'there's a spot in my heart sure no other can own'.

As a reverie, I would add:

I wish I had the gift to tell
The world of things which make hearts swell,
But I can only sigh and try
To make it known how deeply I
Love Scotland . . .

This last decade I have found my dream house—and my partner, too, Fiona—in Gairloch; after noting its attraction some fifty-five years ago. Prior to that, and returning home from the Tropics, I had been wandering through the bitter summers of Life; but then, I came from Camelot to Elysium. And so as the ballad has it . . .

. . . these are bitter summers
And you have taught me to spend them with you . . . Gairloch!

Anyone who gets tired of the Highlands is surely too tired to live. We are shaped and fashioned by what we love. The Highland folk love their country and thus they are shaped; both the old women—the CALLAICHS—and the old men—the BHOAD-ACHS; and in the small world they live in, they cannot understand the pleasures of others who live in the rest of the world. Some paint the Highlands as a region of stagnation and laziness, rather than what it is, namely a country of plain living and high thinking. Generations to come may yet learn that Highland folk can look up to the hills and think with their hearts as in those days of old . . . doing good and reading God's word.

A visit becomes an adventure; it is also the angler's dream (Sutherland in particular), the photographer's paradise, the geologist's treasure chest and the antiquarian's curio shop. If the sun doesn't always shine, it is because God willed it so. If it did, we here would be living in a desert looking upon cactus instead of heather.

*   *   *

During her long captivity in England, Mary Queen of Scots, liked to use the enigmatic motto '*In my end is my beginning*'. Even as she went to her execution to the Great Hall of Fotheringay Castle in February 1587, she still prayed there might be a beginning. 'My end is my beginning'.

This book is not written to any specific formula for any material gain it may bring in, but for the joy of recording all that is best in the Highlands; there being no 'worst'. The pages of this book are fast running out; as the meter said to the shilling 'I am glad you popped in Bob for I was just going out'! And reluctantly I have to conclude; 'to end'. Though what I have written is really but a 'beginning', for I am sure it would not be too hard to carry on from one thing to another, one thought to another, and still there would be something I missed recording, something unsaid, something left out. Something I would have forgotten from memories of the old days. Most of us say there was nothing like the old days. I must confess I liked the old days best—for I was younger then. But everything described today has a different perspective tomorrow. As we grow older, the hours are so precious; so little time left (even in this land where Time is so plentiful) to do the things we would like to do. But perhaps if I carried on and on, beginning again from this end to write further of this land, it might become boring? There is a saying 'you can have too much of a good thing'. So 'tis best to end whilst the going is good, leaving another beginning till later mayhap?

To bring matters very up-to-date, I would refer to the 'hour', up in the far north. The 'hour' is very disturbing—the terror of the night in fact; but the Government seems to be linked with the Common Market idea and Continental time. Daylight and sun seem now in the north to stay with us shorter. In the old days the science of measuring the length of day was by shadows cast by stones. When the shadow cast by a standing stone grew no longer, there was general rejoicing. 'The sun is coming back' was the great cry. The early Christian Church disliking this paganism, fixed the date of the festival of Christmas to approximate to that of the solstice. The rebirth of light and love are still the symbols of Christmastide. The Scottish sailor, however, still utilises the tide, which is governed by the moon—and not by office or governmental hours.

*   *   *

With Scotlands rivers running sparkling to the sea, and with amenities existing to enhance their beauty, everyone can—or should be—thrilled over Scotland and the north; and in turn Scotland thrilled over itself. We have no dust or grime to contend with, and so we only need to clean the windows but twice a year at most.

Finally as Jane Austin says 'there is charity (love) in the adieu'. Live well, love well; 'love your way to longevity', could be an apt Highland saying. Love can't be dead when you are surrounded by so much of everything that matters in the far north-west. Peace, quiet and respect. Surely the goal of everyone? Life is very much alive here, even though in solitude there be an end to ambition; and they say to themselves 'this is my country, the land that begat me; these windy spaces are surely my own'.

Yes, in the Highlands, in the open country, the old High- landers have rosy faces—and the young fair maidens, quiet eyes. And all have a cheerful smile; and such a cheery face is almost as good for a sick person as healthy weather.

*　　　*　　　*

'*For once, he deserved to win.*' This was a remark of a fellow traveller as we sat at tea in a café in the Great St. Bernard Pass, a place which I was visiting when I came back from the East. The reference was to Napoleon's great feat in leading an army of 30,000 men with all its artillery and other equipment into Italy by this breathtaking pass in May 1800. We had come by car. Bonaparte's army had no such mechanical devices to facilitate his expedition. The Great St. Bernard's Pass is part of the mountain road leading from Martiginy in Switzerland to Aosta in Northern Italy. It rises to a height of 8150 feet, nearly three times as high as any of the Highland mountains, and from the time the first snow falls, it remains closed until the warm sun- shine of the next year melts the frozen drifts. Now of course a tunnel goes under the Swiss-Italian border and so there is vehicular connections between the two countries all the year round by this route. Yes, provided that victory be recognised as the due reward of determination and endurance . . . '*he deserved to win*'. I think these four words constitute a fitting epitaph to all those Highland folk who, long ago, had to experience this selfsame determination and endurance; and with God at their side, they deserved to win through.

*　　　*　　　*

Throughout this book, I have tried to give readers as full a picture as I can of all the pearls discovered in one way and another, in this far-off Continent of ours (Sutherland and Wester Ross). With me, some spots seem to have a memory and a living spirit. We do well to keep such places sacred, and to seek what they have to tell us. Scotland is a fine place to be born, and a fine place to die; the problem is, where to spend the intervening years!

Pearls of Peace, oystered in the North-West . . .

> A timeless calm
> Lies on the rugged land
> And settles on the soul. . . .

For who but God could make the day, and gently tuck the night away?

So, BEANNACH LEIBH AN DRASDA, 'Goodbye for the present', PERLES D'OUEST.

Yes, these strings of pearls will still be here when all of us are out beyond th' moors an' beyond th' clouds.

> This is my story,
> This is my song.

THE END

READER'S MEMO